Essentials of

Accounting

Tenth Edition

Essentials of
Accounting

Tenth Edition

Leslie K. Breitner and Robert N. Anthony

University of Washington,   Harvard Business School
Evans School of Public Affairs

Boston   Columbus   Indianapolis   New York   San Francisco   Upper Saddle River
Amsterdam   Cape Town   Dubai   London   Madrid   Milan   Munich   Paris   Montreal   Toronto
Delhi   Mexico City   Sao Paulo   Sydney   Hong Kong   Seoul   Singapore   Taipei   Tokyo

Editorial Director: Sally Yagan
Editor in Chief: Eric Svendsen
Acquisitions Editor: Julie Broich
Editorial Assistant: Christina Rumbaugh
Director of Marketing: Patrice Lumumba Jones
Marketing Manager: Elizabeth Averbeck
Marketing Assistant: Ian Gold
Senior Managing Editor: Judy Leale
Project Manager: Debbie Ryan
Senior Operations Supervisor: Arnold Vila

Operations Specialist: Ben Smith
Senior Art Director: Jayne Conte
Cover Designer: Margaret Kenselarr
Manager, Rights and Permissions: Charles Morris
Cover Art: Getty Images
Full-Service Project Management: Kelli Jauron
Composition: S4Carlisle Publishing Services
Printer/Binder: Bind-Rite Graphics/Robbinsville
Cover Printer: Lehigh-Phoenix Color/Hagerstown
Text Font: Times

Credits and acknowledgments borrowed from other sources and reproduced, with permission, in this textbook appear on appropriate page within text.

Library of Congress Cataloging-in-Publication Data

Breitner, Leslie Pearlman.
  Essentials of accounting / Leslie K. Breitner and Robert N. Anthony.
—10th ed.
    p. cm.
  Previous ed. entered under: Rober N. Anthony.
  ISBN-13: 978-0-13-607182-2
  ISBN-10: 0-13-607182-1
  1. Accounting. I. Anthony, Rober N. (Robert Newton). II.
Title
  HF5635.A6879 2010
  657—dc22

                                2009008676

10 9 8 7 6 5 4 3 2 1

www.pearsonhighered.com

ISBN 10: 0-13-607182-1
ISBN 13: 978-0-13-607182-2

For Professor Robert N. Anthony—In Memory
I am grateful for your wisdom and advice over
the years of our partnership.

—LKB

Contents

Introduction

This book will help you teach yourself the essential ideas of accounting. You will learn what accounting information can—and cannot—tell you about an organization.

Accounting is the principal way of organizing and reporting financial information. Although there are differences in detail, the general structure and rules are similar in most countries and in most types of organizations.

Accounting has been called the language of business. Learning this language is complicated by the fact that many words used in accounting do not mean quite the same thing as they mean in everyday life. When using accounting words, it is important that you understand their accounting meaning.

As in any language, some accounting rules and terms have a single correct meaning, and others are like dialects in that their meaning varies with different users. You will learn to understand and allow for these differences.

HOW TO USE THIS PROGRAM

This program consists of "frames." Each frame asks you to DO something: answer a question, make a calculation, fill in blanks. But these frames are NOT tests. As in most learning experiences, you learn by doing. You should be able to complete most frames without difficulty.

Procedures

- Read each frame in the left-hand column, while covering the right-hand column with the mask provided.

- Write your response in the space provided. Experience has shown that if you don't write your response, you will not retain nearly as much information.

- Check your response by moving the mask so as to uncover the correct response in the right-hand column.

- If your response is correct, go to the next frame. Otherwise, study the frame again and try to understand why you were wrong.

- Some frames refer you to exhibits. These are in the back of the book.

- You will find a post-test for each part at the back of this book, after the exhibits. When you have completed a part, complete the post-test. If you have difficulty with it, review the frames on this topic. For additional challenge and review of concepts you can work through the mini cases at the end of each set of post-tests.

- Do not skip frames. If you have difficulty with a particular point, go back to the frame in which it was first mentioned and review it from there.

- NOTE: Halfway through the book, the pages reverse so that the response column will always be on the right-hand side of the page. At this point you must turn the book over to move forward through the frames.

Technical Conventions

_____ = Fill in the one or more words that are missing.

__ __ __ __ __ = Fill in the letters that are missing, one to each underline.

[Yes / No] = Underline or circle the correct alternative.

Acknowledgments

Dr. Matthew Israel developed the program for the first edition.

Dr. Philip E. Meyer, Boston University, developed the original glossary.

Cameron E. H. Breitner contributed to the development of Part 8.

Cory Sbarbaro helped with the Sarbanes-Oxley Act and its relationship to nonprofit organizations.

David Ozag, Bucknell University and Michael Groomer, Indiana University, and Kelli Jauron of S4Carlisle Publishing Services, provided valuable feedback during the revision process for the tenth edition.

Alice Lawson and Lori Reimann-Garretson helped to write the new mini-cases. I am enormously grateful to both of them, and they know why!

Julie Broich and Kierra Kashickey of Pearson Education were extremely supportive during the revision process for the 10th Edition.

I appreciate the advice and help from all of these people as well as the unending patience of my wonderful husband John.

Essentials of
Accounting

Tenth Edition

## Part 1

Basic Concepts

Learning Objectives

In this part you will learn:

- The nature of the balance sheet.
- The accounting meaning of assets, liabilities, and equity.
- The first five of the nine concepts that govern all accounting:
    - The dual-aspect concept.
    - The money-measurement concept.
    - The entity concept.
    - The going-concern concept.
    - The asset-measurement concept.
- The meaning of the principal items reported on a balance sheet.

1-1. Accounting is a language. The purpose of any language is to convey information. Accounting information is provided by reports called **financial statements.** This program helps you understand what the numbers in the financial statements mean and how they can be used. Please see Exhibit 1 (at the back of this book) to view a sample financial statement. As indicated by the title at the top of the page, this report is called a __ __ __ __ __ __ __ sheet.

balance

> ***On an item like this, fill in one letter for each underline and then compare it with the correct answer, found here.***

NOTE: Be sure to cover up the answers with the mask provided.

12-36. The standard-setting board that defines the IFRS wants to use **fair value** as the measurement basis. It is because the board feels that f__ __ __ v__ __ __ __ measurement meets the characteristics described in Frame 12.35.

fair value

12-37. Obviously, this is an area of [similarity / difference] between IFRS and GAAP.

difference

12-38. There are many areas where GAAP and IFRS differ. For IFRS to become the accepted practice in the United States, the two systems for reporting must converge. Such c __ __ __ __ __ __ __ __ __ e may not fully happen for several more years.

convergence

12-39. The study of accounting is not limited to learning about how to structure f __ __ __ __ __ __ __ __ s __ __ __ __ __ __ __ __ s. Students must learn about many aspects of g __ __ __ __ __ reporting.

financial statements
global

You have completed Part 12 of this program. If you think you understand the material in this part, you should now take Post-Test 12, which is found in the back of this text. If you are uncertain about your understanding, you should review Part 12.

The post-test will serve both to test your comprehension and to review the highlights of Part 12. After taking the post-test, you may find that you are unsure about certain points. You should review these points. Please review the answers to Post-Test 12, following the Post-Tests, at the back of this text.

ELEMENTS OF THE BALANCE SHEET

1-2. A balance sheet gives financial information about an **entity.** The name of the entity that this balance sheet refers to is __ __ __ __ __ __ __ __ __ __ __ __ __ .

Garsden
Company

1-3. An entity is any organization for which financial statements are prepared. A business is an __ __ __ __ __ __ __ ; a college, a government, a church, and a synagogue are also __ __ __ __ __ __ __ __ __ .

entity
entities

1-4. The balance sheet is a snapshot of the financial position of the entity as of one moment in time. As indicated by the heading in Exhibit 1, the balance sheet for Garsden Company reports its financial position as of December 31, __ __ __ __ .

2009

1-5. The date December 31, 2009, means [circle A or B]:

    A. it was prepared on December 31, 2009.

    B. it reports the entity's financial position as of December 31, 2009.

B (*Probably, it was prepared early in 2010.*)

1-6. The Garsden Company balance sheet has two sides. The heading of the left side is A __ __ __ __ __ __ , and the heading of the right side is L __ __ __ __ __ __ __ __ __ __ __ and E __ __ __ __ __ __ . We shall describe the meaning of each side.

Assets
Liabilities   Equity

ASSETS

1-7. Assets are valuable resources owned by the entity. An entity needs cash, equipment, and other resources in order to operate. These resources are its a __ __ __ __ __ __ . The balance sheet shows the amounts of each of these assets as of a certain date.

assets

12-29. The asset-measurement concept is: **If r __ __ __ __ __ e information is available, an asset is measured at its fair value.**

reliable

12-30. You learned in Part 1 that the fair value of most assets is known on the date the asset was acquired because the buyer and the seller agreed on the amount. You learned that if Garsden Company purchased a plot of land in 1999 for $100,000, this land would have been reported on its December 31, 1999, balance sheet as $100,000. Its fair value on December 31, 2009, would be:

A. $100,000

B. More than $100,000

C. Garsden doesn't know

C. *Garsden doesn't know until such time as someone buys the land from it. Any other amount would be subjective.*

12-31. Because entities usually don't know the fair value of their assets, they report them at c __ __ __ .

cost

12-32. So, if reliable information is available, the amount of an asset is measured at its fair value. Otherwise, the measurement is based on its __ __ __ __ .

cost

12-33. Because fair values are difficult to estimate, they are [objective / subjective], whereas costs are [objective / subjective].

subjective

objective

12-34. According to GAAP, most assets are reported as an objective measure, which is __ __ __ __ .

cost

12-35. Recall that we introduced the qualitative characteristics of the IFRS earlier. They are:

u _____y

r _____e

r _____y

c _____y

understandability

relevance

reliability

comparability

1-8. Assets are resources **owned** by Garsden Company. Its employees, although usually its most valuable resource, [are / are not] accounting assets.

are not (*No one owns humans since the abolition of slavery.*)

> **NOTE:** On an item like this, circle the answer of your choice.

LIABILITIES AND EQUITY

1-9. The right side of the balance sheet shows the sources of funds that provided the entity's assets. As the heading indicates, there are two general types of sources, l __ __ __ __ __ __ __ __ __ __ __ and e __ __ __ __ __ __ .

liabilities

equity

1-10. Liabilities are the entity's obligations to outside parties who have furnished resources. These parties are generally called **creditors** because they have extended credit to the entity. As Exhibit 1 indicates, suppliers have extended credit in the amount of $5,602,000 as indicated by the item A __ __ __ __ __ __ __ P __ __ __ __ __ __ .

Accounts Payable

> **NOTE:** Note that the last three "000" are omitted on the balance sheet.

1-11. Creditors have a **claim** against the assets in the amount shown as the liability. For example, a bank has loaned funds to Garsden Company, and therefore has a current claim of $1,000,000 of this amount, as indicated by the item, __ __ __ __ __ __ __ __ __ __ __ __ __ __ __ .

Bank Loan Payable

1-12. Because an entity will use its assets to pay its claims, the claims are claims against __ __ __ __ __ __ . They are claims against all the assets, not any particular asset.

assets

12-24. Bookkeeping uses fairly straightforward rules. Using guiding principles rather than rules calls for judgment. Evidently, today's student [can get by just learning the rules / must learn to think more broadly] about financial accounting.

must learn to think more broadly

GAAP AND IFRS: SIMILARITIES AND DIFFERENCES

12-25. Some of the changes necessary for adoption of the IFRS are minimal, whereas others will take a long time. Evidently, there are s__ __ __ __ __ __ __ __ __ __ s as well as d __ __ __ __ __ __ __ __ __ __ s between GAAP and IFRS. We have already mentioned some of these.

similarities

differences

12-26. As an example, the IFRS framework provides a description of the elements on the balance sheet (statement of financial position) similar to GAAP:

_____ = resources controlled by the entity that provide future economic benefits

asset

_____ = obligations of the entity requiring settlement in the form of cash outflows or outflows of resources that have economic benefits

liabilities

_____ = the residual interest in the assets of the entity after deducting all liabilities

equity

12-27. Note that the names of the financial statements will likely change to reflect the new standards.

B_____ S_____ = Statement of Financial Position

Balance Sheet

I_____ S_____ = Statement of Comprehensive Income

Income Statement

S_____ of C_____ F_____ = Statement of Cash Flows

Statement of Cash Flows

12-28. Let's use an example to illustrate a potential difference between GAAP and IFRS. Recall from Part 1 the asset-measurement concept. The name for what an asset is "worth" is its f __ __ __ __ v __ __ __ __ __ .

fair value

1-13. The other source of the funds that an entity uses to acquire its assets is called **equity.** In Garsden Company, equity investors provided funds for which they received common stock. The total amount supplied by equity investors is called **total paid-in capital.** In Garsden Company, it was $__ __ , __ __ __ ,000. (We shall describe the details in a later part.)

$12,256,000

> **NOTE:** The term is "equity" (singular) not "equities" (plural) even though there are several sources of equity.

1-14. Equity funds also come from a second source, the profits or **earnings** generated by the entity. The amount of these earnings that has not been paid to equity investors in the form of dividends is retained in the entity, and therefore is called __ __ __ __ __ __ __ __ earnings. In Garsden Company, the amount was $__ __ , __ __ __ ,000.

retained
$13,640,000

1-15. Creditors can sue the entity if the amounts due them are not paid. Equity investors have only a *residual claim;* if the entity is dissolved, they get whatever is left after the liabilities have been paid, which may be nothing. Liabilities therefore are a [stronger / weaker] claim against the assets, and equity is a [stronger / weaker] claim.

stronger
weaker

DUAL-ASPECT CONCEPT

1-16. Whatever assets remain after the liabilities are taken into account will be claimed by the equity investors. Consider the case of an entity whose assets total $10,000, and whose liabilities total $4,000. Its equity must be $_____.

$6,000 = ($10,000 – $4,000)

> *A single blank indicates that the answer is one word or, when preceded by the dollar sign as it is here, one amount.*

1-17. (1) Any assets not claimed by creditors will be claimed by equity investors, and (2) the total amount of claims (liabilities + equity) cannot exceed what there is to be claimed. Therefore, the total amount of assets will always be [greater than / equal to / less than] the total amount of liabilities plus equity.

equal to

12-17. Global financial reporting would help to make the qualitative characteristics of comparability easier. Users of financial statements often need to c __ __ __ __ __ e the financial information across many organizations.

compare

12-18. G __ __ __ __ __ __ financial reporting cannot be consistent around the world without a single set of standards. The IFRS attempts to bring together many different sets of standards into a common set of standards.

Global

12-19. If the U.S. systems are more __ __ __ __ __ -based and the IFRS is more __ __ __ __ __ __ __ __ __ __ -based, it will not be easy for all countries to agree on the common set of standards.

rules
principles

12-20. Global financial reporting covers more material than just focusing on the United States. Therefore, students must now learn the basics of both the U.S. system as well as the IFRS. Global financial reporting is also concerned with global economic concepts. Thus, students must study e __ __ __ __ __ __ __ __ s as well as f __ __ __ __ __ __ __ __ __ r __ __ __ __ __ __ __ __ .

economics   financial reporting

12-21. Earlier in the book you learned about T-accounts, the double-entry system, ledgers, and journal entries. Such tools help us to keep the financial records, or books, of the entity. We usually refer to these activities as book__ __ __ __ __ __ __ .

keeping

12-22. In Part 10 you learned about financial statement analysis. Obviously, there's more to accounting than bookkeeping. Financial statement analysis allows us to interpret f __ __ __ __ __ __ __ __ __ s __ __ __ __ __ __ __ __ __ s and give meaning to them.

financial statements

12-23. Global __ __ __ __ __ __ __ __ __ __ reporting should allow us to analyze and c __ __ __ __ __ __ financial statements from different countries. Financial reporting is not only about bookkeeping.

financial
compare

1-18. Here is the balance sheet of Garsden Company, greatly condensed so as to focus on the main elements, and disregarding the thousands:

GARSDEN COMPANY
Balance Sheet as of December 31, 2009
(000 omitted)

Assets		Liabilities & Equity	
Cash	$ 1,449	Liabilities	$12,343
Other Assets	36,790	Equity	25,896
Total	$38,239	Total	$38,239

The total of the left side is $___ , _____ ,000, and the total of the right side is $___ , _____ ,000.

$38,239,000
$38,239,000

1-19. This is another way of saying that total assets must always equal total __ __ __ __ __ __ __ __ __ __ __ __ plus __ __ __ __ __ __ .

liabilities   equity

1-20. The fact that total assets must equal, or **balance,** total liabilities plus equity is why the statement is called a __ __ __ __ __ __ __ __ __ __ __ __ . This equality tells nothing about the entity's financial condition; it always exists unless the accountant has made a mistake.

balance
sheet

1-21. This equality leads to what is called the **dual-aspect concept.** The two aspects to which this concept refers are (1) _____ and (2) _____ plus _____ , and the concept states that these two aspects are always _____ . (In what relation to each other?)

assets
liabilities   equity
equal

1-22. The dual-aspect concept is the first of nine fundamental accounting concepts we shall describe in this program. The concept can be written as an equation, that is, a statement that something is equal to something else. Write this equation, using the words *Assets, Liabilities,* and *Equity:*

_____ = _____ + _____

Assets = Liabilities + Equity

12-11. The underlying assumptions used in the IFRS are similar to what you have already learned. One important difference is that U.S. accounting is __ __ __ __ __ -based whereas the IFRS is __ __ __ __ __ __ __ __ __ __ -based.

rules

principles

12-12. In Part 1 you learned that financial statements are prepared assuming the entity will continue operations in the foreseeable future. (See Frames 1-40 through 1-43.) This concept is called the g __ __ __ __ - c __ __ __ __ __ __ concept.

going-concern

12-13. In Part 4 you learned that transactions are recognized when they occur rather than when cash is received or paid. (See Frames 4-6 through 4-17.) This is called a __ __ __ __ __ l accounting.

accrual

12-14. The underlying assumptions in IFRS are the going-concern and accrual-basis assumptions. Thus, there are [similarities / no connections] to U.S. Generally Accepted Accounting Principles.

similarities

12-15. The IFRS framework describes some qualitative characteristics of financial statements (understandability, relevance, reliability, and comparability). Obviously, an important issue is the ability to c __ __ __ __ __ e financial statements of organizations from different countries. Needless to say, it will be [easy / quite difficult] to be able to achieve this with so many countries in the world.

compare

quite difficult

12-16. When we think of how many countries have financial reporting guidelines, we are thinking of countries around the world, or the g __ __ __ __ . *Sometimes we refer to international reporting as g __ __ __ __ __ reporting.*

globe

global

1-23. Suppose a business had assets totaling $20,000 and liabilities totaling $18,000. Evidently, its equity was $_____.

$2,000 = ($20,000 − $18,000)

Always equal!
The two sides **balance.**

1-24. At the close of business on December 31, 2008, Dowling Company had $2,000 in its bank account. It owned other assets totaling $24,000. The company owed $10,000 to creditors. Its equity was $16,000. Complete the balance sheet for Dowling Company:

DOWLING COMPANY

Balance Sheet as of _____

December 31, 2008

	Assets			Liabilities and Equity	
Cash	$		Liabilities	$	$ 2,000 / $10,000
Other Assets			Equity		24,000 / 16,000
Total	$		Total	$	$26,000 / $26,000

1-25. If Dowling Company prepared a balance sheet as of the beginning of business the next day, January 1, 2009, would it be different from the one you prepared above? [Yes / No]

No (*because nothing changes between the close of business on one day and the beginning of business on the next day*)

1-26. The term "net assets" is sometimes used instead of "equity." It refers to the fact that equity is always the difference between a _____ and l _____. (We shall describe the details in a later part.)

assets

liabilities

NOTE: You will see the term "net assets" instead of "equity" on some balance sheets. We will describe accounting for nonprofit entities later.

12-3. There is a standard set of guidelines in the United States. These guidelines are called **G**enerally **A**ccepted **A**ccounting **P**rinciples. We usually shorten this to __ __ __ __ . GAAP includes the rules, in the form of standards, that accountants follow when they prepare financial statements.

GAAP

12-4. Although the complexity of GAAP is more advanced than this text, it is useful to know that such guiding p __ __ __ __ __ __ __ __ __ s exist.

principles

12-5. Since we follow the guidelines of the U.S. GAAP, [it seems logical / it would not be possible] that other countries have their own versions of __ __ __ __ .

it seems logical

GAAP

12-6. If every country has its own set of guidelines, this would make it [easy / incredibly difficult] to understand the financial statements of other countries.

incredibly difficult

12-7. Many countries have joined together to form a set of accounting standards to make it easier to read and compare f __ __ __ __ __ __ __ __ __ s __ __ __ __ __ __ __ __ __ s.

financial

statements

12-8. IFRS stands for I __ __ __ __ __ __ __ __ __ __ __ __ __ F __ __ __ __ __ __ __ __ R __ __ __ __ __ __ __ __ S __ __ __ __ __ __ __ __ __ . These standards are intended to make it easier for a wide range of users to interpret financial statements.

International Financial Reporting Standards

12-9. The U.S. standards are rules-based. But the IFRS are based on a set of guiding principles. We can conclude that the IFRS are p __ __ __ __ __ __ __ __ __ __ -based.

principles

12-10. The overall framework of the IFRS states that the objective of financial statements should help users to make economic decisions through understanding the f __ __ __ __ __ __ __ __ __ status of an entity.

financial

MONEY-MEASUREMENT CONCEPT

1-27. If a fruit store had $200 in cash, 100 dozen oranges, and 200 apples, could you add up its total assets from this information? [Yes / No]

No (*because you can't add apples and oranges*)

Cash	$200

     100 dozen

     200

—————
Can't add

1-28. To add together objects as different as apples, oranges, automobiles, shoes, cash, supplies, and so on, they must be stated in [different / similar] units.

similar

1-29. Can you add the amounts of apples and oranges if they are stated in terms of money? [Yes / No]

Yes (*You could also add them to get "pieces of fruit," but this is not a useful number for accounting purposes.*)

1-30. The facts that appear in an accounting report are stated in units of money—that is, dollars and cents. This is the **money-measurement concept.** By converting different facts to monetary amounts, we can deal with them [verbally / arithmetically]; that is, we can add one item to another, or we can _____ one item from another.

arithmetically

subtract

1-31. The money-measurement concept states that accounting reports only those facts that can be stated as m __ __ __ __ __ __ __ a __ __ __ __ __ __ .

monetary

amounts

1-32. If facts cannot be expressed in monetary terms, they cannot be reported on a balance sheet. Which of the following facts could be learned by reading a balance sheet of Able Company?

    A. How much cash Able Company has.

    B. The health of the president of Able Company.

    C. How much money Able Company owes.

    D. A strike is beginning at Able Company.

    E. How many automobiles Able Company owns.

A and C (*Not E because the number of automobiles is not a monetary amount.*)

## Part 12

International Financial Reporting Standards (IFRS)

Learning Objectives

In this part you will learn:

- Why we need a set of international standards.
- How the proposed international standards may differ from what you have learned so far in this book.

> **NOTE:** The concepts introduced in this book are basic. They should allow you to understand the nature and use of financial statements. The perspective has been based on U.S. accounting standards. Although it is beyond the introductory nature of this material, we will introduce the emerging role of International Financial Reporting Standards (IFRS) here.

12-1. In this book you have learned many rules that help to define the way financial statements are prepared. This suggests that U.S. accounting is primarily a r __ __ __ __ -based set of standards.

rules

12-2. In almost anything we do, if there is a set of rules, it is clear what we need to do. If there are no formal rules, we must choose what to do based on guidelines or practice. You have learned that some accounting rules may depend on how the accountant applies the rules (FIFO/LIFO accounting, for example). Thus, accounting has both rules and c __ __ __ __ __ __ s. Accounting is definitely not a science.

choices

1-33. Because accounting reports include only facts that can be stated in monetary amounts, accounting is necessarily a(n) [complete / incomplete] record of the status of a business and [does / does not] always give the most important facts about a business.

incomplete

does not

ENTITY CONCEPT

1-34. Accounts are kept for **entities,** rather than for the persons who own, operate, or otherwise are associated with those entities. For example, suppose Green Company is a business entity, and Sue Smith is its owner. Sue Smith withdraws $100 from the business. In preparing financial accounts for Green Company, we should record the effect of this withdrawal on the accounts of [Sue Smith / the entity].

the entity

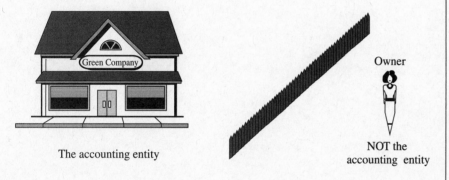

The accounting entity

Owner

NOT the accounting entity

1-35. Sue Smith withdraws $100 from Green Company, of which she is the sole owner. Smith now has $100 more cash, but she has $100 less equity in Green Company. Smith is [better off / worse off / no better or worse off] than she was before.

no better or worse off (*If Smith withdraws $100 from Green Company, of which she is the sole owner, she is just as well off after this withdrawal as before.*)

1-36. What about Green Company? It now has [$100 more / the same amount / $100 less] in assets.

$100 less

1-37. The fact that accounts are kept for entities as distinguished from the persons associated with those entities is called the e __ __ __ __ __ concept.

entity

- The interpretation of ratios is different in nonprofit organizations. Ratios will have meaning only to the extent that both their numerator and denominator are appropriate measurements.

- Nonprofit organizations often have goals that are nonfinancial in nature. We must choose appropriate performance measures to complement the information provided in their financial statements.

You have completed Part 11 of this program. If you think you understand the material in this part, you should now take Post-Test 11, which is found in the back of this text. If you are uncertain about your understanding, you should review Part 11.

The post-test will serve both to test your comprehension and to review the highlights of Part 11. After taking the post-test, you may find that you are unsure about certain points. You should review these points. Please review the answers to Post-Test 11, following the Post-Tests, at the back of this text.

1-38. Owners of some small retail stores (called "mom and pop" stores) may not identify the cost of merchandise they withdraw for personal use, personal telephone calls, and the like. If this is so, then they do not apply the __ __ __ __ __ __ concept. Consequently, the financial statements of these stores are inaccurate.

entity

> **NOTE:** A business may be organized under any one of several legal forms: a corporation, a partnership (two or more owners), or a proprietorship (a single owner). The entity concept applies regardless of the legal status.

1-39. John and Ellen own the John and Ellen Laundry, a partnership. Each takes $1,000 cash from the partnership entity and deposits it into a personal bank account. An accounting report of the financial position of the John and Ellen Laundry would show that:

   A. the change in the entity's equity is zero.

   B. the entity has $2,000 less cash.

   C. the entity has $2,000 less equity.

   D. John and Ellen each have $1,000 more cash.

B and C (*John's and Ellen's personal statements would show that each had $1,000 more cash.*)

> **NOTE:** Municipalities, hospitals, religious organizations, colleges, and other nonprofit or nonbusiness organizations are also accounting entities. Although in this program we focus primarily on businesses, the accounting for nonprofit entities is similar. (We will describe accounting for nonprofit entities later.)

GOING-CONCERN CONCEPT

1-40. Every year some entities go bankrupt or cease to operate. Most entities, however, keep on going from one year to the next. Accounting must assume either that (a) entities are about to cease operations, or (b) they are likely to keep on going. The more realistic assumption for most entities is [(a) / (b)].

(b)

1-41. Accounting assumes that an entity, or **concern,** normally will keep on **going** from one year to the next. This assumption is therefore called the g __ __ __ __ - **concern concept.**

going

11-62. You also learned about the amount of capital tied up in inventory by looking at the inventory turnover ratio. Many nonprofit organizations do not use i _____ in the way that corporations use it. Often the inventory in nonprofits is a supplies inventory rather than a sales inventory. This makes the i _____ t _____ ratio potentially meaningless for performance measurement, too.

inventory

inventory turnover

11-63. A ratio is the relationship between the numerator and the denominator. Before measuring performance by using a r _____, we must ask if both the n __ __ __ __ __ __ __ __ and the d __ __ __ __ __ __ __ __ __ __ have meaning for the analysis we are trying to do. If the answer is no, then another type of p _____ m _____ may be better.

ratio

numerator

denominator

performance

measure

11-64. The financial statements tell only a part of the story about an entity. Since nonprofits have goals that are often nonfinancial in nature, [we can use the same analysis as a for-profit uses / we must develop other measures of performance].

we must develop other measures of performance

KEY POINTS TO REMEMBER

- Some entities have no ownership; we refer to such organizations as nonprofit or not-for-profit organizations.

- Nonprofit organizations have three financial statements, just as for-profit businesses have: the statement of financial position, the statement of activities, and the statement of cash flows.

- Net assets is the portion of the statement of financial position occupied by equity on a balance sheet. The three categories of net assets are unrestricted, temporarily restricted, and permanently restricted.

- Revenues from contributions must be classified as unrestricted, temporarily restricted, or permanently restricted. Revenues from services provided are unrestricted revenues.

- Both realized and unrealized gains on investments are reported as unrestricted revenues.

- Transfers from temporarily restricted funds occur when the funds are used for their specified purpose.

1-42. Specifically, the g __ __ __ __ - c __ __ __ __ __ __ __ concept states that accounting assumes that an entity will continue to operate indefinitely unless there is evidence to the contrary.

going-concern

> **NOTE:** If the entity is not a going concern, special accounting rules apply; they are not discussed in this introductory program.

1-43. Because of the going-concern concept, accounting [does / does not] report what the assets could be sold for if the entity ceases to exist.

does not

> **NOTE:** We next describe the concepts that govern the measurement of asset amounts on the balance sheet. Most monetary assets are reported at their *fair value*, and most nonmonetary assets are reported at an amount that is based on their *cost*. These concepts, and the reasoning behind them, are introduced in this section.

ASSET-MEASUREMENT CONCEPT

1-44. Readers of the balance sheet want to know what the reported assets are worth. In accounting, the name for what an asset is "worth" is its *fair value* (also called *market value*). The Garsden Company balance sheet (Exhibit 1) reported that the company's cash on December 31, 2009, was $1,449,000. This was the f __ __ __ v __ __ __ __ of the asset Cash. We can be reasonably certain that the amount was actually $1,449,000 because the banks in which cash was deposited have reliable records of the amount.

fair value

1-45. Also, we can be reasonably certain that the __ __ __ __ __ __ __ __ __ of marketable securities was $246,000 because a stock exchange publishes a reliable record of the value as of December 31, 2009, for each security that it trades.

fair
value

1-46. In general, an asset is reported at its fair value when reliable information as to its market value is available. Usually, this information is obtained from an outside party. Thus, the concept is: **If reliable information is available, an asset is measured as its __ __ __ __ __ __ __ __ .**

fair
value

11-57. In Exhibit 15b find the amount of the transfer from net assets released from restrictions to unrestricted net assets. The total amount of transfers is $_____, and the net effect of the transfers is [$7,370 / ($7,370) / $0].

$7,370   ($5,995 + $1,375)

$0

11-58. Use the exhibit to show that revenues for the period 2009 increase net assets and expenses decrease net assets. The beginning amount of unrestricted net assets for 2009 is $_____. The total of unrestricted revenues for 2009 is $_____, and the total of unrestricted expenses is $_____. The surplus, or c _____ in n _____ a _____, is $_____. If you add the beginning net assets to the change in net assets, you arrive at the ending unrestricted net assets figure of $_____.

$51,835

$21,804

$16,025   change

net assets $5,779

$57,614

SIMILARITIES

11-59. The financial statements of nonprofit organizations are similar to those of for-profit companies in almost as many ways as they are different. For example, nonprofit organizations are **required** to recognize the c _____ of using up long-lived tangible assets. However, d _____ need not be recognized for certain works of art and historical treasures.

cost   depreciation

11-60. Nonprofit organizations must prepare a statement of cash flows to accompany the statement of f _____ p _____ and the statement of a _____. This statement of cash flows looks very similar to the ones you learned about in Part 9.

financial position

activities

LIMITATIONS OF RATIO ANALYSIS

11-61. In Part 10 you learned to use some tools to measure financial performance. **Equity** investors invest in a business to earn a profit. Non _____ organizations do not have equity investors, so the return on e _____ is [still the best overall measure of performance / somewhat meaningless] for these entities. This does not mean that we should ignore the surplus, or the difference between revenues and expenses.

Nonprofit

equity   somewhat meaningless

1-47. The fair value of most assets is known on the date the asset was acquired because the buyer and the seller agreed on the amount. If Garsden Company purchased a plot of land in 1999 for $100,000, this land would have been reported on its December 31, 1999, balance sheet as $100,000. What was its fair value on December 31, 2009?

    A. $100,000

    B. More than $100,000

    C. Garsden doesn't know.

C *(The fair value may have changed for any number of good reasons.)*

1-48. Because it doesn't know the fair value of the land on December 31, 2009, Garsden would report the amount at $100,000, which was its __ __ __ __ .

cost

1-49. If on December 31, 2009, Garsden owned machinery that it had purchased five years earlier for $50,000 with an estimated life of 10 years, it would probably report the asset amount as [$50,000 / less than $50,000] representing the amount of cost that has not yet been used up. (Calculating this amount involves depreciation, described in Part 7.)

less than $50,000

1-50. In general, land, buildings, equipment, and inventories have this characteristic; their f __ __ __ __ v __ __ __ __ __ cannot be reliably measured except at the time they were acquired. They are reported at __ __ __ __ __ or a number based on cost.

fair value

cost

1-51. The asset-measurement concept combines both types of assets illustrated above. It is: **If reliable information is available, the amount of an asset is measured at its __ __ __ __ __ __ __ __ __ __ . Otherwise the measurement is based on its __ __ __ __ .**

fair value

cost

11-51. To be certain you understand how the transfer process works, re-call the closing process from Part 3. In Part 3 (see Frame 3-62) you learned that [balance sheet / income statement] accounts are temporary accounts and [balance sheet / income statement] accounts are permanent accounts. This will help you to understand how t _____ s work.

income statement

balance sheet

transfers

11-52. You also learned that ultimately revenues [increase / decrease] the equivalent of equity and that expenses [increase / decrease] the equivalent of equity. This, too, will help you to understand how transfers work.

increase

decrease

11-53. Complete the journal entry for a contribution of $5,000 to a non-profit entity in 2009 for a program to take place in 2010.

    Dr. Cash (temporarily restricted) $5,000

        Cr. R _____ s (temporarily restricted) $5,000

Revenues

11-54. Now provide the journal entry to close the temporarily restricted revenue account to net assets at the end of 2009.

Dr. R _____ s (temporarily restricted) .... $_____

    Cr. N _____ A _____ (temporarily restricted) $_____

Revenues $5,000

Net assets $5,000

11-55. In 2010 when the program takes place, the journal entry would be:

Dr. _____ _____ (t_____ r_____) $_____

    Cr. R _____ s (unrestricted) $_____

Net assets (temporarily restricted) $5,000

Revenues $5,000

11-56. At the end of 2010, the un _____ revenues account will close to un _____ n _____ a _____ .

unrestricted

unrestricted net assets

1-52. There are two reasons for measuring some assets at cost. First, estimating fair value of each asset may be expensive and unreliable. If you bought a pair of shoes for $100 in 2008 and asked two friends in 2009 for the shoes' value, they probably would disagree. Even if the estimates were made by professionals, the appraised value of each asset in a company would be [subjective / objective] and [expensive / inexpensive].

subjective *(that is, influenced by personal feelings rather than facts)*
expensive

1-53. Second, many assets are not going to be sold in the near future; they will be used in ongoing operations. The entity and those who use its balance sheet therefore [do / do not] need to know the fair value of these assets. This reason stems from the previous concept, the g _ _ _ _ _ - c _ _ _ _ _ _ _ concept.

do not

going-concern

1-54. To summarize, the two reasons that accounting focuses on costs, rather than on fair values for some assets, are:

1. fair values are difficult to estimate; that is, they are [objective / subjective], whereas costs are [objective / subjective], and

2. the _ _ _ _ _ - _ _ _ _ _ _ _ _ concept makes it unnecessary to know the market value of many assets; we assume the assets will be used in future operations rather than being sold immediately.

subjective
objective
going-concern

1-55. The decision of whether an asset is accounted for at fair value or at cost is usually made at the time the asset is acquired. For example, if a shoe retailer purchased an inventory of shoes for $1,000, they would be accounted for at (or recorded at) $1,000, which was their _ _ _ _ _ . If the retailer expected to sell the shoes for at least $1,500, they would be reported on the balance sheet at [$1,000 / $1,500 / somewhere between $1,000 and $1,500].

cost

$1,000 *(Any higher amount is a subjective opinion.)*

11-45. If the financial statements for Mercer Community Services are typical for nonprofits like Mercer, it is [customary that fees from services make up the majority of unrestricted revenues / customary that alternative sources of revenue make up the majority of unrestricted revenues / too difficult to tell from the information provided].

customary that alternative sources of revenue make up the majority of unrestricted revenues *(If the statements are typical, this would be the case.)*

TRANSFERS

11-46. As you learned earlier, sometimes contributions from donors are recorded in the category of t _____ ly restricted. This means that there is a designated **purpose** for the contribution specified by the d _ _ _ _ _ .

temporarily

donor

11-47. Funds must remain in the temporarily restricted category of n _ _ a _ _ _ _ _ s until the accounting period when they are used for their designated p _ _ _ _ _ _ _ .

net assets

purpose

11-48. As restricted funds are used for their designated purpose, they must be transferred from their holding pattern to the unrestricted category on the statement of activities. This t _ _ _ _ _ _ _ of funds allows the reader to see that the entity has used funds held for a specific purpose.

transfer

11-49. Current operating activities of a nonprofit entity are found in the unrestricted revenues and expenses on the s _____ of a _____ s. Therefore, contributions for activities that are to take place in the future will not be recorded in the unrestricted portion of the statement of activities. Rather, they will stay in the category of temporarily restricted n _ _ a _ _ _ _ _ s until such time as they are used.

statement

activities

net assets

11-50. Although the total amount of net assets will not change as a result of a transfer, the individual categories will change. Evidently the sum total of all t _ _ _ _ _ _ _ _ s must be zero.

transfers

1-56. Monetary assets are those that have a claim on a specified amount of money. Cash, securities, and bonds mentioned earlier are [monetary / nonmonetary] assets. Land, buildings, equipment, and inventory are [monetary / nonmonetary] assets. In general, but with some exceptions described in later parts, **monetary assets are reported at fair value; nonmonetary assets are reported at cost or an amount based on cost.**

monetary

nonmonetary

1-57. Accounting does not report what many of the individual assets are worth, that is, their f __ __ __ v __ __ __ __ . Accounting therefore [does / does not] report what the whole entity is worth. Those who criticize accounting for its failure to report an entity's "worth" do not appreciate that to do so would be difficult, subjective, and usually unnecessary.

fair value
does not

REVIEW OF ACCOUNTING CONCEPTS

1-58. The asset-measurement concept is the fifth of the nine fundamental accounting concepts. The first five are:

1. dual-aspect concept
2. money-measurement concept
3. entity concept
4. going-concern concept
5. asset-measurement concept

The dual-aspect concept is:

__ __ __ __ __ __ __ =

__ __ __ __ __ __ __ __ __ __ __ __ + __ __ __ __ __ __ __ .

Assets =
Liabilities + Equity

The money-measurement concept is:
Accounting reports only facts that can be expressed in m __ __ __ __ __ __ __ __ a __ __ __ __ __ __ __ .

monetary amounts

The entity concept is:
Accounts are kept for e __ __ __ __ __ __ __ __ as distinguished from the p __ __ __ __ __ __ __ who own those entities.

entities

persons

11-39. Sometimes the organization does not sell stocks or bonds that have increased in value but decides to hold them for the future. At the end of each accounting period, the organization must determine the market value of these investments. Although the gain, if there is one, is not realized unless the stock is sold, it must be reported as revenue. This unr _____ ed gain is just as much a part of revenues on the statement of activities as d __ __ __ __ __ __ __ s and i __ __ __ __ __ __ t or other realized g __ __ __ s.

unrealized
dividends
interest   gains

11-40. The financial statements for Mercer Community Services in Exhibits 15a and b are typical of those for a nonprofit organization. Evidently Mercer had investments that provided income and realized and un _____ ed gains.

unrealized

11-41. Also, evidently there were restrictions on some of the investment i __ __ __ __ __ . The income on Mercer's long-term investments was [unrestricted / temporarily restricted / permanently restricted / some of each].

income
some of each

11-42. Mercer apparently had both unr _____ ed and realized g _____ s on its long-term investments. In Exhibit 15b, the total net realized and unrealized gains on all categories of long-term investments is $_____.

unrealized
gains

$7,900,000

11-43. From Exhibit 15b, the total amount of revenue that Mercer received from fees from its services was $_____. This is _____% of the total unrestricted revenues for the period ending June 30, 2009.

$2,700,000
12.4%

11-44. Unrestricted revenues from contributions amounted to _____% of the total unrestricted revenues for the period ending June 30, 2009.

19.8%

The going-concern concept is:

Accounting assumes that an e _ _ _ _ _ will continue to operate | entity

i _ _ _ _ _ _ _ _ _ _ _ _ . | indefinitely

The asset-measurement concept is:

Accounting focuses on the _ _ _ _ _   _ _ _ _ _ _ of monetary | fair value

assets and on the _ _ _ _ of nonmonetary assets. That is, it focuses | cost

on how we measure assets on the balance sheet.

BALANCE SHEET ITEMS

1-59. Refer to Exhibit 1. This is the balance sheet we introduced

earlier. It reports the amounts of a _ _ _ _ _ _ , | assets

l _ _ _ _ _ _ _ _ _ _ _ _ , and e _ _ _ _ _ _ of Garsden | liabilities   equity

Company as of _____ . | December 31, 2009

1-60. Remember that the note "($000 omitted)" means that the numbers

are reported in thousands of dollars. For example, the number reported

for Cash, $1,449, means that the amount of cash was $_____ . | $1,449,000

This is common practice. It is done to make the numbers easier to read;

users are not interested in the details of the last three digits.

1-61. Recall also that the total of the assets always equals the total of the

liabilities plus equity. Total assets were $_____ , and total lia- | $38,239,000

bilities plus equity were $_____ . | $38,239,000

1-62. Most items on a balance sheet are summaries of more detailed ac-

counts. For example, the cash is probably located in a number of separate

bank accounts, in cash registers, and in petty cash boxes. The total of all

the cash is $_____ , rounded to the nearest thousand dollars. | $1,449,000 (*NOT $1,449*)

11-34. This means that in addition to revenues from operating activities and from contributions, revenues from i _ _ _ _ _ _ _ _ _ s will also appear as increases in unrestricted net assets. This can make the interpretation of the financial statements of a nonprofit organization very challenging.

investments

11-35. The investment portion of an organization's assets derived from donations is called an endowment. An endowment can earn a return for the organization in several different ways. Funds invested in bonds or put into a bank earn i _ _ _ _ _ _ _ t. Interest income is thus a source of revenue from an endowment.

interest

11-36. Unless the use of interest earned is restricted, it will be reported as r _____ in the statement of a _ _ _ _ _ _ _ _ _ s.

revenue   activities

11-37. Funds may also be invested in stocks of private entities. Recall from earlier parts that some companies pay dividends to shareholders. Although a nonprofit organization does not have s _____ s or owners, it can own stock in another company as an investment. D _____ s earned from stock investments will also be reported as r _____ in the statement of activities, according to accounting regulations.

shareholders

Dividends

revenues

11-38. Investments may be made in stocks that don't pay d _ _ _ _ _ _ _ _ s or in bonds that don't pay i _ _ _ _ _ _ _ t. Investors hope that such investments will result in higher stock or bond prices at some time in the future.

dividends   interest

ASSETS

1-63. Assets are valuable resources. Let's make this idea more specific. In order to count as an __ __ __ __ __ in accounting, an item must pass three tests.

asset

1-64. The first requirement is that the item must be **controlled** by the entity. Usually this means that the entity must **own** the item. If Able Company rents a building owned by Baker Company, this building [is / is not] an asset of Able Company. The building [is / is not] an asset of Baker Company.

is not

is

NOTE: Certain leased items, called capital leases, are assets and are an exception to this rule. They are described in Part 7.

An asset   Not an asset

1-65. In accounting, the employees of an entity are not assets because the entity does not _____ them. However, if a baseball club owns a contract in which a player agrees to provide services, the contract [is / is not] an asset.

own

is (*The asset is the contract, not the player, and it is an asset only if it passes the third test, in Frame 1-67.*)

1-66. The second requirement is that the item must be **valuable** to the entity. Which of these would qualify as assets of a company that sells dresses?

 A. The company's right to collect amounts owed by customers.

A, B, and D

 B. Regular dresses held for sale.

 C. Dresses that no one wants because they have gone out of style.

 D. A cash register in working condition.

 E. A cash register that doesn't work and can't be repaired.

11-29. If a donor imposes a r __ __ __ __ __ __ __ __ __ __ __ n on a contribution, the revenue from that contribution will ultimately increase t _____ r _____ed net assets or p _____ r _____ed net assets.

restriction

temporarily restricted   permanently restricted

11-30. Since revenues from services provided and revenues from contributions (with no restrictions) can both be considered un _____, both types of revenues will appear together on a statement of unrestricted activities.

unrestricted

NOTE: The classification of revenues and expenses within the three categories of net assets does not preclude the organization from incorporating additional classifications or explanations within a statement of activities. For example, within a category of net assets, the nonprofit organization may distinguish between operating and nonoperating items.

11-31. Some contributions do not qualify as revenues. For example, contributions of works of art, historical treasures, and similar assets need not be recognized as r _____ s if the donated items are added to collections held for public exhibition, education, or research to further public service rather than financial gain.

revenues

11-32. Apparently, the accounting for many transactions for nonprofit organizations [is straightforward and easy / is more complex than for-profit accounting].

is more complex than for-profit accounting

11-33. Some nonprofits have funds invested in a way that will provide dividend, interest, or noncash returns. According to accounting regulations for nonprofit organizations, the gains and losses on such investments must be reported as increases or d _____ in unrestricted net assets unless their use is temporarily or permanently restricted by the donor or by the law.

decreases

1-67. The third requirement is that the item must have been acquired at a **measurable cost.** Jones Company bought a trademark from another company for $1 million; this trademark [is / is not] an asset of Jones Company.

is

1-68. By contrast, if Jones Company has built up an excellent reputation because of the consistently high quality of its products, this reputation [is / is not] an asset in accounting, even though it may be worth many millions of dollars.

is not

1-69. To summarize, for an item to be listed as an asset, it must meet three requirements:

1. It must be __ __ __ ed or c __ __ __ __ __ __ __ __ ed by the entity;

    owned   controlled

2. It must be v __ __ __ __ __ __ __ __ to the entity; and

    valuable

3. It must have been acquired at a m __ __ __ __ __ __ __ __ __
   c __ __ __ .

    measurable

    cost

NOTE: Assets are divided into two main categories—current and noncurrent—and liabilities also are divided into these categories. They are introduced in the following section and explained in more detail in Part 2.

1-70. Current assets are cash and other assets that are expected to be converted into cash or used up in the near future, usually within one year. Groceries on the shelves of a grocery store [are / are not] current assets. The store building [is / is not] a c __ __ __ __ __ __ __ a __ __ __ __ __ . On the balance sheet, current assets are usually reported separately from noncurrent assets. They are expected to be converted to cash within a year.

are

is not   current asset

PLEASE DON'T PEEK: If you look at the answer before writing your response, you will lose much of the educational value.

1-71. Current assets consist of c __ __ __ __ and of assets that are expected to be converted into c __ __ __ __ or used up within a short period, usually within _____ _____ (how long?).

cash

cash

one year

1-72. As the name suggests, assets that are expected to be useful for longer than one future year are called [current / noncurrent] assets.

noncurrent

11-24. The classification of net assets is thus either r _____ or
u _____ , depending on the intentions of the d __ __ __ __ __ .

restricted

unrestricted   donor

> **NOTE:** It is important to understand the intentions of donors because they
> affect how organizations can subsequently use funds. There are more com-
> plications with respect to the classification of net assets that go beyond the
> scope of this introductory text.

REVENUES, EXPENSES, AND INVESTMENTS

11-25. Revenues are realized for nonprofits in much the same way as
they are in corporations. Remember the r _____ concept,
which states that r __ __ __ __ __ __ __ is recognized when goods and
services are [paid for / delivered]. So when a nonprofit organization
provides services, it recognizes the revenue associated with the service
provided.

realization

revenue

delivered

11-26. The distinction between a revenue and an inflow of c __ __ __ is
treated much the same way as it would be in a corporation. If services are
provided in 2009 but are not paid until 2010, the revenue is recognized in
[2009 / 2010] in keeping with the realization concept. When this happens, the account called a _____ r _____ is debited
in 2009 with the accompanying credit to sales revenue.

cash

2009
accounts receivable

11-27. Revenues from contributions are different from revenues earned
on services provided. Recall that all revenues ultimately increase net
assets (similar to their role in increasing equity in a corporation). In a
nonprofit, revenues are considered i _____ in unrestricted
n _____ a _____ unless the use of the assets received is limited to a specific purpose.

increases

net assets

11-28. Similarly, expenses are considered d _____ in unrestricted net assets.

decreases

LIABILITIES

1-73. The right-hand side of the Garsden Company balance sheet lists the company's liabilities and equity. These can be regarded either as c _ _ _ _ _ against the assets or as the s _ _ _ _ _ _ from which the assets were acquired. The claims of creditors and other outside parties are called l _ _ _ _ _ _ _ _ _ _ .

claims   sources

liabilities

1-74. In Exhibit 1, the first category of liabilities is _____ liabilities. As you might expect from the discussion of current assets, current liabilities are claims that become due within a [short / long] time, usually within _____ _____ (how long?).

current

short
one year

1-75. As we have seen, Garsden Company has obtained funds by borrowing, and $_____ of this debt is not due to be repaid until after December 31, _____. This amount is therefore a [current / noncurrent] liability.

$2,000,000
2010
noncurrent

1-76. Liabilities are claims against all the assets. The $5,602,000 of accounts payable on the Garsden Company balance sheet is a claim against [the current assets of $22,651,000 / the total assets of $38,239,000].

the total assets of $38,239,000

CURRENT RATIO

1-77. The current assets and current liabilities indicate the entity's ability to meet its current obligations. A measure of this ability is the **current ratio,** which is the ratio of **current** assets to **current** liabilities. For Garsden Company, the current ratio is:

$$\frac{\text{current assets}}{\text{current liabilities}} = \frac{\$ \boxed{}}{\$ \boxed{}} = \boxed{}^* \text{ to } 1$$

$$\frac{\$22,651,000}{\$\ 9,519,000} = 2.4 \text{ to } 1$$

_____
* Carry this amount to one decimal place.

11-18. Sometimes assets are donated for specific uses in a designated accounting period. Once used for the special purpose for which they were intended, they are no longer available. Thus, for the temporary period when they are not being used, the organization may invest them. These assets are called t _ _ _ _ _ _ _ _ _ ly restricted assets.

temporarily

11-19. U _ _ _ _ _ _ _ _ _ _ _ _ ed net assets are those that result from profitable operating activities or from donations with no r _____ s.

Unrestricted

restrictions

11-20. There are many examples of assets in each of the three categories. If a donor gave land to an organization to use as part of ongoing operations, this donation would fit into the category of [permanently restricted / temporarily restricted / unrestricted] net assets because the purpose of the donation would be for the permanent future operations of the organization.

permanently restricted

11-21. Likewise, the donation of works of art to a museum would be considered permanently restricted n _____ a _____.

net assets

11-22. The donation of funds for a specific program to take place in May 2010, however, would fit into the category of [permanently restricted / temporarily restricted / unrestricted] net assets because the funds [would continue to be available indefinitely / would be used up after the program ended]. Until May 2010, however, the funds should not be used for other purposes.

temporarily restricted

would be used up after the program ended

11-23. If you receive a phone call from someone asking you to donate funds to your college and you agree to do so, those funds would probably fit into the category of [permanently restricted / temporarily restricted / unrestricted] net assets. Unless you specify that your donation is to be saved for a specific purpose, or saved indefinitely and invested for a monetary return, it would show on the statement of financial position in the category u _____ n _____ a _____.

unrestricted

unrestricted net assets

1-78. In Garsden's industry, a current ratio of at least 2 to 1 is desirable. Garsden Company [does / does not] pass this test.

does

EQUITY

1-79. Equity consists of capital obtained from sources that are not liabilities. As Exhibit 1 indicates, there are two sources of equity capital: (1) $12,256,000, which is labeled Total _____ - _____ _____ and (2) $13,640,000, which is labeled _____ _____.

Paid-in

Capital   Retained

Earnings

1-80. Paid-in capital is the amount of capital supplied by equity investors. They own the entity. The details of how this item is reported depends on the type of organization. Garsden Company is a corporation, and its owners receive *shares* of common _____ as evidence of their ownership. They are therefore called s __ __ __ __ holders. Other forms of ownership will be described in Part 8.

stock

share (or stockholders)

1-81. The paid-in capital is reported as two separate amounts: $1,000,000, which is labeled _____ _____, and $11,256,000, labeled Additional _____ - _____ _____. The reasons for this distinction are described in Part 8. The important number is the total amount paid in by the shareholders, which is $_____.

Common Stock

Paid-in Capital

$12,256,000

1-82. Individual shareholders may sell their stock to someone else, but this has no effect on the balance sheet of the corporation. The market price of shares of Apple, Inc. stock changes almost every day; the amount of paid-in capital reported on the Apple, Inc. balance sheet [does / does not] reflect these changes. This is consistent with the e __ __ __ __ __ __ concept; transactions between individual shareholders do not affect the entity.

does not

entity

1-83. The other equity item, $13,640,000, shows the amount of equity that has been *earned* by the profitable operations of the company and that has been *retained* in the entity; hence the name, R __ __ __ __ __ __ __ __ E __ __ __ __ __ __ __ __ .

Retained

Earnings

11-13. Nonprofit organizations are [the same as / very different from] corporations with respect to their purpose or m _ _ _ _ _ n. If we seek to measure their performance using only the monetary amounts, we would neglect important aspects of their mission and goals. Therefore, the f _____ s _____ limit the information we have for measuring performance to those that can be expressed in m _ _ _ _ _ _ _ _ amounts.

	very different from
	mission
	financial statements
	monetary

11-14. Some of a nonprofit's g _ _ _ _ s can be measured by using financial statement information. For nonprofits, however, the surplus is not always an appropriate m _____. Performance measures need to be tied to goals and therefore [are the same / are likely to be different] for nonprofit organizations.

	goals
	measure
	are likely to be different

> **NOTE:** Tools like the Balanced Scorecard have been developed to help focus on many more perspectives related to a company's performance than the financial perspective. We will not explore the Balanced Scorecard in this introductory text.

NET ASSETS

11-15. One important difference in a balance sheet or statement of financial position of a nonprofit is the term n _ _ assets. This term represents the portion of the statement that is occupied by e _____ in a corporation.

	net
	equity

11-16. Net assets are classified based on the existence or absence of restrictions imposed by those who provide the funds. Three types of net assets must be reported on a statement of financial position for a nonprofit entity. The types are distinguished according to the level of **restriction** imposed on them by donors. The three types are:

1. permanently r _ _ _ _ _ _ _ _ ed net assets
2. temporarily restricted n _____ a _____
3. unr _ _ _ _ _ _ _ _ ed net assets

	restricted
	net assets
	unrestricted

11-17. Some assets are donated so that they are maintained **permanently** by an institution rather than used up. Usually the donors allow the institution to use income generated from investing these assets. While the income can support general operating activities, the assets themselves cannot be spent. Such assets fit into the category of p _ _ _ _ _ _ _ _ _ ly restricted net assets.

	permanently

1-84. Retained earnings represents those amounts that have been retained in the entity after part of the company's earnings (i.e., profits) have been paid to shareholders in the form of dividends. Complete the following equation:

Retained Earnings = [ ] – [ ] .

Earnings – Dividends

1-85. Retained earnings are additions to equity that have accumulated since the entity began, not those of a single year. Therefore, unless Garsden Company has been in business only one year, the $13,640,000 shown as Retained Earnings as of December 31, 2009, reflects [one / all previous] year(s) of operations.

all previous

1-86. The amount of retained earnings shows the amount of capital generated by operating activities. It is **not** cash. Cash is an asset. On December 31, 2009, the amount of Cash was $_____. The amount of retained earnings was $_____.

$1,449,000

$13,640,000

1-87. Always keep in mind the fundamental accounting equation:

[ ] = [ ] + [ ] .

Assets = Liabilities + Equity

The right-hand side of the balance sheet shows the *sources* of capital. The capital itself exists in the form of __ __ __ __ __ __ , which are reported on the left-hand side.

assets

KEY POINTS TO REMEMBER

- The assets of an entity are the things of value that it owns.

- The sources of funds used to acquire assets are:

    1. liabilities and
    2. equity.

- Liabilities are sources from creditors.

11-8. Nonprofit entities also have three basic financial statements. The status report for a nonprofit is similar to the [income statement / balance sheet] and is called a s _ _ _ _ _ _ _ _ t of financial position. The flow report is similar to the [income statement / balance sheet] and is called a statement of activities. The third statement, called a s _ _ _ _ _ _ _ _ _ t of c _ _ _ _ _ _ f _ _ _ _ _ _ _ s, has the same name in a nonprofit entity.

balance sheet
statement
income statement

statement cash flows

11-9. Just like the b _ _ _ _ _ _ _ s _ _ _ _ _ _, the statement of financial position reports amounts for the organization's a _ _ _ _ _ _, l _ _ _ _ _ _ _ _ _ _ _ _, and equivalent of e _ _ _ _ _ _. Since there is no equity or ownership in a nonprofit, this last term is the **net difference** between the assets and the liabilities and is called n _ _ a _ _ _ _ _ _.

balance sheet

assets liabilities

equity

net assets

11-10. In a corporation, the operating **expenses** (or activities) portrayed on the income statement cause equity to increase or decrease. Similarly, in a nonprofit, the statement of a _ _ _ _ _ _ _ _ _ s causes changes in net assets.

activities

11-11. Finally, a nonprofit entity reports the change in its **cash** and cash equivalents in a [balance sheet / income statement / statement of cash flows].

statement of cash flows

DIFFERENT MISSIONS AND GOALS

11-12. A primary goal of a corporation is to earn a p _ _ _ _ _ _. The financial statement that measures this best is the [balance sheet / income statement / statement of cash flows.] You learned earlier that a good analysis must incorporate information from [the income statement alone / the balance sheet and the income statement / all three financial statements] because all of the financial statements together provide information on different aspects of financial performance.

profit
income statement

all three financial statements

- Equity consists of (1) funds obtained from equity investors, who are owners, and (2) retained earnings, which result from the entity's profitable operation.

- Creditors have a strong claim on the assets. They can sue if the amounts due them are not paid. Equity investors have only a residual claim.

- Total assets equal the total of liabilities plus equity. This is the dual-aspect concept.

- The amounts of assets, liabilities, and equity as of one point in time are reported on the entity's balance sheet.

- Accounting reports only those facts that can be stated in monetary amounts. This is the money-measurement concept.

- Business accounts are kept for entities, rather than for the persons who own, operate, or otherwise are associated with those entities. This is the entity concept.

- Accounting assumes that an entity will continue to operate indefinitely. This is the going-concern concept.

- Monetary assets are reported at their fair value; other assets are reported at a number based on cost. This is the asset-measurement concept.

- Assets are valuable items that are owned or controlled by the entity and that were acquired at a measurable cost. Goodwill is not an asset unless it was purchased.

- Current assets are cash and other assets that are expected to be converted into cash or used up in the near future, usually within one year.

- Current liabilities are obligations due in the near future, usually within one year.

- The current ratio is the ratio of current assets to current liabilities.

- Equity consists of paid-in capital (which in a corporation is represented by shares of stock) plus earnings retained since the entity began. It does not report the market value of the stock. Retained earnings is not cash; it is part of the owners' claim on the assets.

You have completed Part 1 of this program. If you think you understand the material in this part, you should now take Post-Test 1, which is found at the back of this text. If you are uncertain about your understanding, you should review Part 1.

The post-test will serve both to test your comprehension and to review the highlights of Part 1. After taking the post-test, you may find that you are unsure about certain points. You should review these points before going on to Part 2. Please review the answers to Post-Test 1, following the Post-Tests, at the back of this text.

11-3. Some examples of organizations with no **ownership** are museums, hospitals, colleges and universities, private schools, research organizations, churches and synagogues, cultural organizations, foundations, social service organizations, and advocacy groups. Although these organizations may be very different from one another, they all share one common trait. They do not have shareholders or o __ __ __ __ s.

owners

11-4. Nonprofit organizations are also exempt from paying taxes in most states. The regulations to determine nonprofit status may differ from state to state. To qualify as a n __ __ __ __ __ __ __ __ t organization, application must be made to the governing body in the state in which the organization resides.

nonprofit

11-5. In Part 2 you learned that the terms "profit," "earnings," and "income" all have the same meaning. They refer to the **excess** of r __ __ __ __ __ __ s over e __ __ __ __ __ __ s. Nonprofit organizations can have the equivalent of profitable operations however. To simplify, for nonprofit entities we often just use the term "surplus," or e __ __ __ __ __ of revenues less expenses.

revenues   expenses

excess

11-6. Remember that the Equity section of the balance sheet reports the amount of capital that the for-profit entity has obtained from two different sources:

1. The amount paid in by the owner(s), which is called P _____ - _____ C _____.

Paid-
in Capital

2. The amount of income that has been retained in the entity, which is called R _____ E _____.

Retained Earnings

11-7. Since no dividends are paid in nonprofit organizations, the retained earnings are equal to the accumulated s __ __ __ __ __ __ __ s. Some nonprofit organizations do receive contributions from persons outside the entity. They are not called **paid-in capital** but are indeed sources of c _____.

surpluses

capital

## Part 2

Balance Sheet Changes; Income Measurement

Learning Objectives

In this part you will learn:

- The meaning of the principal items reported on a balance sheet.
- How several types of transactions change the amounts reported on the balance sheet.
- The nature of income and the income statement.

NOTE: Assets are divided into two main categories—current and noncurrent—and liabilities also are divided into these categories. They are explained in the following section.

CURRENT ASSETS

2-1. Current assets are cash and other assets that are expected to be converted into cash or used up in the near future, usually within __ __ __ __ __ __ __ __ .

one
year

2-2. Securities are stocks and bonds. They give valuable rights to the entity that owns them. The U.S. Treasury promises to pay stated amounts of money to entities that own treasury bonds. Therefore, U.S. Treasury Bonds owned by Garsden Company [are / are not] assets of Garsden Company.

are

## Part 11

Nonprofit Financial Statements

Learning Objectives

In this part you will learn:

• The nature of nonprofit or not-for-profit organizations.

• How financial statements of nonprofit organizations are different.

• How equity differs from net assets.

• Why ratio analysis for nonprofits may be different.

NONPROFIT ORGANIZATIONS

11-1. In earlier parts you learned that when revenues are greater than expenses, the result of such **profitable** operations is net i _ _ _ _ _ _   income
or p _ _ _ _ _ _ . You learned also that the Equity section of the balance sheet reports the amount of capital that the entity has obtained from   profit
its shareholders or o _ _ _ _ _ s, as well as the income that has been re-   owners
tained in the account called r _ _ _ _ _ _ _ d e _ _ _ _ _ _ _ s.   retained earnings

11-2. Some entities have no ownership. Such entities do not obtain capital from shareholders and do not pay d _ _ _ _ _ _ _ _ . These entities   dividends
are called nonprofit or not-for-p _ _ _ _ _ _ organizations. For our   profit
purposes, both of these terms have the same meaning.

2-3. Marketable securities are securities that are expected to be converted into cash within a year. An entity owns these securities so as to earn a return on funds that otherwise would be idle. Marketable securities are [current / noncurrent] assets.

current

> **NOTE:** Investments in safe, very short-term funds, such as money market funds, are often included in the cash item rather than in marketable securities. The item is then called "cash and cash equivalents."

2-4. An **account receivable** is an amount that is owed to the business, usually by one of its customers, as a result of the ordinary extension of credit. A customer's monthly bill from the electric company would be an a __ __ __ __ __ __ __ r __ __ __ __ __ __ __ __ __ __ of the electric company until the customer paid the bill.

account receivable

2-5. Inventories are goods being held for sale, as well as supplies, raw materials, and partially finished products that will be sold upon completion. For example, a truck owned by an automobile dealer for resale to its customers [is / is not] inventory. A truck owned by an entity and used to transport its own goods [is / is not] inventory.

is

is not

2-6. In Exhibit 1 the inventories of Garsden Company are reported as $_____.

$10,623,000

2-7. An entity's burglar alarm system is valuable because it provides protection against loss. The burglar alarm system is an asset. Would a fire insurance policy that protects the entity against losses caused by fire damage also be an asset? [Yes / No]

Yes

2-8. Entities buy fire insurance protection ahead of the period that the insurance policy covers. When they buy the insurance policy, they have acquired an a __ __ __ __ __ . Because the policy covers only a short period of time, the asset is a [current / noncurrent] asset. Insurance protection can't be touched. It is an **intangible** asset.

asset

current

KEY POINTS TO REMEMBER

- The financial statements do not tell the whole story about an entity because they report only past events, do not report market values, and are based on judgments and estimates. Nevertheless, they provide important information.

- Financial statements are analyzed by using ratios, rather than absolute dollar amounts. These ratios are compared with those for the same entity in the past, with those for similar entities, or with standards based on judgment.

- An overall measure of performance is return on equity (ROE). It takes into account both profitability and the capital used in generating profits. Another overall measure is return on permanent capital, or return on investment, which is the ratio of profits (adjusted for interest and taxes) to total permanent capital.

- An entity with a low profit margin can provide a good return on equity investment if it has a sufficiently high capital turnover.

- In addition to information about profitability, financial statements provide information about the entity's liquidity and solvency.

- ROE can be broken down into three distinct components. This is the DuPont ratio analysis.

- Quality of earnings analysis helps investors and analysts to identify "red flags" or warnings. This type of analysis is often used to determine the riskiness of stocks. It goes beyond a simpler and more usual financial performance analysis.

- The Sarbanes-Oxley Act of 2002 (SOX) is complex and detailed. In essence it is a law designed to increase disclosure of all material events that could affect financial reporting. Furthermore it defines unethical and unlawful behavior that could give rise to criminal and civil penalties.

You have completed Part 10 of this program. If you think you understand the material in this part, you should now take Post-Test 10, which is at the back of this text. If you are uncertain about your understanding, you should review Part 10.

The post-test will serve both to test your comprehension and to review the highlights of Part 10. After taking the post-test, you may find that you are unsure about certain points. You should review these points before going on to Part 11. Please review the answers to Post-Test 10, following the Post-Tests, at the back of this text.

2-9. Prepaid expenses is the name for intangible assets that will be used up in the near future; that is, they are intangible [current / noncurrent] assets. (The reason for using the word "expense" will be explained in Part 5.) Exhibit 1 shows that Garsden Company had $_____ of prepaid expenses on December 31, 2009.

current

$389,000

NONCURRENT ASSETS

2-10. Tangible assets are assets that can be touched; they have physical substance. Buildings, trucks, and machines are t __ __ __ __ __ __ __ assets. They are also [current / noncurrent] assets.

tangible

noncurrent

2-11. As indicated by the first item listed under Noncurrent Assets in Exhibit 1, the usual name for tangible, noncurrent assets is _____, _____, and _____. Because they are noncurrent, we know that these assets are expected to be used in the entity for more than _____ _____ (how long?).

Property   Plant   Equipment

one year

2-12. Exhibit 1 shows the [cost / market value] of property, plant, and equipment to be $26,946,000. It shows that a portion of the cost of this asset has been subtracted from the original cost because it has been "used up." This "used-up" portion is labeled _____ _____ and totals $_____.

cost

Accumulated

Depreciation $13,534,000

2-13. After this amount is subtracted, the asset amount is shown as $_____. This is the amount of cost that [has / has not] been used up. (In Part 7, we shall explain this amount further.)

$13,412,000   has not

2-14. The other noncurrent asset items are **intangible assets**; that is, they have no physical substance, except as pieces of paper. The Investments item consists of securities, such as bonds. Evidently Garsden Company does not intend to turn these investments into cash within _____ _____ (how long?). If these securities were expected to be turned into cash within that period, they would be listed as a current asset, M __ __ __ __ __ __ __ __ __ __ S __ __ __ __ __ __ __ __ __ __ .

one

year

Marketable Securities

10-118. Simply put, Sarbanes-Oxley addresses the following:

- Establishment of a Public Company Accounting Oversight Board (PCAOB) under the SEC to oversee public accounting firms and issue accounting standards
- New standards for corporate boards of directors
- New standards for accountability and criminal penalties for corporate management
- New independence standards for external auditors

With new standards and rules set by the PCAOB we can be confident of [more detailed / less detailed] annual reports from public companies. Such reports will include a focus on internal controls and ethical behaviors for financial officers. One can hope that SOX will help to increase public c__ __ __ __ __ __ __ __ __ .

> more detailed
>
> confidence

10-119. "Whistle blowers" are those who have publicly exposed undesirable or unlawful behavior by companies. This term comes from the notion that blowing a whistle calls attention to something. SOX also provides extended w__ __ __ __ __ __ b__ __ __ __ __ protection to employees who disclose private information about their employers as long as those disclosures are within the law.

> whistle blower

> **NOTE:** While nonprofit organizations are currently not required to adhere to the majority of SOX regulations, they must comply with regulations related to document destruction and whistle blower protection. Many nonprofit organizations are starting to implement policies that follow the spirit of SOX.

10-120. SOX has also made it a crime to destroy or conceal documents that might be used in official proceedings. Presumably company officials will now be discouraged from such behavior. Because such tampering is a c__ __ __ __ __ __ __ __ activity, penalties and jail may be the result.

> criminal

10-121. In summary, SOX has provided the oversight and structure to encourage annual reports that are [easier to read / more comprehensive and detailed]. In so doing the new law requires the behavior and disclosure on the part of management to increase public confidence and t__ __ __ __ __ .

> trust

2-15. The next noncurrent asset reported is titled **Patents and Trademarks.** These are rights to use patents and rights to valuable brand names or logos (such as "ADVIL"). Because they are assets, we know that

1. they are v __ __ __ __ __ __ __ ,   valuable
2. they are o __ __ __ __ by Garsden Company, and   owned
3. they were acquired at a measurable c __ __ __ .   cost

2-16. Goodwill, the final item on the asset side, has a special meaning in accounting. It arises when one company buys another company and pays more than the value of its net identifiable assets. Grady Company bought Baker Company, paying $1,400,000 cash. Baker Company's identifiable assets were judged to be worth $1,500,000, and Grady became responsible for Baker's liabilities, which totaled $500,000. Complete the following calculation:

Baker's identifiable assets	$ _____	$1,500,000
less liabilities	_____	$500,000
Net identifiable assets	_____	$1,000,000
Grady paid Baker	$ 1,400,000	
Therefore, goodwill was	_____	$400,000

CURRENT LIABILITIES

2-17. In Exhibit 1, the first category of liabilities is _____ liabilities. As you might expect from the discussion of current assets, current liabilities are claims that become due within a [short / long] time, usually within _____ _____ (how long?).

current

short
one year

2-18. The first current liability listed in Exhibit 1 is _____ _____. These are the opposite of Accounts Receivable; that is, they are amounts that [the company owes to its suppliers / are owed to the company by its customers].

Accounts
Payable

the company owes to its suppliers

10-113. Sarbanes-Oxley is a law passed in _____ to strengthen corporate governance and restore investor confidence. The law is complex. It specifies corporate responsibilities and criminal penalties for noncompliance with the standards. Company management and boards of directors must now be familiar with the details of SOX.

2002

10-114. The Sarbanes-Oxley Act was an enormous change to federal securities laws in the United States. It came in response to the collapse of Enron (and other companies) and the related accounting scandal by Enron's auditor, Arthur Andersen. Public companies are now required to submit annual reports of their internal accounting controls to the Securities and Exchange Commission (SEC). Evidently, company management and boards of directors must now be familiar with the details of the S_____-O_____ Act (SOX).

Sarbanes-Oxley

10-115. All companies should be concerned about **governance** (authority and control). Since SOX generally affects only publicly traded companies, it is about corporate g_____. SOX affects U.S. companies as well as foreign companies operating in the U_____ S_____.

governance

United States

10-116. The Sarbanes-Oxley Act is detailed and technical. Most issues related to **compliance** are well beyond the introductory nature of this book. However, there are some general areas related to SOX that we will examine. Since SOX is **law** it is critical that companies know how to conform or make their operations c_____.

compliant

10-117. The costs of noncompliance may be great. They may include both civil and criminal penalties. Since managers concerned with **internal** operations are not generally experts in SOX compliance, they often hire e_____ consultants to help identify areas of potential noncompliance. Evidently those who are experts in SOX must understand both the a_____ issues and the l_____ ones.

external

accounting   legal

2-19. In December 2008, Green Company sold a personal computer to Brown Company for $3,000. Brown Company agreed to pay for it within 60 days. On their December 31, 2008, balance sheets, Green Company would report the $3,000 as Accounts [Receivable / Payable] and Brown Company would report the $3,000 as Accounts [Receivable / Payable].

Receivable

Payable

2-20. The next item, titled: **Bank Loan Payable,** is reported separately from Accounts Payable because the debt is evidenced by a promissory n __ __ __ . Which statement is true?

note

A. Garsden owes the bank $1,000,000.
B. Garsden will pay the bank $1,000,000.
C. Both A and B are true.

A (*Although most liabilities will be paid, the balance sheet does not promise this.*)

NOTE: Amounts owed to employees and others for services they have provided but for which they have not been paid are listed as **Accrued Liabilities.** They will be described in Part 5.

2-21. Estimated Tax Liability is the amount owed to the government for taxes. It is shown separately from other liabilities, both because the amount is large and also because the exact amount owed may not be known as of the date of the balance sheet. In Exhibit 1 this amount is shown as $_____. It is a current liability because the amount is due within _____ _____ (how long?).

$1,541,000

one year

2-22. Two items under **Long-term Debt** are shown as liabilities. One, labeled "current portion," amounts to $_____. The other, listed under noncurrent liabilities, amounts to $_____. Evidently, the total amount of long-term debt is $_____.

$500,000

$2,000,000

$2,500,000

2-23. The $500,000 is shown separately as a current liability because it is due within _____ _____ (how soon?), that is, before December 31, _____. The remaining $2,000,000 does not become due until after December 31, _____.

one year

2010

2010

10-110. You learned that financial statements tell only a part of the story of a company. **Red flags** or warnings about a company's financial condition that might not show in a typical ratio analysis might be detected in a q_ _ _ _ _ _ _   o_   e_ _ _ _ _ _ _ _ analysis. Warning signals are often identified early in the analysis to help direct the focus of the analysis. Thus, one reason for thinking about a company's quality of earnings is to detect r_ _ _   f_ _ _ _ _ . While detecting red flags is useful for investors and analysts, this process is very subjective. It is usually the [final step / the beginning of a more detailed] analysis.

quality of earnings

red flags

the beginning of a more detailed

10-111. Quality-related red flags should not be ignored. They may suggest potential problems not indicated by a more typical r_ _ _ _ analysis. This means that investors and analysts must understand fully the accounting practices as well as the nature and behavior of financial statement items to be able to detect red flags.

ratio

10-112. Below are some typical quality-related **red flags.** Indicate for each whether you would look at the balance sheet, income statement, neither, or both to detect the red flag.

	Balance Sheet	Income Statement	Both	Neither
A. An unusually long audit report or one that indicates a change in auditors				
B. An increase in Accounts Receivable not consistent with the past				
C. A one-time source of income				
D. An increase in borrowing				
E. A slowdown of the inventory turnover rate				

A. Neither *(because the audit report covers all three financial statements [balance sheet, income statement and statement, of cash flows] and might indicate disagreement between the auditor and management)*
B. Balance sheet *(because the company might encourage sales by allowing customers more time to pay)*
C. Income statement *(because the company might be encouraged to sell an asset to increase its profits)*
D. Balance sheet *(because the company might be having problems financing its activities from internally generated funds)*
E. Both *(because sales, inventory, or production problems might be developing)*

NOTE: If you are unclear about any of these items, please review the earlier parts of this chapter related to ratios and their interpretation.

THE SARBANES-OXLEY ACT OF 2002

NOTE: Most of us heard about the collapse of Enron Corporation and related accounting scandals. However, even experienced financial analysts were unable to forecast these events through an examination of the financial statements of companies like Enron. The American Competitive and Corporate Accountability Act of 2002, commonly known as the Sarbanes-Oxley Act (SOX), was passed into law in the wake of corporate financial scandals. Its primary purpose was to strengthen corporate governance and rebuild trust in the corporate sector.

NONCURRENT LIABILITIES

2-24. Suppose the $500,000 current portion was paid in 2010, and an additional $600,000 of debt became due in 2011. On the balance sheet as of December 31, 2010, the current portion of long-term debt would be reported as $_____, and the noncurrent liability would be reduced to $_____.

$600,000

$1,400,000

> **NOTE:** Although a single **liability** may have both a current portion and a noncurrent portion, a single asset is not always so divided. Prepaid Insurance of $2,000, covering protection for two future years, is usually reported as a current asset of $2,000.

> **NOTE:** The other noncurrent liability, Deferred Income Taxes, will be described in Part 7.

EQUITY

2-25. Recall that equity consists of capital obtained from sources that are not liabilities. The two sources of equity capital for Garsden Company are total _____ - _____ _____ and _____ _____.

paid-in capital

retained earnings

2-26. Recall also that the amount of equity that has been *earned* by the profitable operations of the company and that has been *retained* in the entity is called _____ _____.

retained earnings

BALANCE SHEET CHANGES

2-27. The amounts of assets, liabilities, and equity of an entity [remain constant / change from day to day]. Therefore, the amounts shown on its balance sheet also [remain constant / change].

change from day to day

change

2-28. Although a balance sheet must be prepared at the end of each year, it can be prepared more often. In this part, you will be asked to prepare a balance sheet at the end of each day. We shall consider a business named Evergreen Market, owned by a proprietor, Steve Smith. The **entity** here is [Steve Smith / Evergreen Market].

Evergreen Market

> **NOTE:** Evergreen Market is a proprietorship with a single owner. We can refer to it as a sole proprietorship. **Proprietorships** don't have retained earnings. Equity is represented simply as **Capital.**

10-109. Use the exhibits below to indicate whether you think the earnings would be considered high or low.

    A. Consistent and conservative accounting policies:

	High-Quality Earnings	Low-Quality Earnings
FIFO and straight-line depreciation		
LIFO and accelerated depreciation		

A. Low/High *(because LIFO and accelerated depreciation result in lower earnings)*

    B. Net income (earnings) from recurring activities:

	High-Quality Earnings	Low-Quality Earnings
Earnings from activities other than the company's basic business activity		
Earnings from the ongoing fundamental business of the company		

B. Low/High *(because net income is not indicative of future earnings and is not predictable)*

    C. Sales resulting in timely cash inflows:

	High-Quality Earnings	Low-Quality Earnings
Revenues received in cash at the time (or near) of sale		
Revenues that stay in Accounts Receivable for long periods of time		

C. High/Low *(because of earnings that are not potentially distributable in cash are not what most investors seek)*

    D. Appropriate debt and capital structure levels:

	High-Quality Earnings	Low-Quality Earnings
Increasing levels of debt relative to equity		
Debt levels consistent with the industry and ability of the company to meet its obligations		

D. Low/High *(because higher debt may mean it will be more difficult to obtain additional debt financing in the future or the interest rate will likely be higher than the present debt)*

    E. Stable and predictable earnings:

	High-Quality Earnings	Low-Quality Earnings
Current and recent earnings that are good indicators of future earnings streams		
Current and recent earnings that fluctuate, are from foreign operations, or are from extraordinary events		

E. High/Low *(because investors want to be more certain of future earnings rather than to anticipate surprises)*

2-29. On January 2, Smith started Evergreen Market by opening a bank account in its name and depositing $10,000 of his money in it. In the assets column of the following balance sheet, enter the amount of cash that Evergreen Market owned at the close of business on January 2.

EVERGREEN MARKET
Balance Sheet as of January 2

Assets	Liabilities & Equity
Cash . . . . $	

$10,000

2-30. Cash is money on hand and money in bank accounts that can be withdrawn at any time. On January 2, if Steve Smith deposited $8,500 in the bank instead of $10,000 and kept $1,500 in the cash register, its cash at the close of business on January 2 would be _____.

$10,000

2-31. Recall that a name for equity capital is "paid-in capital" in a corporation. Since Evergreen Market is a sole proprietorship, record this in the space below as of the close of business on January 2.

EVERGREEN MARKET
Balance Sheet as of January 2

Assets	Liabilities & Equity
Cash $10,000	Smith, _____ . . $

Smith, Capital $10,000

2-32. This balance sheet tells us how much cash [Evergreen Market / Steve Smith] had on January 2. The separation of Evergreen Market from Steve Smith, the person, is an illustration of the e __ __ __ __ __ concept.

Evergreen Market

entity

> **NOTE:** An entity owned by one person, such as Evergreen Market, is called a **proprietorship.** In proprietorships, the equity item is labeled with the proprietor's name: "Steve Smith, Capital." This is simply a variation in terminology from that of a corporation, not a difference in concepts.

10-104. You have learned that not all revenues are received in c_ _ _ at the time of a sale. You have also learned that not all expenses are paid out in c_ _ _ at the time they are incurred. Therefore, net income [is / is not] necessarily a good indicator of c_ _ _ earnings.

cash

cash   is not
cash

10-105. Investors often equate "real earnings" with those that generate **cash** from year to year. For these investors r_ _ _ e_ _ _ _ _ _ _ may be more important than n_ _ i_ _ _ _ _ when determining profitability.

real
earnings   net
income

10-106. You have also learned that the statement of cash flows indicates cash flow from o_ _ _ _ _ _ _ _ _ activities, from i_ _ _ _ _ _ _ _ _ activities and from f_ _ _ _ _ _ _ _ _ activities. Investors think of **real earnings** as normal, recurring operating activities that generate _ _ _ _ . Obviously the statement of c_ _ _ f_ _ _ _ is a(n) [extremely useful / somewhat unnecessary] part of financial statement analysis.

operating
investing   financing

cash
cash flows   extremely useful

10-107. Since investors and analysts look for different things in their analyses, there are no commonly agreed-upon standards for a q_ _ _ _ _ _ of e_ _ _ _ _ _ _ _ analysis. Some of the ratios you calculated earlier may be part of a quality of earnings analysis.

quality of earnings

10-108. Some of the characteristics of companies with high quality of earnings are:
   A. Consistent and conservative accounting p_ _ _ _ _ _ _ _

policies

   B. Net income (earnings) from recurring rather than one-time e_ _ _ _ _ _

events

   C. Sales revenues that result in cash i_ _ _ _ _ _ _ sooner rather than later

inflows

   D. Debt that is appropriate for the business, capital s_ _ _ _ _ _ _ _ _ _ , and industry

structure

   E. Earnings that are stable, predictable, and indicative of future e_ _ _ _ _ _ _ _ levels.

earnings

2-33. On January 2, Evergreen Market received $10,000 cash from Steve Smith. To record the effect of this event on the financial condition of the entity, you made _____ (how many?) changes in the balance sheet. After you made these changes, the balance sheet [did / did not] balance. This is an illustration of the d __ __ __ - a __ __ __ __ __ concept.

two

did

dual-aspect

2-34. A total should always be given for each side of the balance sheet. Complete the following balance sheet.

BROWN COMPANY
Balance Sheet as of June 30, 2008

Assets		Liabilities & Equity	
Cash	$50,000	Accounts Payable	$10,000
		Brown, Capital	40,000

	$		$

Total $50,000 Total $50,000

2-35. The totals of the above balance sheet [are equal by coincidence / are necessarily equal].

are necessarily equal

2-36. Amounts on a balance sheet are generally listed with the most current items first. Correct the following list to make it in accord with this practice.

Liabilities (as of December 31, 2008):

Bank Loan Payable (due next October)

Accounts Payable (due in 60 days)

Long-term Debt

Accounts Payable

Bank Loan Payable

Long-term Debt

2-37. When an entity borrows money, it may sign a written promise to repay. Such a written promise is termed a **note.** For example, if Business A borrows money from Business B, signing a note, Business A will record a [note receivable / note payable] on its balance sheet, and Business B will record a [note receivable / note payable].

note payable

note receivable

10-99. Information found in the financial statements has limitations. Sometimes investors want to dig deeper to evaluate the **quality** of a company's net income (earnings) or other reported financial data. A q＿＿＿＿＿＿ of e＿＿＿＿＿＿＿＿ analysis typically allows an analyst to evaluate performance in a more comprehensive way than simple ratio analysis.

quality   earnings

10-100. Typically, ratio analysis involves the use of accounting data as reported. Since accountants have choices when preparing financial statements, the data presented could look different if different c＿＿＿＿＿＿ had been made. To evaluate the q＿＿＿＿＿＿ of a company's earnings, analysts often make adjustments to the reported numbers. This does not mean that the reported numbers are incorrect!

choices   quality

10-101. Golden Company's net income might be exactly the same as Silver Company's net income. Golden Company's revenues and expenses might all come from regular and recurring business activities. Silver Company's revenues might come partially from a one-time event not expected to happen again in the future. An analyst would likely say that Golden Company's earnings are a [higher / lower] quality than Silver Company's earnings.

higher

10-102. Evergreen Company turns its revenues into cash inflows within 30 days on a regular basis. River Company allows its customers to buy on credit and they typically don't collect these accounts receivable for many months. The current ratios of both companies might be identical. Investors are likely to say that River Company's current assets are of a [higher / lower] quality than Evergreen's.

lower

10-103. Analysts and investors use indicators other than the performance ratios described earlier to evaluate the quality of a company's reported earnings. Not all analysts define q＿＿＿＿＿＿ of earnings in the same way. Therefore a quality of earnings analysis is [an exact science / a very subjective process].

quality
a very subjective process

2-38. On January 3, Evergreen Market borrowed $5,000 cash from a bank, giving a note therefor.

Change the following January 2 balance sheet so that it reports the financial condition on January 3. In making your changes, cross out any material to be changed and write the corrections like this:

15,000

~~10,000~~

EVERGREEN MARKET
Balance Sheet as of January 2

Assets		Liabilities & Equity	
		.... $	
Cash $10,000		Smith, Capital $10,000	
Total $10,000		Total $10,000	

EVERGREEN MARKET 3
Balance Sheet as of January ~~2~~

Assets		Liabilities & Equity	
		Note payable $5,000	
Cash ...... **15,000** ~~$10,000~~		Smith, Capital $10,000	
Total ..... ~~$10,000~~ **15,000**		Total .... ~~$10,000~~ **15,000**	

2-39. To record the effect of the event of January 3, you made _____ (how many?) change(s) to the balance sheet (not counting the new totals and the new date) that were necessary. The change(s) [did / did not] affect the equality that had existed between assets and liabilities + equity.

two

did not

2-40. On January 4, Evergreen Market purchased and received inventory costing $2,000, paying cash.

Change the following January 3 balance sheet so that it reports the financial condition on January 4. Strike out any items that must be changed, and write the corrections above (or below) them.

EVERGREEN MARKET
Balance Sheet as of January 3

Assets		Liabilities & Equity	
Cash $15,000		Note Payable .... $ 5,000	
....		Smith, Capital 10,000	
		Total $15,000	

EVERGREEN MARKET 4
Balance Sheet as of January ~~3~~

Assets		Liabilities & Equity	
Cash .:..... **13,000** ~~$15,000~~		Note Payable .... $ 5,000	
Inventory $2,000		Smith, Capital 10,000	
Total $15,000		Total $15,000	

10-96. In summary, the DuPont system of ratios breaks the __ __ __ down into _____ (how many?) parts.

p_____ m_____

a_____ t_____

f_____ l_____

ROE

3

profit margin

asset turnover

financial leverage

10-97. Profit margin measures_____efficiency.

Asset turnover measures_____ _____efficiency.

The equity multiplier measures_____ _____.

Together these are the components of __ __ __.

operating

asset use

financial leverage

ROE

10-98. Financial analysts form their opinions about a company partly by studying ratios such as those we have presented. They also study the details of the financial statements, including the notes that accompany these statements. They obtain additional information by conversations and visits because they realize that the financial statements tell [only part of the / the whole] story about the company.

only part of the

> **NOTE:** Any of dozens of other ratios may be used for various purposes in analyzing the profitability and financial condition of a business. Those described here are the ones in most general use. Others give a more detailed picture of the important relationships.

QUALITY OF EARNINGS

> **NOTE: Quality of earnings** is a term used most often by investors or analysts interested in evaluating a stock, a set of securities, or even just the financial statements of a company. It involves analysis that goes beyond the ratio analysis introduced earlier in this chapter.

2-41. The event of January 4 required two changes on the balance sheet, even though [only one / both] side(s) of the balance sheet was (were) affected.

only one

2-42. Each event that is recorded in the accounting records is called a **transaction.** When Evergreen Market received $10,000 from Steve Smith and deposited it in its bank account, this qualified as a _____ under the definition given earlier because it was "an event that was

__ __ __ __ __ __ __ __ in the __ __ __ __ __ __ __ __ __ __ __

__ __ __ __ __ __ __."

transaction

recorded   accounting

records

2-43. Each transaction you recorded has caused at least _____ (how many?) change(s) on the balance sheet (not counting the changes in the totals and in the date), even when only one side of the balance sheet was affected. This is true of all transactions, and this is why accounting is called a [single / double / triple]-entry system.

two

double

2-44. Earlier we described the fundamental accounting equation, assets = liabilities + equity. If we were to record only *one* aspect of a transaction, this equation [would / would not] continue to describe an equality.

would not

2-45. The fundamental accounting equation, which is _____ = _____ + _____, was also referred to in Part 1 as the d__ __ __ -aspect concept.

assets

liabilities   equity

dual

NOTE: When a business sells merchandise for $300 that had cost it $200, the profit of $100 represents an increase of $100 in equity. As we saw in Part 1, the Retained Earnings item is used to record changes in equity arising from the operation of the business. These facts will help you in analyzing the transactions that follow.

10-90. Now consider Black Company and Blue Company. Calculate the ROE for each company.

Black Company	Blue Company
Profit margin = 2%	Profit margin = 20%
Asset turnover = 6.25	Asset turnover = .625
Leverage ratio = 2.0	Leverage ratio = 2.0

Black Company's ROE = 25%

Blue Company's ROE = 25%

10-91. Black Company and Blue Company have [exactly the same / very different] profit margin and asset turnover ratios. They have [exactly the same / very different] ROEs.

very different

exactly the same

10-92. Black Company has a [higher / lower] profit margin than Blue Company. Blue Company has a [higher / lower] asset turnover than Black Company. But they have the same __ __ __.

lower

lower

ROE

10-93. You can see that there are _____ (how many?) components that give rise to the calculation of ROE?

3

10-94. Without the use of debt (the equity multiplier or the leverage ratio), Black Company and Blue Company's ROE would be:

$$\text{Profit Margin} \times \text{Asset Turnover} =$$

12.5%   12.5%

(Note that both companies have the same ROE but they achieve it in very different ways.)

10-95. We can see that by using leverage, a company can generate a higher return on equity, but with greater risk for the investor. This suggests that there is a tradeoff between r_____ and r_____.

risk   return

(In either order)

NOTE: The risk/return tradeoff is more complex than what is presented here. However, this should serve as a basic introduction to what would be covered on this subject in a finance course.

2-46. On January 5, Evergreen Market sold merchandise for $300, receiving cash. The merchandise had cost $200.

Change the following January 4 balance sheet so that it reports the financial condition on January 5. (If you cannot do this frame, skip to the next without looking at the answer to this one.)

EVERGREEN MARKET
Balance Sheet as of January 4

Assets		Liabilities & Equity	
Cash	$13,000	Note Payable	$ 5,000
Inventory	2,000	Smith, Capital	10,000
		[ ] ... [ ]	
Total	$15,000	Total	$15,000

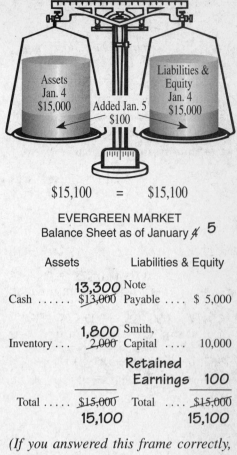

$15,100 = $15,100

EVERGREEN MARKET
Balance Sheet as of January ~~4~~ 5

Assets		Liabilities & Equity	
Cash	**13,300** ~~$13,000~~	Note Payable	$ 5,000
Inventory	**1,800** ~~2,000~~	Smith, Capital	10,000
		Retained Earnings	**100**
Total	~~$15,000~~ **15,100**	Total	~~$15,000~~ **15,100**

(If you answered this frame correctly, skip to Frame 2-53.)

2-47. On January 5, Evergreen Market sold merchandise for $300 cash that cost $200.

To record this transaction, let's handle its individual parts separately. Change the date. Then, record only the amount of cash after the receipt of the $300. (Disregard, for the moment, any other changes, including changes in totals.)

EVERGREEN MARKET
Balance Sheet as of January 4

Assets		Liabilities & Equity	
Cash	$13,000	Note Payable	$ 5,000
Inventory	2,000	Smith, Capital	10,000
Total	$15,000	Total	$15,000

EVERGREEN MARKET
Balance Sheet as of January ~~4~~ 5

Assets		Liabilities & Equity	
Cash	**13,300** ~~$13,000~~	Note Payable	$ 5,000
Inventory	2,000	Smith, Capital	10,000
Total	$15,000	Total	$15,000

10-85. The DuPont system of ratios allows us to separate the components of the return on e _____. Fill in the blanks below to show how this works and enter the numerator and denominator for each on lines 14–16 of Exhibit 14.

equity

Profit Margin $\times$ Asset Turnover $\times$ Equity Multiplier = ___ ___ ___

$$\frac{\rule{2cm}{0.4pt}}{\rule{2cm}{0.4pt}} \times \frac{\rule{2cm}{0.4pt}}{\rule{2cm}{0.4pt}} \times \frac{\rule{2cm}{0.4pt}}{\rule{2cm}{0.4pt}} = \frac{\text{Net Income/}}{\text{Equity}}$$

ROE

Net Income/Sales Revenue

Sales Revenue/Assets

Assets/Equity

10-86. It is easy to see that two companies may achieve the same ___ ___ ___ in very different ways. Some ways are more attractive to investors for different reasons. A company with a lot of debt, for example, is [riskier than / not as risky as] a company with little or no debt.

ROE

riskier than

10-87. A highly leveraged company is one with high levels of d __ __ __. Generally speaking, such a company poses more r_____ to investors because of the potential to go bankrupt if it cannot pay back the debt.

debt

risk

10-88. Sam Company has the following financial data:

Sales Revenues	$55,000
Net Income	$8,000
Assets	$50,000
Equity	$25,000

Use the three components to arrive at ROE.

Profit Margin $\times$ Asset Turnover $\times$ Equity Multiplier = ROE

Profit Margin = Net Income ÷ Sales Revenue = $8,000 ÷ $55,000 = 14.5%

Asset Turnover = Sales Revenue ÷ Assets = $55,000 ÷ $50,000 = 1.1

Equity Multiplier = Assets ÷ Equity = $50,000 ÷ $25,000 = 2.0

ROE = 32%

10-89. What if Sam Company had no debt? The ROE would then be:

14.5% $\times$ 1.1 = 16%

(Note that while the profit margin is usually expressed as a percent, the asset turnover and equity multiplier are usually presented as a number. In this case, Sam Company turns its assets over, on average, 1.1 times in the accounting period.)

2-48. On January 5, Evergreen Market sold merchandise for $300 cash that cost $200. Merchandise that had cost $200 was removed from its inventory.

Record the amount of inventory after this transaction.

EVERGREEN MARKET
Balance Sheet as of January ~~4~~ 5

Assets		Liabilities & Equity	
	13,300		
Cash	~~$13,000~~	Note Payable	$ 5,000
Inventory	2,000	Smith, Capital	10,000
Total	$15,000	Total	$15,000

EVERGREEN MARKET
Balance Sheet as of January ~~4~~ 5

Assets		Liabilities & Equity	
	13,300	Note	
Cash	~~$13,000~~	Payable	$ 5,000
	1,800	Smith,	
Inventory	~~2,000~~	Capital	10,000
Total	$15,000	Total	$15,000

2-49. On January 5, Evergreen Market sold merchandise for $300 cash that cost $200.

Now total the assets as of the close of business on January 5, and show the new total.

EVERGREEN MARKET
Balance Sheet as of January ~~4~~ 5

Assets		Liabilities & Equity	
	13,300		
Cash	~~$13,000~~	Note Payable	$ 5,000
	1,800		
Inventory	~~2,000~~	Smith, Capital	10,000
Total	$15,000	Total	$15,000

EVERGREEN MARKET
Balance Sheet as of January ~~4~~ 5

Assets		Liabilities & Equity	
	13,300	Note	
Cash	~~$13,000~~	Payable	$ 5,000
	1,800	Smith,	
Inventory	~~2,000~~	Capital	10,000
Total	~~$15,000~~ **15,100**	Total	$15,000

2-50. On January 5, Evergreen Market sold merchandise for $300 cash that cost $200.

EVERGREEN MARKET
Balance Sheet as of January ~~4~~ 5

Assets		Liabilities & Equity	
	13,300		
Cash	~~$13,000~~	Note Payable	$ 5,000
	1,800		
Inventory	~~2,000~~	Smith, Capital	10,000
Total	~~$15,000~~ **15,100**	Total	$15,000

Evidently the transaction of January 5 caused a net [decrease / increase] of $_____ in the assets of Evergreen Market from what they had been at the close of business on January 4.

increase

$100

10-79. The leverage ratio is Assets ÷ Equity. What is the leverage ratio for Page Company?

$$\frac{\underline{\hspace{2cm}}}{\underline{\hspace{2cm}}} =$$

100/100 = 1

10-80. In a company with no liabilities (no debt), the leverage ratio will always be 1 because Total a_____ is equal to Total l_____ and E_____.

assets   liabilities

Equity

10-81. Now consider that Page Company has taken out a loan. Here is its new balance sheet.

Page Company

Assets - $200   Liabilities = $100
                                       Equity   = $100
_____   _____

200   200

 Total Assets =   Total Liabilities and Equity =

10-82. The leverage ratio is now:

$$\frac{\underline{\hspace{2cm}}}{\underline{\hspace{2cm}}} =$$

200/100 = 2

10-83. Evidently, as an organization takes on debt its leverage ratio [increases / decreases]. With zero debt the leverage ratio can never be lower than _____. This means that even a small amount of debt will make the leverage ratio greater than _____.

1

1

10-84. It is possible for a company with low efficiency ratios to increase its ROE by taking on debt. This works by breaking down the ROE into three components and multiplying the impact of debt on ROE. Thus, the leverage ratio is sometimes called the equity m __ __ __ __ __ __ __ __r.

multiplier

2-51. On January 5, Evergreen Market sold merchandise for $300 that cost $200. The assets of the entity increased by $100. The increase was the result of selling merchandise at a profit. As we learned in Part 1, profitable operations result in an increase in equity, specifically in the item R _____ E _____.

Retained Earnings

> **NOTE:** In most proprietorships, the Retained Earnings account will simply be included in the capital account. We show it separately here for learning purposes.

2-52. On January 5, Evergreen Market sold merchandise for $300 that cost $200. Add $100 of Retained Earnings and show the new total of the right-hand side.

EVERGREEN MARKET
Balance Sheet as of January ~~4~~ 5

Assets		Liabilities & Equity	
	13,300		
Cash	~~$13,000~~	Note Payable	$ 5,000
	1,800		
Inventory	~~2,000~~	Smith, Capital	10,000
Total	~~$15,000~~ 15,100	Total	$15,000

EVERGREEN MARKET
Balance Sheet as of January ~~4~~ 5

Assets		Liabilities & Equity	
	13,300	Note	
Cash	~~$13,000~~	Payable	$ 5,000
	1,800	Smith,	
Inventory	~~2,000~~	Capital	10,000
		Retained Earnings	**100**
Total	~~$15,000~~ 15,100	Total	~~$15,000~~ 15,100

2-53. On January 6, Evergreen Market purchased merchandise for $2,000 and added it to its inventory. It agreed to pay the vendor within 30 days.

Change the following January 5 balance sheet so that it reports the financial condition on January 6. Recall that an obligation to pay a vendor is called an "Account Payable." Be sure to change the totals.

EVERGREEN MARKET
Balance Sheet as of January 5

Assets		Liabilities & Equity	
			$
Cash	$13,300		
Inventory	1,800	Note Payable	5,000
		Smith, Capital	10,000
		Retained Earnings	100
Total	$15,100	Total	$15,100

EVERGREEN MARKET
Balance Sheet as of January ~~5~~ 6

Assets		Liabilities & Equity	
		Accounts Payable	**$2,000**
Cash	$13,300		
	3,800	Note	
Inventory	~~1,800~~	Payable	5,000
		Smith, Capital	10,000
		Retained Earnings	100
Total	~~$15,100~~ 17,100	Total	~~$15,100~~ 17,100

In the next frame we will see another way to arrive at the ROE. It is called the **DuPont Identity** or **DuPont Analysis,** developed by the DuPont Company many years ago.

10-75. In Frame 10-26 we looked at the profit margin. Recall that the profit margin is:

_____ _____

_____

_____ _____

Net Income ÷ Sales Revenue

The profit margin helps to measure operating efficiency.

10-76. We might also be interested in other efficiencies, such as the use of a company's assets. The **asset turnover ratio** measures how effectively a company uses assets to generate sales revenues. Thus, the asset turnover ratio is:

S _____ R _____

Sales Revenue

_____

A _____

Assets

10-77. Both the profit margin and the asset turnover ratios are efficiency ratios. They measure o _____ efficiency and a _____ u ___ efficiency.

operating

asset   use

10-78. The financial leverage ratio is a measure of how much debt (leverage) a company has relative to the rest of the balance sheet. Consider the following example.

Page Company

Assets = $100	Liabilities = 0
	Equity = $100
_____	_____
Total Assets =	Total Liabilities and Equity =

100   100

2-54. On January 7, merchandise costing $500 was sold for $800, which was received in cash.

Change the following January 6 balance sheet so that it reports the financial condition on January 7.

EVERGREEN MARKET
Balance Sheet as of January 6

Assets		Liabilities & Equity	
Cash	$13,300	Accounts Payable	$ 2,000
Inventory	3,800	Note Payable	5,000
		Smith, Capital	10,000
		Retained Earnings	100
Total	$17,100	Total	$17,100

EVERGREEN MARKET
Balance Sheet as of January ~~6~~ 7

Assets		Liabilities & Equity	
Cash	**14,100** ~~$13,300~~	Accounts Payable	$ 2,000
Inventory	**3,300** ~~3,800~~	Note Payable	5,000
		Smith, Capital	10,000
		Retained Earnings	**400** ~~100~~
Total	~~$17,100~~ **17,400**	Total	~~$17,100~~ **17,400**

2-55. On January 8, merchandise costing $600 was sold for $900. The customer agreed to pay $900 within 30 days. (Recall that when customers buy on credit, the entity has an asset called "Accounts Receivable.")

Change the following January 7 balance sheet so that it reports the financial condition on January 8.

EVERGREEN MARKET
Balance Sheet as of January 7

Assets		Liabilities & Equity	
Cash	$14,100	Accounts Payable	$ 2,000
	...	Note Payable	5,000
Inventory	3,300	Smith, Capital	10,000
		Retained Earnings	400
Total	$17,400	Total	$17,400

EVERGREEN MARKET
Balance Sheet as of January ~~7~~ 8

Assets		Liabilities & Equity	
Cash	$14,100	Accounts Payable	$ 2,000
Accounts Receivable 900		Note Payable	5,000
Inventory	**2,700** ~~3,300~~	Smith, Capital	10,000
		Retained Earnings	**700** ~~400~~
Total	~~$17,400~~ **17,700**	Total	~~$17,400~~ **17,700**

10-70. The return on permanent capital is the same in both companies, as you can see for yourself in the following calculation.

	EBIT margin	× Capital turnover	= Return on permanent capital	
Supermarket	0._____	× _____ times	= _____ %	$0.04 \times 10 = 40\%$
Electronics store	0._____	× _____ times	= _____ %	$0.20 \times 2 = 40\%$

TESTS OF FINANCIAL CONDITION

> **NOTE:** A business must be concerned with more than profitability. It must also maintain a sound financial condition. This means that it must be able to pay its debts when they come due.

10-71. Ability to meet current obligations is called **liquidity.** The ratio of current assets to current liabilities, called the _____ ratio, is a widely used measure of liquidity.

current

10-72. Solvency measures the entity's ability to meet all its obligations when they come due. If a high proportion of permanent capital is obtained from debt, rather than from equity, this increases the danger of insolvency. The proportion of debt is indicated by the d __ __ __ r __ __ __ __ __ .

debt ratio

DUPONT ANALYSIS

10-73. As you learned earlier, the return on e__ __ __ __ __ __ is an important measure of an organization's success. One of the primary uses of ratio analysis is to compare organizations. But two organizations with the same R __ __ may not really be the same.

equity

ROE

10-74. Do you remember the ROE formula?

_____ _____

_____

_____

Net Income ÷ Equity

2-56. On January 9, Evergreen Market purchased a one-year insurance policy for $200, paying cash. (Recall that the right to insurance protection is an asset. For this asset, use the term "Prepaid Insurance.")

Change the following January 8 balance sheet so that it reports the financial condition on January 9.

EVERGREEN MARKET
Balance Sheet as of January 8

Assets		Liabilities & Equity	
Cash	$14,100	Accounts Payable	$ 2,000
Accounts Receivable	900	Note Payable	5,000
Inventory	2,700	Smith, Capital	10,000
		Retained Earnings	700
Total	$17,700	Total	$17,700

EVERGREEN MARKET
Balance Sheet as of January 8̶ 9

Assets		Liabilities & Equity	
Cash ...... **13,900** $~~14,100~~		Accounts Payable	$ 2,000
Accounts Receivable .	900	Note Payable	5,000
Inventory ...	2,700	Smith, Capital	10,000
Pre-paid Insurance	**200**	Retained Earnings ...	700
Total	$17,700	Total	$17,700

2-57. On January 10, Evergreen Market purchased two lots of land of equal size for a total of $10,000. It thereby acquired an asset, land. It paid $2,000 in cash and gave a 10-year mortgage for the balance of $8,000. (Use the term "Mortgage Payable" for the liability.)

Change the following January 9 balance sheet so that it reports the financial condition on January 10.

EVERGREEN MARKET
Balance Sheet as of January 9

Assets		Liabilities & Equity	
Cash	$13,900	Accounts Payable	$ 2,000
Accounts Receivable	900	Note Payable	5,000
Inventory	2,700	Smith, Capital	10,000
Prepaid Insurance	200	Retained Earnings	700
Total	$17,700	Total	$17,700

EVERGREEN MARKET
Balance Sheet as of January 8̶ 10

Assets		Liabilities & Equity	
Cash ...... **11,900** $~~13,900~~		Accounts Payable	$ 2,000
Accounts Receivable ..	900	Note Payable	5,000
Inventory ...	2,700	**Mortgage Payable**	**8,000**
Prepaid Insurance ..	200	Smith, Capital	10,000
Land	**10,000**	Retained Earnings ...	700
Total ..... $~~17,700~~ **25,700**		Total .... $~~17,700~~ **25,700**	

10-68. For example, consider the following results for a supermarket and an electronics store, each with $10 million of sales revenue.

	Supermarket	Electronics
	(000 omitted)	
Sales revenue	$10,000	$10,000
EBIT	400	2,000
Permanent capital	1,000	5,000

The EBIT margin for the supermarket is only

$$\frac{\$\boxed{}}{\$\boxed{}} = \underline{}\%$$

$$\frac{\$400}{\$10,000} = 4\%$$

and for the electronics store it is

$$\frac{\$\boxed{}}{\$\boxed{}} = \underline{}\%$$

$$\frac{\$2,000}{\$10,000} = 20\%$$

The ratio for the electronics store is much [lower / higher].

higher

10-69. However, the electronics store has more expensive fixtures, a larger inventory, and a lower inventory turnover than the supermarket, so its capital turnover is lower. Calculate the capital turnover of each.

	Sales	÷ Permanent Capital	= Capital turnover	
Supermarket	$_____	÷ $_____	= _____ times	$10,000 ÷ $1,000 = 10 times
Electronics store	$_____	÷ $_____	= _____ times	$10,000 ÷ $5,000 = 2 times

2-58. On January 11, Evergreen Market sold one of the two lots of land for $5,000. The buyer paid $1,000 cash and assumed $4,000 of the mortgage; that is, Evergreen Market was no longer responsible for this half of the mortgage payable.

Change the following January 10 balance sheet so that it reports the financial condition on January 11.

EVERGREEN MARKET
Balance Sheet as of January 10

Assets		Liabilities & Equity	
Cash	$11,900	Accounts Payable	$ 2,000
Accounts Receivable	900	Note Payable	5,000
Inventory	2,700	Mortgage Payable	8,000
Prepaid Insurance	200	Smith, Capital	10,000
Land	10,000	Retained Earnings	700
Total	$25,700	Total	$25,700

EVERGREEN MARKET
Balance Sheet as of January ~~10~~ 11

Assets		Liabilities & Equity	
Cash	**12,900** ~~$11,900~~	Accounts Payable	$ 2,000
Accounts Receivable ..	900	Note Payable	5,000
Inventory ...	2,700	Mortgage Payable	**4,000** ~~8,000~~
Prepaid Insurance ..	200	Smith, Capital	10,000
Land	**5,000** ~~10,000~~	Retained Earnings ...	700
Total	~~$25,700~~ **21,700**	Total	~~$25,700~~ **21,700**

2-59. On January 12, Smith received an offer of $15,000 for his equity in Evergreen Market. Although his equity was then only $10,700, he rejected the offer. This means that the store had already acquired goodwill with a market value of $4,300.

What changes, if any, should be made in the January 11 balance sheet so that it reports the financial condition on January 12? _____

_____

The balance sheet is unchanged from that of January 11, except for the date. In accordance with the asset measurement concept, goodwill is an asset only when it has been paid for. The balance sheet does not usually show the *fair value* of the entity.

10-64. Another way of finding the return on permanent capital is to multiply the EBIT margin ratio by the capital turnover. Calculate this relationship.

EBIT margin (Frame 10-59)	×	Capital turnover (Frame 10-62)	=	Return on permanent capital
[ ] %	×	[ ]	=	[ ] %

$14\% \times 1.8 = 25\%$

10-65. This formula suggests two fundamental ways in which the profitability of a business can be improved:

1. [Increase / Decrease] the EBIT margin ratio.

2. [Increase / Decrease] the capital turnover.

Increase

Increase (*If you had difficulty in following these relationships, try some numbers of your own.*)

COMMENTS ON PROFITABILITY MEASUREMENT

10-66. In the previous analysis, we used ratios because absolute dollar amounts are [rarely / often] useful in understanding what has happened in a business.

rarely

10-67. Also, we focused on *both* income and the capital used in earning that income. Focusing on just one of these elements can be [just as good / misleading].

misleading

2-60. On January 13, Smith withdrew for his personal use $200 cash from the Evergreen Market bank account, and he also withdrew merchandise costing $400.

Change the following January 12 balance sheet so that it shows the financial condition on January 13.

EVERGREEN MARKET
Balance Sheet as of January 12

Assets		Liabilities & Equity	
Cash	$12,900	Accounts Payable	$ 2,000
Accounts Receivable	900	Note Payable	5,000
Inventory	2,700	Mortgage Payable	4,000
Prepaid Insurance	200	Smith, Capital	10,000
Land	5,000	Retained Earnings	700
Total	$21,700	Total	$21,700

> **NOTE:** In corporations, withdrawals are recorded in an account called "Dividends." We will discuss this later.

2-61. On January 14, Smith learned that the person who purchased the land on January 11 for $5,000, sold it for $8,000. The lot still owned by Evergreen Market was identical in value with this other plot.

What changes, if any, should be made in the January 13 balance sheet so that it reports the financial condition on January 14? _____

_____

EVERGREEN MARKET
Balance Sheet as of January ~~12~~ 13

Assets		Liabilities & Equity	
Cash	**12,700** ~~$12,900~~	Accounts Payable	$ 2,000
Accounts Receivable	900	Note Payable	5,000
Inventory	**2,300** ~~2,700~~	Mortgage Payable	4,000
Prepaid Insurance	200	Smith, Capital	10,000
Land	5,000	Retained Earnings	**100** ~~700~~
Total	~~$21,700~~ **21,100**	Total	~~$21,700~~ **21,100**

None. The balance sheet is identical to that of January 13, except for the date. As required by the asset-measurement concept, the land continues to be shown at its historical cost because it is a nonmonetary asset.

10-60. The permanent capital as of December 31, 2009, is the debt capital (i.e., noncurrent liabilities) of \$_____,000 plus the equity capital of \$_____,000, a total of \$_____,000. The return on permanent capital is found by dividing EBIT by this total. Calculate the return on permanent capital.

$$\frac{\underline{\hspace{2cm}}}{\underline{\hspace{1cm}}\ \ \underline{\hspace{1cm}}} = \frac{\boxed{\$\qquad}}{\boxed{\$\qquad}} = \boxed{\qquad}\ \%$$

\$40

\$130   \$170 (= \$40 + \$130)

$$\frac{\text{EBIT}}{\text{Permanent capital}} = \frac{\$42}{\$170} = 25\%$$

10-61. Copy the numerator and denominator of the return on permanent capital on Line 4 of Exhibit 14.

Numerator: EBIT (Earnings before interest and taxes)
Denominator: Permanent capital

10-62. Another ratio shows how much sales revenue was generated by each dollar of permanent capital. This ratio is called the **capital turnover** ratio. Calculate it for Chico Company.

$$\text{Capital turnover} = \frac{\text{Sales revenue}}{\text{Permanent capital}} = \frac{\boxed{\$\qquad}}{\boxed{\$\qquad}} = \boxed{\qquad}\ \text{times}$$

$$\frac{\$300}{\$170} = 1.8\ \text{times}$$

Copy the numerator and denominator of this ratio on Line 13 of Exhibit 14.

Numerator: Sales revenue
Denominator: Permanent capital

10-63. American manufacturing companies have a capital turnover ratio of roughly two times on average. A company that has a large capital investment in relation to its sales revenue is called a **capital-intensive** company. A capital-intensive company, such as a steel manufacturing company or a public utility, has a relatively [high / low] capital turnover.

2-62. On January 15, Evergreen Market paid off $2,000 of its bank loan, giving cash (disregard interest).

Change the following January 14 balance sheet so that it reports the financial condition on January 15.

EVERGREEN MARKET
Balance Sheet as of January 14

Assets		Liabilities & Equity	
Cash	$12,700	Accounts Payable	$ 2,000
Accounts Receivable	900	Note Payable	5,000
Inventory	2,300	Mortgage Payable	4,000
Prepaid Insurance	200	Smith, Capital	10,000
Land	5,000	Retained Earnings	100
Total	$21,100	Total	$21,100

> **NOTE:** Remember that in corporations, the Capital account will be stated as Paid-in Capital.

EVERGREEN MARKET
Balance Sheet as of January ~~14~~ 15

Assets		Liabilities & Equity	
Cash	**10,700** ~~$12,700~~	Accounts Payable	$ 2,000
Accounts Receivable	900	Note Payable	**3,000** ~~5,000~~
Inventory	2,300	Mortgage Payable	4,000
Prepaid Insurance	200	Smith, Capital	10,000
Land	5,000	Retained Earnings	100
Total	~~$21,100~~ **19,100**	Total	~~$21,100~~ **19,100**

2-63. On January 16, Evergreen Market was changed to a corporation. Steve Smith received 100 shares of common stock in exchange for his $10,100 equity in the business. He immediately sold 25 of these shares for $4,000 cash.

What changes, if any, should be made in the January 15 balance sheet so that it reports the financial condition on January 16? _____
_____

> **NOTE:** Any conceivable transaction can be recorded in terms of its effect on the balance sheet, just as you have done in this section. Although we shall describe techniques, refinements, and shortcuts in later parts, none of them changes this basic fact.

The "Smith, Capital" account will change to "Paid-in Capital" and the date will change. Changing the organization to a corporation did not affect any amount on the balance sheet. (The name of the entity was changed to, say, Evergreen Market Corporation, but this does not affect the numbers.) Steve Smith's sale of the stock did not affect the entity, Evergreen Market. The Evergreen Market is now a corporation with one shareholder.

10-56. We have focused on return on equity (ROE) as an overall measure of performance. Another useful measure is the **return on permanent capital.** This shows how well the entity used its capital, without considering how much of its permanent capital came from each of the two sources: d __ __ __ and e __ __ __ __ __ . This ratio is also called **return on investment (ROI).**

debt   equity

10-57. The *return* portion of this ratio is *not* net income. Net income includes a deduction for interest expense, but interest expense is the return on debt capital. Therefore, net income [understates / overstates] the return earned on all permanent capital. Also, income tax expense is often disregarded to focus on pretax income.

understates

10-58. The return used in this calculation is **earnings before** the deduction of **interest** and **taxes** on income. It is abbreviated by the first letters of the words in boldface, or __ __ __ __ .

EBIT

10-59. As with other income statement numbers, Earnings Before Interest and Taxes (EBIT) is expressed as the percentage of sales revenue. This gives the **EBIT margin.** Calculate it for Chico Company.

$$\frac{\text{EBIT}}{\text{Sales revenue}} = \frac{\$\boxed{}}{\$\boxed{}} = \boxed{} \% \ \text{EBIT margin}$$

$$\frac{\text{EBIT}}{\text{Sales revenue}} = \frac{\$42}{\$300} = 14\% \ \text{EBIT margin}$$

Enter the numerator and denominator of the EBIT margin ratio on Line 7 of Exhibit 14.

Numerator: EBIT
Denominator: Sales revenue

INCOME MEASUREMENT

> Please turn to Exhibit 2. It is a summary of the transactions for Evergreen Market that you analyzed in Frames 2-33 through 2-55. We shall focus on the transactions that affected equity.

2-64. As explained in Part 1, an entity's equity increases for either of two reasons. One is the receipt of capital from owners. On January 2, Evergreen Market received $10,000 from Steve Smith, its owner. You recorded this as an increase in _____ and an increase in the equity item, Smith, C _____.

Cash

Smith, Capital

2-65. The other source of an increase in equity is the profitable operation of the entity. Transactions that increase profit also increase the equity item, R _____ E _____. Refer to the transactions for January 3 through 8. In the following table, show the dollar amount of the change in Retained Earnings, if any, that resulted from each transaction. If the transaction had no effect on Retained Earnings, put an X in the "No effect" column.

Retained Earnings

> **NOTE:** Remember that Retained Earnings is *not* the same as the Capital account!

RETAINED EARNINGS

Date	Nature	Increased by	No effect
3	Borrowing	$	
4	Purchase		
5	Sale		
6	Purchase		
7	Sale		
8	Sale		
	Total	$	

RETAINED EARNINGS

Date	Nature	Increased by	No effect
3	Borrowing	$	X
4	Purchase		X
5	Sale	100	
6	Purchase		X
7	Sale	300	
8	Sale	300	
	Total	$ 700	

OTHER MEASURES OF PERFORMANCE

10-50. Another measure of performance is **earnings per share.** As the name suggests, the ratio is simply the total _____ for a given period, divided by the number of _____ of common stock outstanding.

earnings (*or* net income)

shares

10-51. Exhibit 10 shows that the earnings (i.e., net income) of Chico Company in 2009 was $_____ and that the number of shares outstanding during 2009 was _____. Therefore, earnings per share was $_____.

$24,000

4,800

$5 (= $24,000 ÷ 4,800)

10-52. On line 2 of Exhibit 14 enter the numerator and denominator of the earnings-per-share ratio.

Numerator: Net income
Denominator: Number of shares outstanding

10-53. Earnings per share is used in calculating another ratio—the **price-earnings ratio.** It is obtained by dividing the average market price of the stock by the earnings per share. If the average market price for Chico Company stock during 2009 was $35, then the price-earnings ratio is the ratio of $35 to $5, or _____ to 1.

7 (= $35 ÷ $5)

10-54. On line 3 of Exhibit 14, enter the numerator and denominator of the price-earnings ratio.

Numerator: Average market price
Denominator: Earnings per share

10-55. Price-earnings ratios of many companies are published daily in the financial pages of newspapers. Often, the ratio is roughly 9 to 1, but it varies greatly depending on market conditions. If investors think that earnings per share will increase, this ratio could be much higher—perhaps 15 to 1. Apparently, investors are willing to pay [more / less] per dollar of earnings in a growing company, as long as the risk of doing so is not excessive.

more

2-66. As can be seen from the table in Frame 2-65, three of these transactions did not affect Retained Earnings. Borrowing money [does / does not] affect Retained Earnings. The purchase of merchandise [does / does not] affect Retained Earnings. The sale of that merchandise, however, [does / does not] affect Retained Earnings.

does not

does not

does

2-67. The amount by which equity increased as a result of operations during a period of time is called the **income** of that period. You have just calculated that the total increase during the period January 2 through 8 was $_____, so Evergreen Market's i __ __ __ __ __ for that period was $_____.

$700   income

$700

2-68. The amount of income and how it was earned is usually the most important financial information about a business entity. An accounting report called the **income statement** explains the income of a period. Note that the income statement is for a [period of time / point in time], in contrast with the other statement, the b__ __ __ __ __ __ s __ __ __ __ , which is for a [period of time / point in time].

period of time

balance

sheet   point in time

2-69. The $700 increase in Retained Earnings during the period is reported on the i __ __ __ __ __ s __ __ __ __ __ __ __ __ . That statement explains *how* this increase occurred.

income statement

2-70. To understand how the income statement does this, let's look at the January 5 transaction for Evergreen Market. On January 5, Evergreen Market sold for $300 cash some merchandise that had cost $200. This caused equity (Retained Earnings) to [increase / decrease] by $_____.

increase

$100

> **NOTE:** Recall that in a proprietorship, Retained Earnings will be included in the owner's Capital account.

2-71. On January 5, Evergreen Market sold merchandise for $300 cash that had cost $200. This transaction consists of two separate events: (1) the sale, which, taken by itself, [increased / decreased] Retained Earnings by $300, and (2) the decrease in inventory, which, taken by itself, [increased / decreased] Retained Earnings by $200.

increased

decreased

10-45. The final ratio we will use in examining capitalization is the **debt ratio.** As explained in Part 8, this is the ratio of debt capital to total permanent capital. Noncurrent liabilities are d ___ ___ ___ capital, and noncurrent liabilities plus equity are t ___ ___ ___ ___ p ___ ___ ___ ___ ___ ___ ___ ___ capital. Calculate the debt ratio for Chico Company.

debt
total
permanent

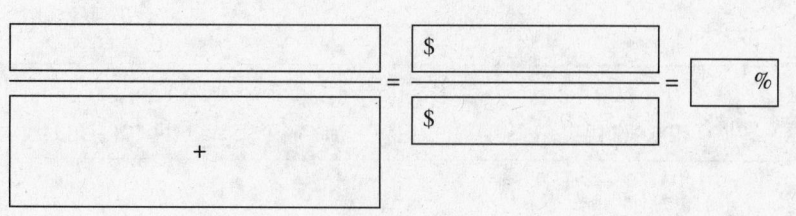

$$\frac{\text{Noncurrent liabilities}}{\text{Noncurrent liabilities} + \text{Equity}} = \frac{\$40}{\$40 + \$130} = 24\%$$

10-46. Copy the numerator and denominator of the debt ratio on Line 12 of Exhibit 14.

Numerator: Noncurrent liabilities
Denominator: Noncurrent liabilities + Equity

10-47. The larger the proportion of permanent capital that is obtained from debt, the smaller is the amount of equity capital that is needed. If Chico had obtained $85,000 of its $170,000 permanent capital from debt, its debt ratio would have been _____%, and its ROE would have been [higher / lower] than the 18.5% shown in Exhibit 13.

50%
higher

10-48. A high debt ratio results in a [more / less] risky capital structure than does a low debt ratio.

more

10-49. In several of the calculations above, we used balance sheet amounts taken from the ending balance sheet. For some purposes, it is more informative to use an **average** of beginning and ending balance sheet amounts. Chico Company had $130,000 of equity at the end of 2009. If it had $116,000 at the beginning of 2009, its *average* equity during 2009 was $_____. Since its net income in 2009 was $24,000, its return on *average* equity investment was _____%.*

$123,000
19.5% (= $24,000 ÷ $123,000)

_____
* one decimal place.

2-72. Taken by itself, the increase in Retained Earnings resulting from operations is called a **revenue.** When Evergreen Market sold merchandise for $300, the transaction resulted in $300 of _____.

revenue

2-73. And taken by itself, the associated decrease in Retained Earnings is called an **expense.** When Evergreen Market transferred merchandise to the customer, the transaction reduced inventory and resulted in $200 of _____.

expense

2-74. Thus, when Evergreen Market sold merchandise for $300 that cost $200, the effect of the transaction on Retained Earnings can be separated into two parts: a _____ of $_____ and an _____ of $_____.

revenue $300
expense $200

2-75. In accounting, revenues and expenses are recorded separately. From Exhibit 2, calculate the revenues and expenses for the period January 2 through 8 by completing the following table:

Date	Revenues	Expenses
5	$	$
7		
8		
Total	$	$

$ 300 $ 200

800   500

900   600

$2,000 $1,300

10-40. Calculate the current ratio for Chico Company.

$$\frac{\underline{\qquad\qquad}\quad\underline{\qquad\qquad}}{\underline{\qquad\qquad}\quad\underline{\qquad\qquad}} = \frac{\boxed{\$\qquad\qquad}}{\boxed{\$\qquad\qquad}} = \boxed{\qquad}$$

$$\frac{\text{Current assets}}{\text{Current liabilities}} = \frac{\$140}{\$60} = 2.3$$

10-41. Copy the numerator and the denominator of the current ratio on Line 10 of Exhibit 14.

Numerator: Current assets
Denominator: Current liabilities

10-42. If Chico Company decreased its current ratio to 1.5 by increasing its current liabilities, this would [increase / decrease] its ROE. However, such a low current ratio would [increase / decrease] the possibility that Chico would be unable to pay its current liabilities when they come due.

increase

increase

> **NOTE:** The numbers used here to calculate the current ratio are amounts as of the end of the year. Seasonal factors may greatly affect the current ratio during the year. For example, a department store may increase its inventory in the fall in anticipation of holiday business, and its current ratio therefore decreases. Similar limitations affect the other measures discussed in this part.

10-43. A variation of the current ratio is the **quick ratio** (also called the **acid-test ratio**). In this ratio, inventory is often excluded from the current assets, and the remainder is divided by current liabilities. This is a more stringent measure of immediate bill-paying ability than the current ratio. Calculate this ratio for Chico Company:

$$\frac{\text{Current assets} - \text{Inventory}}{\text{Current liabilities}} = \frac{\boxed{\$\qquad -\qquad}}{\boxed{\$\qquad}} = \boxed{\qquad} \text{ times}$$

$$\frac{\$140 - \$60}{\$60} = 1.3$$

10-44. Copy the numerator and the denominator of the quick ratio on Line 11 of Exhibit 14.

Numerator: Current assets – Inventory
Denominator: Current liabilities

2-76. You can now prepare an income statement. Its heading shows the name of the accounting entity, the title of the statement, and the period covered. Complete the heading for Evergreen Market's income statement for January 2–8:

EVERGREEN MARKET

[   ]   Statement   Income

for the period   [   ]   January 2–8

2-77. The income statement reports revenues and expenses for the period and the difference between them, which is income. Label the amounts in the following income statement for Evergreen Market.

EVERGREEN MARKET

Income Statement
for the period January 2–8

[   ] . . . . $2,000   Revenues

[   ]   1,300   Expenses

[   ] . . . . $ 700   Income

Revenues	$2,000

=

Expenses	$1,300	+	Income	$700

2-78. As the name suggests, Retained Earnings refers to the amount of income that has been r _____ in the entity. On January 13, Smith withdrew $600 of assets for his personal use. This reduced R _____ E _____ by $_____.

retained

Retained Earnings $600

10-36. The amount of capital tied up in inventory can be examined by calculating the **inventory turnover ratio.** Since inventory is recorded at cost, this ratio is calculated in relation to cost of sales, rather than to sales revenue.

Calculate the inventory turnover ratio for Chico Company (refer to Exhibit 13 if necessary).

$$\frac{\text{Cost of sales}}{\text{Inventory}} = \frac{\$\boxed{}}{\$\boxed{}} = \boxed{} \text{ times}$$

$$\frac{\text{Cost of sales}}{\text{Inventory}} = \frac{\$180}{\$60} = 3 \text{ times}$$

10-37. Copy the numerator and the denominator of the inventory turnover ratio on Line 9 of Exhibit 14.

Numerator: Cost of sales
Denominator: Inventory

10-38. If Chico Company had maintained an inventory of $90,000 to support $180,000 cost of sales, its inventory turnover would have been _____ (how many?) times, rather than three times. With this change, its ROE would have been [higher / lower] than the 18.5% shown in Exhibit 13.

two

lower

10-39. The **current ratio** is another way of examining the current section of the balance sheet. In an earlier part we pointed out that if the ratio of current assets to current liabilities is too low, the company might not be able to pay its bills. However, if the current ratio is too high, the company would not be taking advantage of the opportunity to finance current assets with current l __ __ __ __ __ __ __ __ __ s. Additional current liabilities would [increase / decrease] its ROE. Equity inevitably would be lower; otherwise, the balance sheet would not balance.

liabilities

increase

2-79. No other changes in Retained Earnings occurred. Complete the following table:

Retained Earnings, January 2	$ 0	
Income	+ _____	700
Withdrawal	− _____	600
Retained Earnings, January 13	$ _____	100

The amount of Retained Earnings calculated [does / does not] equal the amount shown on the balance sheet of January 13.

does

2-80. Assume that in the remainder of January, Evergreen Market had additional income of $800 and there were no additional withdrawals. Since Retained Earnings was $100 as of January 13, it would be $_____ on January 31. Thus, the amount of Retained Earnings on a balance sheet is:

$900

A. the amount earned in the current period.

B. the total amount retained since the entity began operations.

B

2-81. The terms **profit, earnings,** and **income** all have the same meaning. They are the differences between the r _ _ _ _ _ _ _ _ _ of an accounting period and the e _ _ _ _ _ _ _ _ of that period. In nonprofit organizations, the term **surplus** refers to profit.

revenues

expenses

> **NOTE:** Some people use the term **income** when they mean **revenue;** this can be confusing.

> **NOTE:** In later parts, we shall describe various revenue and expense items, such as sales revenue, interest revenue, salary expense, and rent expense. These explain in more detail the reasons for the change in Retained Earnings during a period.

2-82. Remember that the equity section of the balance sheet reports the amount of capital that the entity has obtained from two different sources:

1. The amount paid in by the owner(s), which is called P _____ - _____ C _____ or simply C _____.

   Paid-in Capital

   Capital

2. The amount of income that has been retained in the entity, which is called R _____ E _____.

   Retained Earnings

10-31. If Stimson Company could reduce its equity to $500,000, while still maintaining its net income of $60,000, its ROE would become _____%. Evidently, with net income held constant, Stimson Company can increase its ROE by [increasing / decreasing] its equity.

12% ($60,000 ÷ $500,000)

decreasing

10-32. Since total assets always equal liabilities plus equity, equity can be decreased only if (1) assets are [increased / decreased], (2) liabilities are [increased / decreased], or (3) there is some combination of these two types of changes.

decreased

increased

10-33. For example, Stimson Company's equity would be decreased by $100,000 (to $500,000) if assets were decreased by $40,000 (to $960,000) and liabilities were [increased / decreased] by $_____ (to $_____). If equity was $500,000 and net income was $60,000, ROE would be

increased

$60,000 $460,000

$$ \frac{\$\boxed{}}{\$\boxed{}} = \boxed{} \% $$

$$ \frac{\$60,000}{\$500,000} = 12\% $$

10-34. In earlier parts, two ratios for measuring current assets were described. One related to accounts receivable and was called the **days' sales uncollected.** It shows how many days of sales revenue are tied up in accounts receivable.

Calculate days' sales uncollected for Chico Company.

$$ \frac{\text{Accounts receivable}}{\text{Sales revenue} \div 365} = \frac{\$\boxed{}}{\$\boxed{} \div 365} = \boxed{} \text{ days' sales uncollected} $$

$$ \frac{\text{Accounts receivable}}{\text{Sales revenue} \div 365} = \frac{\$40}{\$300 \div 365} = 49 \text{ days} $$

10-35. Copy the numerator and the denominator of the days' sales uncollected on Line 8 of Exhibit 14.

Numerator: Accounts receivable
Denominator: Sales revenue ÷ 365

2-83. The two financial statements may be compared to two reports on a reservoir. One report may show how much water *flowed through* the reservoir during the period, and the other report may show how much water *was in* the reservoir as of the end of the period. Similarly, the [balance sheet / income statement] reports flows during a period of time, whereas the [balance sheet / income statement] reports status as of a point of time.

income statement

balance sheet

Thus, the income statement may be called a [flow / status] report, and the balance sheet may be called a [flow / status] report.

flow

status

2-84. Note also that withdrawals by owners (which are called dividends in a corporation) [are / are not] expenses. They [do / do not] appear on the income statement. They [do / do not] reduce income. They [do / do not] decrease retained earnings.

are not   do not

do not

do

KEY POINTS TO REMEMBER

The following diagram summarizes how assets are reported.

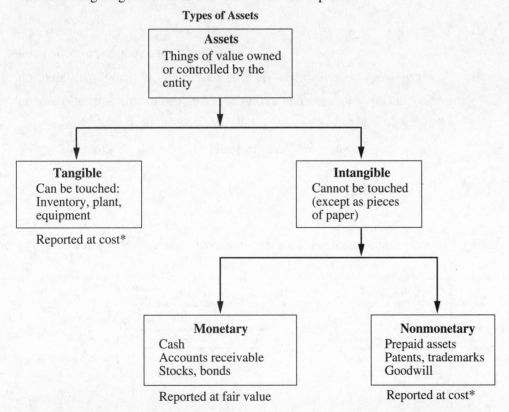

---

*Historical cost less depreciation or amortization

10-26. The **profit margin percentage** is a useful number for analyzing net income. You calculated it in an earlier part. Calculate it for Chico Company.

Net income / Sales revenue = [$] / [$] = [ ] % profit margin

$$\frac{\text{Net income}}{\text{Sales revenue}} = \frac{\$24}{\$300} = 8\%$$

10-27. Copy the numerator and denominator of the profit margin percentage on Line 6 of Exhibit 14.

Numerator: Net income
Denominator: Sales revenue

10-28. Statistics on the average profit margin percentage in various industries are published and can be used by Chico Company as a basis for comparison. Statistics on the average *dollar* amount of net income are not published. Such statistics [are / are not] useful because sheer size is not a good indication of profitability.

are not

TESTS OF CAPITAL UTILIZATION

10-29. The bottom section of the diagram in Exhibit 13 shows the main components of Chico Company's capital. The information is taken from its [income statement / balance sheet]. We shall examine ratios useful in understanding these components.

balance sheet

10-30. As background for this analysis, let's examine some relationships in Stimson Company, which has the following condensed balance sheet:

Assets	Liabilities and Equity	
	Total liabilities	$400,000
	Total equity	600,000
Total $1,000,000	Total	$1,000,000

If net income was $60,000, Stimson Company's return on equity (ROE) was Net income ÷ Equity, or _____ %.

10% (= $60,000 ÷ $600,000)

- Current assets are cash and assets that are expected to be converted into cash or used up in the near future, usually within one year.

- Current liabilities are obligations due in the near future, usually within one year.

- Marketable securities are current assets; investments are noncurrent assets.

- A single liability may have both a current portion and a noncurrent portion.

- Equity consists of capital (which in a corporation is represented by shares of stock plus paid-in capital) plus earnings retained since the entity began. It does not report the market value of the stock. Retained earnings is not cash; it is part of the owners' claim on the assets.

- Every accounting transaction affects at least two items and preserves the basic equation: Assets = Liabilities + Equity. Accounting is a double-entry system.

- Some events are not transactions; they do not affect the accounting amounts. Examples in this part were: a change in the value of land, "goodwill" that was not purchased, and changing the entity from a proprietorship to a corporation.

- Other events affect assets and/or liabilities but have no effect on equity. Examples in this part were borrowing money, purchasing inventory, purchasing insurance protection, acquiring an asset, giving a mortgage, buying land, selling land at its cost, and repaying a bank loan.

- Still other events affect equity as well as assets and/or liabilities. Revenues are increases in equity resulting from operations during a period. Expenses are decreases. Their net effect is shown in the equity item called Retained Earnings. Equity also increases when owners pay in capital, and equity decreases when owners withdraw capital, but these transactions do not affect income.

- A sale has two aspects: a revenue aspect and an expense aspect. Revenue results when the sale is made, whether or not cash is received at that time. The related expense is the cost of the merchandise that was sold. The income of a period is the difference between the revenues and expenses of that period.

You have completed Part 2 of this program. If you think you understand the material in this part, you should now take Post-Test 2, which is found at the back of this text. If you are uncertain about your understanding, you should review Part 2.

The post-test will serve both to test your comprehension and to review the highlights of Part 2. After taking the post-test, you may find that you are unsure about certain points. You should review these points before going on to Part 3. Please review the answers to Post-Test 2, following the Post-Tests, at the back of this text.

10-22. One factor that affects net income is gross margin. In an earlier part, you calculated the **gross margin percentage.** Calculate it for Chico Company.

$$\frac{\text{Gross margin}}{\text{Sales revenue}} = \frac{\$\boxed{} *}{\$\boxed{}} = \boxed{}\% \text{ gross margin}$$

> **NOTE**: If you have difficulty with this or other calculations, refer to Exhibit 13, where the amounts are calculated.

$$\frac{\text{Gross margin}}{\text{Sales revenue}} = \frac{\$120}{\$300} = 40\%$$

10-23. On Line 5 of Exhibit 14, write the name of the numerator and of the denominator of the gross margin percentage.

Numerator: Gross margin
Denominator: Sales revenue

10-24. Gross margin percentages vary widely. A profitable supermarket may have a gross margin of only 15%. Many manufacturing companies can have gross margins of about 35%. Compared with these numbers, the gross margin of Chico Company is [low / high].

high

> **NOTE**: Since companies even in the same industry can differ widely, it is often misleading to generalize about financial statistics.

10-25. A high gross margin does not necessarily lead to a high net income. Net income is what remains after expenses have been deducted from the gross margin, and the higher the expenses, the [higher / lower] the net income.

lower

## Part 3

Accounting Records and Systems

Learning Objectives

In this part you will learn:

- The nature of the account and how entries are made to accounts.
- The meaning of debit and credit.
- Use of the ledger and the journal.
- The closing process.
- Items reported on the income statement.
- Accounting with the computer.

THE ACCOUNT

3-1. In Part 2 you recorded the effect of each transaction by changing the appropriate items on a balance sheet. Erasing the old amounts and writing in the new amounts [would / would not] be a practical method for handling the large number of transactions that occur in most entities.

would not

3-2. Instead of changing balance sheet amounts directly, accountants use a device called an **account** to record each change. In its simplest form, an account looks like a large letter T, and it is therefore called a _____ -account.

T

> **NOTE:** As a matter of accounting custom, the name of an account is treated as a proper noun; that is, the first letter is capitalized.

10-18. Chico Company's net income in 2009 was $24,000. Paul Company's net income in 2009 was $50,000. From this information we cannot tell which company performed better. Why not?

10-19. Paul Company's equity was $1,000,000. Its net income in 2009 was $50,000. Its ROE was therefore

$$\frac{\boxed{\$ }}{\boxed{\$ }} = \underline{}\%$$

$$\frac{\$50,000}{\$1,000,000} = 5\%$$

Chico Company with an ROE of 18.5% performed [better / worse] than Paul Company.

better

10-20. The comparison of Chico Company's dollar amount of net income with Paul's dollar amount [did / did not] provide useful information. The comparison of their **ratios** or **percentage**s was [useful / not useful]. Useful comparisons involve r _____ s or p _____ s.

did not

useful

ratios

percentages

FACTORS AFFECTING RETURN ON EQUITY

10-21. Ratios help explain the factors that influenced return on equity.

> **NOTE:** Some ratios were explained in earlier parts. We shall review these ratios and introduce others, using the financial statements of Chico Company in Exhibit 10 and the diagram of these factors in Exhibit 13. These ratios are to be summarized in Exhibit 14.

We have already described the return on equity ratio, which is:

$$\frac{\text{(numerator) Net income}}{\text{(denominator) Equity}} = \text{Return on Equity}$$

Copy the numerator and denominator of this ratio on Line 1 of Exhibit 14.

Numerator: Net income
Denominator: Equity

3-3. The title of the account is written on top of the T. Draw a T-account and title it "Cash."

```
                Cash
          _____|_____
                  |
                  |
                  |
```

3-4. Following is how a T-account looks at the beginning of an accounting period.

```
                Cash
    _____
    Beg. bal. 10,000 |
                     |
                     |
                     |
```

Evidently the amount of cash at the beginning of the accounting period was $_____.

$10,000

> **NOTE**: Although the amounts are in dollars, the dollar sign is not used.

3-5. Transactions that affect the Cash account during the accounting period can either **increase** cash or **decrease** cash. Thus, one side of the T-account is for __ __ __ __ __ __ __ __ s, and the other side is for __ __ __ __ __ __ __ __ s.

increases
decreases (either order)

3-6. Increases in cash add to the beginning balance. Because the beginning balance is recorded on the left side of the T-account, increases in cash are recorded on the [left / right] side of the T-account. Decreases are recorded on the [left / right] side.

left
right

10-13. In 2009, Chico Company had net income of $24,000, and its equity on December 31, 2009, was $130,000. Calculate its ROE for 2009.

N _____ i _____ | $ _____ |

—————————————————— = ——————————— = | %* | ROE

E _____ | $ _____ |

_____

* one decimal place

$$\frac{\text{Net income}}{\text{Equity}} = \frac{\$24,000}{\$130,000} = 18.5\% \text{ ROE}$$

10-14. In order to judge how well Chico Company performed, its 18.5% ROE must be compared with something. If in 2008 Chico Company had an ROE of 20%, we can say that its performance in 2009 was [better / worse] than in 2008. This is the **historical** basis of comparison.

worse

10-15. If in 2009 another company had an ROE of 15%, Chico's ROE was [better / worse] than the other company's. Or if in 2009 the average ROE of companies in the same industry as Chico was 15%, Chico's ROE was [better / worse] than the industry average. This is the **external** basis of comparison. If the other company is thought to be the best-managed company in the industry, this comparison is called **benchmarking.**

better

better

10-16. Finally, if from our experience we judge that a company like Chico should have earned an ROE of 20% in 2009, we conclude that Chico's ROE was [better / worse] than this **judgmental standard.**

worse

10-17. Most comparisons are made in one or more of the three ways described above. Give the meaning of each.

1. **Historical:** comparing the entity with _____

   its own performance in the past

2. **External:** comparing the entity with _____

   another entity's performance or industry averages

3. **Judgmental:** comparing the entity with _____

   a standard based on our judgment

3-7. Here is the T-account for Cash.

Cash

(Increases)	(Decreases)
Beg. bal. 10,000	

Record in the above T-account the effect of the following transactions on Cash:

A. The entity received $300 cash from a customer.

B. The entity borrowed $5,000 from a bank.

C. The entity paid $2,000 cash to a supplier.

D. The entity sold merchandise for $800 cash.

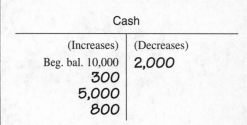

Cash

(Increases)	(Decreases)
Beg. bal. 10,000	*2,000*
300	
5,000	
800	

3-8. At the end of an accounting period, the increases are added to the beginning balance, and the total of the decreases is subtracted from it. The result is the **new balance.** Calculate the new balance for the Cash account shown below.

Cash

(Increases)	(Decreases)
Beg. bal. 10,000	2,000
300	
5,000	
800	
Total	Total
New balance	

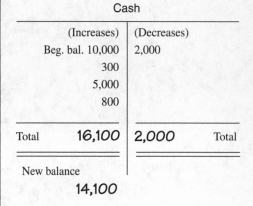

Cash

(Increases)	(Decreases)
Beg. bal. 10,000	2,000
300	
5,000	
800	
Total *16,100*	*2,000* Total
New balance	
14,100	

3-9. The amount of the above Cash shown on the balance sheet at the end of the accounting period was $_____. The beginning balance of Cash in the next accounting period will be $_____.

$14,100

$14,100

10-8. The opinion says that the auditors [prepared / audited] the financial statements and that these statements are the responsibility of [the auditors / management].

audited

management

10-9. The opinion further states that the financial statements [accurately / fairly] present the financial results.

fairly
(Because judgments and estimates are involved, no one can say that the financial statements are entirely accurate.)

10-10. In the last paragraph of the opinion, the auditors assure the reader that the statements were prepared in conformity with g _____ a _____ a _____ p _____.

generally
accepted accounting principles

> **NOTE:** Exhibit 12 is an example of a **clean** or **unqualified** opinion. If any of the above statements cannot be made, the auditors call attention to the exceptions in what is called a **qualified** opinion. A qualified opinion can be a serious matter. If the qualification is significant, securities exchanges can suspend trading in the company's stock.

OVERALL FINANCIAL MEASURES OF PERFORMANCE

> **NOTE:** Although they have **limitations,** financial statements usually are the most useful source of information about an entity. We shall focus first on what they tell about its overall **performance.**

10-11. Equity investors (i.e., shareholders) invest money in a business in order to earn a profit, or **return,** on that equity. Thus, from the viewpoint of the shareholders, the best overall measure of the entity's performance is the r _ _ _ _ _ _ that was earned *on* the entity's e _ _ _ _ _ _. (This is abbreviated ROE.)

return   equity

10-12. The accounting name for the profit or return earned in a year is n _ _ i _ _ _ _ _ _.

net income

Return on equity is the percentage obtained by dividing n _ _ i _ _ _ _ _ _ by e _ _ _ _ _ _.

net
income   equity

RULES FOR INCREASES AND DECREASES

3-10. In the T-account for Cash, increases are recorded on the [left / right] side. This is the rule for all asset accounts; that is, increases in _____ accounts are recorded on the _____ side.

left

asset   left

3-11. Suppose Brown Company received $300 cash from Ellen Jones to settle her account receivable. In the T-account below, the increase in Brown Company's cash that results is recorded on the [left / right] side. Enter the amount.

left

Cash	
(Increases)	(Decreases)
Beg. bal. 10,000	

Cash	
(Increases)	(Decreases)
Beg. bal. 10,000	
300	

3-12. Ellen Jones, a customer of Brown Company, paid $300 cash to settle the amount she owed. The Cash account increased by $300. Jones no longer owed $300, so the A _ _ _ _ _ _ _ _ R _ _ _ _ _ _ _ _ _ _ account decreased by $300. In the T-account below, enter the name of this second account that must be changed to complete the record of the transaction.

Accounts

Receivable

Cash				
(Increases)	(Decreases)		(Increases)	(Decreases)
Beg. bal. 10,000			Beg. bal. 2,000	
300				

Accounts Receivable

3-13. Accounts Receivable is an asset account. The dual-aspect concept requires that if the asset account, Cash, increases by $300, the change in the other asset account, Accounts Receivable, must be a(n) . . . [increase / decrease] of $300.

decrease

10-3. Third, the balance sheet does not show the [cost / fair value] of nonmonetary assets. In accordance with the a __ __ __ __ __ - m __ __ __ __ __ __ __ __ __ __ concept, plant assets are reported at their [unexpired cost / fair value].

fair value
asset
measurement
unexpired cost

Also, depreciation is a write-off of [cost / fair value]. It is *not* an indication of changes in the real value of plant assets. The balance sheet [does / does not] show the entity's "net worth."

cost

does not

10-4. Fourth, the accountant and management have some latitude in choosing among alternative ways of recording an event in the accounts. An example of flexibility in accounting is that in determining inventory values and cost of sales, the entity may use the L __ __ __, F __ __ __ __, or average cost methods. Such choices [have no bearing on / definitely impact the company's net income].

LIFO   FIFO
definitely impact the company's net income

10-5. Fifth, many accounting amounts are estimates. In calculating the depreciation expense of a plant asset, for example, one must estimate its s __ __ __ __ __ __ __ l __ __ __ __ and its r __ __ __ __ __ __ __ __ v __ __ __ __ __ .

service life   residual
value

AUDITING

10-6. All large companies and many small ones have their accounting records examined by independent, certified public accountants. This process is called **auditing,** and the independent accountants are called __ __ __ __ tors.

auditors

10-7. After completing their examination, the __ __ __ __ __ __ __ __ s write a report giving their opinion. This o __ __ __ __ __ __ __ is reproduced in the company's annual report. A typical opinion is shown in Exhibit 12.

auditors
opinion

3-14. Record the change in Accounts Receivable resulting from the $300 payment in the account below.

Accounts Receivable	
(Increases)	(Decreases)
Beg. bal. 2,000	

Accounts Receivable	
(Increases)	(Decreases)
Beg. bal. 2,000	*300*

3-15. The decrease in accounts receivable was recorded on the [left / right] side of the Accounts Receivable account. This balanced the [left / right] -side amount for the increase in Cash.

right

left

3-16. Another customer of Brown Company settled an $800 Account Receivable by paying $600 cash and giving a note for $200. Record this transaction in the Brown Company's accounts, given below.

Cash	
(Increases)	(Decreases)
Beg. bal. 10,000	
300	

Accounts Receivable	
(Increases)	(Decreases)
Beg. bal. 3,000	300

Notes Receivable	
(Increases)	(Decreases)
Beg. bal. 1,000	

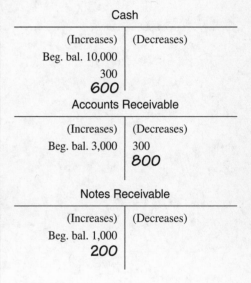

Cash	
(Increases)	(Decreases)
Beg. bal. 10,000	
300	
600	

Accounts Receivable	
(Increases)	(Decreases)
Beg. bal. 3,000	300
	800

Notes Receivable	
(Increases)	(Decreases)
Beg. bal. 1,000	
200	

3-17. As you can see, accounting requires that each transaction give rise to [equal / unequal] totals of left-side and right-side amounts. This is consistent with the fundamental equation: A __ __ __ __ __ = L __ __ __ __ __ __ __ __ __ __ __ + E __ __ __ __ __ .

equal

Assets

Liabilities + Equity

3-18. An **increase** in any asset account is always recorded on the left side. Therefore, since the totals of left-side and right-side amounts must equal each other, a **decrease** in any asset must always be recorded on the [left / right] side.

right

## Part 10

Analysis of Financial Statements

Learning Objectives

In this part you will learn:

- The limitations of financial statement analysis.
- The nature and limitations of auditing.
- An approach to analyzing financial statements.
- Overall financial measures of performance.
- Other ratios used in financial statement analysis.
- The Du Pont system of ratios.
- How to detect high- vs. low-quality earnings.
- The basics of the Sarbanes-Oxley Act of 2002.

LIMITATIONS OF FINANCIAL STATEMENT ANALYSIS

> **NOTE:** In this part, we shall describe how information in financial statements is **used.** Before doing this, let's review the reasons that accounting cannot provide a **complete picture** of the status or performance of an entity.

10-1. One limitation is suggested by the word **financial;** that is, financial statements report only events that can be measured in m __ __ __ __ ary amounts.

| monetary

10-2. A second limitation is that financial statements are historical; that is, they report only events that [have happened / will happen], whereas we are also interested in estimating events that [have happened / will happen]. The fact that an entity earned $1 million last year [definitely predicts / is not necessarily an indication of] what it will earn next year.

| have happened
| will happen
| is not necessarily an indication of

3-19. Black Company borrowed $700 from Northwest Bank, signing a note.

Black Company's Cash account [increased / decreased] by $700, and its Notes Payable account, which is a liability account, [increased / decreased] by the same amount.

increased
increased

3-20. Black Company borrowed $700 from Northwest Bank, signing a note.

The $700 increase in Black Company's cash is recorded on the [left / right] side of its Cash account. In order to show equal totals of right-side and left-side amounts, the corresponding change in the Notes Payable account is recorded on the [left / right] side. Record the two amounts of this transaction in the accounts below.

left

right

Cash			Notes Payable	
(Increases)	(Decreases)			

Cash	
(Increases)	(Decreases)
700	

Notes Payable	
	700

3-21. Because left-side and right-side amounts must have equal totals, and because increases in assets are always recorded on the left side, increases in liability accounts, such as notes payable, are always recorded on the [left / right] side.

right

- The statement of cash flows shows the net increase or decrease in cash that must equal the difference between beginning and ending cash.

- The cash flow from operating activities is found by adjusting net income for (1) depreciation expense and (2) changes in noncash current assets and current liabilities.

- Depreciation expense is not a cash flow. Because it decreases net income, it is added back to net income in order to arrive at the cash flow from operating activities.

- In general, investing activities include the acquisition of new fixed assets and the proceeds of selling fixed assets.

- In general, financing activities include obtaining funds from long-term borrowing, repayment of these borrowings, and obtaining funds from issuance of additional stock.

- GAAP has specific requirements for determining which cash flows are classified as investing activities and which are classified as financing activities, but statement users need not memorize these rules because they are evident from the statement itself.

- When a company is growing or when it is experiencing financial crisis, it may pay more attention to the statement of cash flows than to the income statement. Cash flows from sustainable operating activities are often a focus for analysts.

You have completed Part 9 of this program. If you think you understand the material in this part, you should now take Post-Test 9, which is found at the back of this text. If you are uncertain about your understanding, you should review Part 9.

The post-test will serve both to test your comprehension and to review the highlights of Part 9. After taking the post-test, you may find that you are unsure about certain points. You should review these points before going on to Part 10. Please review the answers to Post-Test 9, following the Post-Tests, at the back of this text.

3-22. Similarly, because **decreases** in assets are always recorded on the *right* side, **decreases** in liabilities are always recorded on the [left side / right side].

left side

Show which side of the Notes Payable account is used to record increases and which side is used to record decreases by filling in the boxes below.

Notes Payable

	700

Notes Payable	
(Decreases)	(Increases)
	700

3-23. As the equation Assets = Liabilities + Equity indicates, the rules for equity accounts are the same as those for liability accounts, that is:

Equity accounts increase on the [left / right] side.

right

Equity accounts decrease on the [left / right] side.

left

3-24. One way to remember the above rules is to visualize the two sides of the balance sheet.

Asset accounts are on the *left* side of the balance sheet, and they increase on the [left / right] side.

left

Liability and equity accounts are on the *right* side of the balance sheet, and they increase on the [left / right] side.

right

3-25. The reasoning used in the preceding frames follows from the basic equation: _____ = _____ + _____ .

Assets = Liabilities + Equity

> **NOTE:** Sometimes you will see a balance sheet where liabilities and equity appear below the assets section. This is a matter of preference on the part of the reporting entity.

USES OF THE STATEMENT OF CASH FLOWS

9-62. A forecast of cash flows helps management and other users of financial information to estimate future needs for cash. For example, when a company is growing, the increase in its accounts receivables, inventory, and fixed assets may require [more / less] cash. Therefore, although growth may result in additional profits, it may [generate the need for / provide] additional cash.

more

generate the need for

9-63. When a company is in financial difficulty, it may pay [more / less] attention to its cash flow statement than to its income statement. It pays bills with cash—not net income.

more

9-64. Lenders want to know if cash flows are adequate to pay i _____ t on debt and to repay the p _____ when it becomes due.

interest   principal

> **NOTE:** Analysts generally want to know how much of the annual cash flows come from **sustainable** operating activities.

9-65. Similarly, shareholders want to know about the adequacy of cash flow to pay d _ _ _ _ _ _ _ s.

dividends

> **NOTE:** A number that is useful for these purposes is called **free cash flow.** It is calculated by subtracting from the cash flow expected from operating activities: (1) the cash needed to purchase normal fixed asset replacements, (2) the cash required to pay long-term debt that is coming due, and (3) normal dividend payments. The difference indicates the amount of cash, if any, that the company is likely to have available (1) to provide a cushion against unforeseen cash outflows and (2) to provide for other spending that it might like to undertake.

KEY POINTS TO REMEMBER

- A required financial statement, the statement of cash flows, reports the changes in balance sheet accounts as positive or negative impacts on cash during the accounting period.

- The statement has three sections: cash flow from operating activities, cash flow from investing activities, and cash flow from financing activities.

DEBIT AND CREDIT

3-26. In the language of accounting, the left side of an account is called the **debit** side, and the right side is called the **credit** side. Thus, instead of saying that increases in cash are recorded on the left side of the Cash account and decreases are recorded on the right side, accountants say that increases are recorded on the _____ side and decreases are recorded on the _____ side.

debit

credit

3-27. Debit and **credit** are also verbs. To record an increase in cash, you _____ the Cash account. To record a decrease in cash, you _____ the Cash account. Instead of saying, "Record an increase on the left side of the Cash account," the accountant simply says, "_____ Cash."

debit

credit

Debit

3-28. Increases in all asset accounts, such as the Cash account, are recorded on the [debit / credit] side. To increase an asset account, you [debit / credit] the account.

debit

debit

3-29. The rules we just developed in terms of "left side" and "right side" can now be stated in terms of debit and credit.

Increases in assets are [debits / credits].	debits
Decreases in assets are [debits / credits].	credits
Increases in liabilities are [debits / credits].	credits
Decreases in liabilities are [debits / credits].	debits
Increases in equity are [debits / credits].	credits
Decreases in equity are [debits / credits].	debits

3-30. In everyday language the word **credit** sometimes means "good" and **debit** sometimes means "bad." In the language of accounting, debit means only [left / right], and credit means only [left / right].

left   right

> **NOTE:** As you can see from Frame 3-29, debits are sometimes increases (when asset accounts are involved) and sometimes decreases (when liability or equity accounts are involved).

> **NOTE:** Generally Accepted Accounting Principles (GAAP) classify other types of cash flows as either investing or financing. The investing category includes both making investments and disposition of investments; for example, sale of an item of PPE is classified as an investing activity, as is the acquisition of an item of plant. Similarly, the financing category includes the repayment of borrowings, as well as cash received from loans. Some people consider cash inflow and outflow related to interest and dividends to be financing activities. Accounting standards suggest, however, that they be included in operating activities. Because the statement of cash flows shows how each item is classified, users do not need to memorize these GAAP rules.

9-58. An investing activity [is / is not] always a cash outflow, and a financing activity [is / is not] always a cash inflow.

is not

is not

COMPLETING THE STATEMENT OF CASH FLOWS

9-59. Calculate the increase in cash by summing the three categories in Exhibit 11, and enter this total. Note that the $_____,000 net increase in cash [equals / does not equal] the change in the Cash balance as reported on the two balance sheets of Chico Company.

13

equals

9-60. To reconcile the statement of cash flows with the balance sheet, there is a section at the bottom. The net increase or decrease in c_____ must equal the d__ __ __ __ __ __ __ce between beginning and ending cash. Enter these amounts at the bottom of Exhibit 11.

cash   difference

7   20

9-61. The cash flow statement shows that although net income was $_____,000 in 2009, Cash increased by only $_____,000. Operating activities generated $_____,000 in cash; $_____,000 of this cash was used to pay dividends. The remaining additional cash inflow was used to acquire new PPE. The cost of the new assets was $_____,000; $_____,000 of this cost was financed by additional borrowing, and cash was used for the remainder. From the cash inflows, $_____,000 remained in the Cash account. This is a simple, but useful, way to tell the "cash flow story" of an organization.

24   13

29   10

12

6

13

3-31. The word **debit** is abbreviated as "Dr.," and the word **credit** is abbreviated as "Cr." Label the two sides of the Cash account below with these abbreviations.

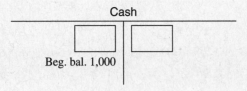

Cash

Beg. bal. 1,000

NOTE: In practice, these labels are not shown in the accounts, but we shall use them in the next frames, to help you fix them in your mind.

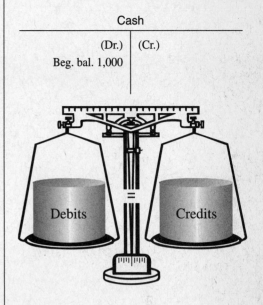

Cash

	(Dr.)	(Cr.)
Beg. bal. 1,000		

Debits = Credits

3-32. Exhibit 3 shows the accounts for Green Company, arranged as they would appear on a balance sheet. The sum of the debit balances is $_____, and the sum of the credit balances is $_____.

$18,000

$18,000

3-33. These totals are equal in accordance with the d __ __ __ - a __ __ __ __ __ concept.

dual-

aspect

9-54. As shown in Exhibit 10, Chico Company had a liability, mortgage bonds. The amount was $_____,000 at the beginning of 2009 and $_____,000 at the end of 2009. The increase of $_____,000 showed that Chico Company issued bonds of this amount. This was a(n) [investing / financing] activity. It represented a(n) [increase / decrease] in cash. Enter this amount in Exhibit 11.

34

40 6

financing

increase

> **NOTE:** Similar to the transaction in Frame 9-51, the amount of new bonds issued may have been more than $6,000. Part of the new issue may have been used to pay off existing bonds. The issuance and redemption of bonds are financing activities.

9-55. The borrowings reported in the financing section are both short-term and long-term borrowings. Whereas short-term borrowings often appear as current liabilities, changes in them are usually reported in the section on Cash Flow from F _____ A _____.

Financing Activities

> **NOTE:** For example, the current portion of long-term debt is a current liability. For the purpose of cash flow analysis, it is reported as a financing activity.

9-56. Issuance of additional shares of a company's stock is also a financing activity. Exhibit 10 shows that Chico Company's Paid-in Capital was $_____ at the beginning of 2009 and $_____ at the end of 2009. Evidently, the company [did / did not] issue additional stock in 2009.

$60,000 $60,000

did not

9-57. Dividends paid are sometimes classified as a financing activity. Exhibit 10 shows that Chico Company paid $_____,000 of dividends in 2009. Enter this amount in Exhibit 11. Then enter the total of the financing activities in Exhibit 11. Note that although it is common to find dividend activity in the financing activities section, such activity is required by Generally Accepted Accounting Principles (GAAP) to be included in the first section—Cash Flows from Operating Activities.

10

3-34. Record the following transactions in the accounts of Exhibit 3. Record increases in assets on the debit side and make sure that in each transaction the debit and credit amounts are equal.

    A. Inventory costing $600 was purchased for cash.

    B. Inventory costing $400 was purchased on credit.

    C. Green Company paid $300 to a creditor.

    D. Green Company received $500 in cash from a credit customer.

ACCOUNTS FOR GREEN COMPANY

Assets	Liabilities and Equity

Cash

	(Dr.)	(Cr.)	
Beg. bal.	1,000	600 (A)	
		500	300 (C)

Accounts Payable

	(Dr.)	(Cr.)	
(C)	300	2,000	Beg. bal.
		400 (B)	

Accounts Receivable

	(Dr.)	(Cr.)	
Beg. bal.	3,000	500 (D)	

Paid-in Capital

	(Dr.)	(Cr.)	
		7,000	Beg. bal.

Inventory

	(Dr.)	(Cr.)
Beg. bal.	4,000	
	600 (A)	
	400 (B)	

Retained Earnings

	(Dr.)	(Cr.)	
		9,000	Beg. bal.

Other Assets

	(Dr.)	(Cr.)
Beg. bal.	10,000	

3-35. Now calculate the new balances for each account and enter them in the accounts of Exhibit 3.

The new balances are:
Cash .... 600 Dr.
Accounts Receivable ..... 2,500 Dr.
Inventory .... 5,000 Dr.
Other Assets .... 10,000 Dr.
Accounts Payable .... 2,100 Cr.
Paid-in Capital .... 7,000 Cr.
Retained Earnings .... 9,000 Cr.

3-36. The total of the new balances of the asset accounts is $_____. The total of the new balances of the liability and equity accounts is $_____. Also, the total of the debit balances equals the total of the _____ balances.

$18,100

$18,100

credit

CASH FLOW FROM INVESTING AND FINANCING ACTIVITIES

9-49. Exhibit 11 shows that in addition to cash flow from operating activities, there are two other categories on a statement of cash flows: cash flow from _____ activities and cash flow from _____ activities.

investing

financing

9-50. When a company invests in additional property or plant, the amount involved is a cash [inflow to / outflow from] the company.

outflow from

> **NOTE:** The amount may not be an immediate decrease in cash because the payment of cash may have been offset by borrowing an equal amount. Nevertheless, it is recorded as a cash outflow, and the amount of the borrowing is recorded separately as a financing activity.

9-51. As shown in Exhibit 10, Chico Company had PPE at the beginning of 2009 that had cost $_____,000. It had $_____,000 of PPE at the end of 2009. The increase of $_____,000 was a(n) [investing / financing] activity in 2009. Enter this amount in Exhibit 11. (The parentheses indicate that this was a cash outflow.)

108   120

12   investing

> **NOTE:** The amount of new plant acquired may have been more than $12,000, say $15,000; the difference of $3,000 would represent cash obtained from the sale of existing plant. Both transactions are investing activities. However, we cannot obtain a breakdown of the amount from the available information. Organizations often provide this breakdown for us on the statement of cash flows or elsewhere in the notes to their financial statements.

9-52. Similarly, if the PPE account decreased, representing the sale of plant assets, there would have been an [inflow / outflow] of cash. Thus, companies may _____ cash to purchase property, plant, and equipment and they may sell property, plant, and equipment to get _____.

inflow

use

cash

9-53. Companies may also obtain cash by issuing debt securities, such as bonds. Issuing debt securities is a(n) . . . [investing / financing] activity.

financing

NOTE: If you answered Frames 3-35 and 3-36 correctly, go to Frame 3-37. If you are not comfortable with these frames, each transaction is repeated in more detail in the following frames. These frames use the approach of first deciding on the effect of the transaction on cash, or on an asset like cash, and then making the second part of the entry as an offsetting debit or credit.

3-36a. "Inventory costing $600 was purchased for cash." There was a decrease in Cash; so there was a [debit / credit] to Cash. The other entry must be a [debit / credit]. It was a [debit / credit] to Inventory; it was an increase in that asset account.

credit

debit   debit

3-36b. "Inventory costing $400 was purchased on credit." There was an increase in Inventory, which is an asset, as is cash, so there was a [debit / credit] to Inventory. The other entry must be a [debit / credit]. It was a [debit / credit] to Accounts Payable; it was an increase in that liability account.

debit

credit

credit

3-36c. "Green Company paid $300 to a creditor." There was a decrease in Cash; so there was a [debit / credit] to Cash. The other entry must be a [debit / credit]. It was a [debit / credit] to Accounts Payable; it was a decrease in that liability account.

credit

debit   debit

3-36d. "Green Company received $500 in cash from a credit customer." There was an increase in Cash; so there was a [debit / credit] to Cash. The other entry must be a [debit / credit]. It was a [debit / credit] to Accounts Receivable; it was a decrease in that asset account.

debit

credit   credit

NOTE: Notice that after each transaction where the debits equal the credits, the fundamental accounting equation remains: Assets = Liabilities + Equity. Therefore, the balance sheet is always in balance.

9-43. Note that the $_____,000 adjustment for Depreciation Expense is [larger than / smaller than / about the same as] the net amount of all the working capital account adjustments. This is the case in some companies, especially manufacturing companies, that have relatively large amounts of fixed assets.

6

larger than

9-44. As a shortcut, therefore, some analysts arrive at the operating cash flow simply by adding Depreciation Expense to Net Income. They disregard changes in the working capital accounts on the assumption that these changes net out to a minor amount. This shortcut may give the impression that depreciation is a cash flow. Such an impression is [approximately correct / dead wrong]. Also, since the statement of cash flows is a required financial statement, it is a good idea to read it and obtain the operating cash flow information directly from it.

dead wrong

SUMMARY OF OPERATING ADJUSTMENTS

9-45. If the total amount of working capital (excluding cash) did not change, and if there are no noncash expenses, such as depreciation, cash flow from operations will be [lower than / the same as / higher than] net income.

the same as

9-46. If the net amount of the working capital accounts (excluding cash) decreased, cash flow from operations will be [lower than / higher than] net income.

higher than

9-47. If the net amount of the working capital accounts (excluding cash) increased, cash flow from operations will be [lower than / higher than] net income.

lower than

9-48. If there was depreciation expense, cash flow from operations will be [lower than / the same as / higher than] net income.

higher than

> **NOTE:** When analyzing the impact on cash from changes in working capital accounts, we must be careful to exclude the cash account from this calculation.

3-37. Because the total of the debit entries for any transaction should always equal the total of the credit entries, it is [difficult / easy] to check the accuracy with which bookkeeping is done. (We owe this ingenious arrangement to Venetian merchants, who invented it more than 500 years ago.)

easy

INCOME STATEMENT ACCOUNTS

3-38. The accounts in Exhibit 3 were for items that appear on the balance sheet. Accounts are also kept for items that appear on another financial statement, the i __ __ __ __ __ statement. As we saw in Part 2, this statement reports the revenues and the expenses of an accounting period and the difference between them, which is net i __ __ __ __ __ .

income

income

> **NOTE:** In Part 2, we referred to the increase in Retained Earnings as "income." From here on, we shall use the technically correct name: "net income." Net income is the bottom line of the income statement. Various subtotals of income, such as *gross income* and *operating income,* are used in practice.

3-39. Revenues are [increases / decreases] in equity during a period, and expenses are [increases / decreases] in equity.

increases

decreases

3-40. For equity accounts, increases are recorded as [debits / credits]. Because revenues are increases in equity, revenues are recorded as [debits / credits].

credits

credits

3-41. Similarly, decreases in equity are recorded as [debits / credits]. Because expenses are decreases in equity, expenses are recorded as [debits / credits].

debits

debits

NET EFFECT OF WORKING CAPITAL CHANGES

9-39. In summary, an increase in current assets means that [more / less] of the cash inflow was tied up in accounts receivable, inventory, and/or other current assets, with a corresponding [increase / decrease] in Cash. This is why, in times when cash is low, a business tries to keep the other current assets as [high / low] as feasible.

more

decrease

low

9-40. An increase in current liabilities means that [more / less] cash was freed up. The cash not paid to suppliers is still in the C _____ account. This is why, in times when cash is low, a business tries to keep current liabilities as [high / low] as feasible.

more

Cash

high

9-41. Users of financial statements need to understand these relationships, but there is no need to memorize them. The cash flow statement gives the net effect of each of the four types of adjustments in working capital items. Complete the following summary of them:

Change	Adjustment to Net Income	
Decrease in a current asset	add	
Increase in a current asset	[add / subtract]	subtract
Increase in a current liability	[add / subtract]	add
Decrease in a current liability	[add / subtract]	subtract

> **NOTE:** Remember that these adjustments are made to convert the net income number to a cash basis. The net income number, as reported on the income statement, is *not changed.*

9-42. Complete the "Cash Flow from Operating Activities" section of Exhibit 11. (Remember that numbers in parentheses are subtracted.) The cash flow from operating activities was $_____,000.

29

3-42. The complete set of rules for making entries to accounts is as follows:

Increases in assets are [debits / credits].

Decreases in assets are [debits / credits].

Increases in liabilities and equity are [debits / credits].

Decreases in liabilities and equity are [debits / credits].

Increases in revenues are [debits / credits].

Increases in expenses are [debits / credits].

debits
credits
credits
debits
credits
debits

NOTE: It is important that you learn these rules; they govern all accounting transactions. Also, although this may seem strange, it is a fact that both increases in assets (which are good things) and increases in expenses (which are not so good) are debits. That's the way it has to be, in order to maintain the basic equation. Remember that *debit* simply means left and *credit* means right.

THE LEDGER AND THE JOURNAL

3-43. A group of accounts, such as those for Green Company in Exhibit 3, is called a ledger. There is no standard form, so long as there is space to record the d __ __ __ __ s and c __ __ __ __ __ s to each account. In Exhibits 4 and 5 we return to Evergreen Market, the same company we examined in Part 2. Exhibit 5 is the _____ of Evergreen Market.

debits   credits

ledger

3-44. In practice, transactions are not recorded directly in the ledger. First, they are written in a record such as Exhibit 4. The title of Exhibit 4 shows that this record is called a _____. The record made for each transaction is called a _____ entry.

journal

journal

3-45. As Exhibit 4 shows, for each journal entry, the account to be [debited / credited] is listed first, and the [Dr. / Cr.] amount is entered in the first of the two money columns. The account to be [debited / credited] is listed below, and is indented. The [Dr. / Cr.] amount is entered in the second money column.

debited   Dr.

credited

Cr.

9-34. This follows from the fundamental accounting equation:

_____ = _____ + _____ . To keep this equation in balance, a decrease in Accounts Receivable would necessarily mean an equal [increase / decrease] in Cash, if these were the only two accounts involved.

Assets = Liabilities + Equity

increase

9-35. This makes sense because if everything else remains the same, a decrease in Accounts Receivable means the company received more c ___ ___ ___ payments during the accounting period compared to last period's Accounts Receivable.

cash

NOTE: A change in a current asset may not have an immediate effect on Cash. For example, an increase in Inventory may be accompanied by an increase in Accounts Payable. However, the ultimate effect on Cash for each separate transaction is as described, and the effect from the other accounts will be considered when we analyze those accounts.

ADJUSTMENTS FOR CHANGES IN CURRENT LIABILITIES

9-36. Changes in current liabilities have the opposite effect on Cash than changes in current assets. An increase in a current liability requires that the net income amount be adjusted to a cash basis by [adding to it / subtracting from it]. A decrease in a current liability requires that the adjustment be a(n) [addition / subtraction].

adding to it

subtraction

9-37. Exhibit 10 shows that Accounts Payable [increased / decreased] by $_____,000. Therefore, net income is adjusted to a cash basis by [adding / subtracting] this amount. Enter this change in Exhibit 11.

decreased

3

subtracting

9-38. Exhibit 10 shows that Accrued Wages [increased / decreased] by $_____,000. Therefore, net income is adjusted to a cash basis by [adding / subtracting] this amount. Enter this change in Exhibit 11.

increased

4

adding

3-46. On January 8, merchandise costing $600 was sold for $900, and the customer agreed to pay $900 within 30 days. Using the two journal entries for January 7 as a guide, record the two parts of this transaction in the journal. (If you are not sure about how to record this transaction, go to Frame 3-47.)

8	Accounts Receivable	.....	900	
	Revenues	....		900
8	Expenses	....	600	
	Inventory	....		600

(If you did this correctly, jump ahead to Frame 3-49.)

3-47. On January 8, merchandise costing $600 was sold for $900, and the customer agreed to pay $900 within 30 days.

The first part of this transaction is that the business earned **revenues** of $900, and an asset, **Accounts Receivable,** increased by $900. Record this part of the transaction by completing the blanks below.

Dr. [ ] 900

Cr. [ ] 900

Dr.   Accounts Receivable 900

Cr.   Revenues 900

> **HINT:** If you are uncertain as to whether a particular account is to be debited or credited, you usually can find out by referring to the other account in the entry. For example, the entry to Accounts Receivable is an increase in an asset, which is a debit, so the entry to Revenues must be a credit.

3-48. On January 8, merchandise costing $600 was sold for $900, and the customer agreed to pay $900 within 30 days.

The other part of this transaction is that the business had an **expense** of $600 because its **Inventory** was decreased by $600. Record this part of the transaction by completing the blanks below.

Dr. [ ] 600

Cr. [ ] 600

Dr.   Expenses 600

Cr.   Inventory 600

9-28. Because the increase in Cash was [more than / less than] the amount of Revenues, we must [add to / subtract from] net income the amount that Cash was greater than Revenues. As shown above, this was $_____,000. Enter this amount in Exhibit 11.

more than
add to

2

9-29. If Accounts Receivable had increased during the period, the adjustment of net income would be the opposite; that is, an increase in a non-cash current asset leads to an adjustment that [adds to / subtracts from] net income in order to find the cash flow from operations.

subtracts from

9-30. As shown in Exhibit 10, the beginning balance in Inventory was $_____,000, and the ending balance was $_____,000, which shows that this asset [increased / decreased] by $_____,000 during the year. This change had the opposite effect on Cash than the change in Accounts Receivable. Therefore, we must [add to / subtract from] net income to arrive at the change in cash. Enter the $4,000 in Exhibit 11.

56   60
increased   4

subtract from

9-31. If the balance in a working capital account is unchanged, the inflow to Cash [is / is not] the same amount as revenue, and an adjustment [is / is not] necessary.

is
is not

9-32. To summarize, we must analyze changes in the balance sheet accounts to determine their impact on Cash. We are interested in the w _____ c _____ accounts to prepare the "cash flows from o __ __ __ __ __ __ __ __ __ activities" section of the statement of cash flows.

working capital
operating

9-33. An easy way to remember whether the impact on Cash (and hence the adjustment to net income) is an addition or a subtraction is to pretend that only that one account and Cash exist. For example, if Cash and Accounts Receivable were the only accounts, a decrease in Accounts Receivable would have to mean a(n) [increase / decrease] in Cash.

increase

3-49. Journal entries are transferred to the l __ __ __ __ __ (as in Exhibit 5). This process is called **posting.** The entries through January 7 have already been posted to the ledger, as indicated by the check mark opposite each one. Post the journal entries for January 8 to the proper ledger accounts in Exhibit 5, and make check marks on Exhibit 4 to show that you have posted them.

ledger

Accounts Receivable		Revenues	
900			300
			800
			900

Inventory		Expenses	
2,000	200	200	
2,000	500	500	
	600	**600**	

3-50. To summarize, any transaction requires at least (how many?) _____ changes in the accounts. These changes are recorded first in the [ledger / journal]. They are then posted to the [ledger / journal].

two

journal   ledger

THE CLOSING PROCESS

3-51. The Revenues account in Exhibit 5 reports [increases / decreases] in Retained Earnings during the period, and the Expenses account reports [increases / decreases] in Retained Earnings. As we know, the difference between revenues and expenses is the net i __ __ __ __ __ of the period.

increases

decreases

income

3-52. The net income for the period is an increase in the equity account, R __ __ __ __ __ __ __ __ E __ __ __ __ __ __ __ __ . Net income is added to this account by a series of journal entries called **closing entries.**

Retained Earnings

3-53. In order to do this, we first must find the balance in the account that is to be closed. What is the balance in the Revenues account in Exhibit 5? $_____.

$2,000 (= $300 + $800 + $900)

9-25. Consider what the account balances would have been if Chico Company had revenue of $300,000 but had received $302,000 cash from customers. Enter the $302,000 in the T-accounts shown below and find the account balances.

```
                        Cash
   Beg. bal.          7
                                                            302
   From customer [      ]
   ════════════════════════  ════════════════════════
   End. bal.    [      ]                                    309

                 Accounts Receivable
   Beg. bal.         42   From customer [      ]            302

   Sale             300
   ════════════════════════  ════════════════════════
   End. bal.    [      ]                                    40

                      Revenues
                          Sale          300
```

9-26. The above accounts show that in this situation, the ending balance of Cash would have been [$2,000 larger than / $2,000 smaller than / the same as] the Cash balance when cash receipts equaled sales revenues, as shown in Frame 9-22. The Accounts Receivable balance would have been [$2,000 larger than / $2,000 smaller than / the same as] the balance when cash receipts equaled sales revenues. Revenues in 2009 would still have been $300,000.

$2,000 larger than

$2,000 smaller than

9-27. This example shows that if the ending balance in Accounts Receivable was *less* than its beginning balance, the increase in Cash would be [more than / less than / the same as] the amount of Revenues. Part of the increase in Cash would be the result of decreasing Accounts Receivable. Put another way, Cash increased partly because more old customers paid their bills and partly because of sales to new customers. This is what happened in Chico Company.

more than

3-54. An entry is made that reduces the balance in the account to be closed to zero and records the same amount in the Retained Earnings account. Because the Revenues account has a [Dr. / Cr.] balance, the entry that reduces Revenues to zero must be on the other side; that is, it must be a [Dr. / Cr.].

Cr.

Dr.

3-55. In Exhibit 4, write the journal entry that closes the $2,000 balance in the Revenues account to the Retained Earnings account. (Date it January 8, the end of the accounting period.)

| 8 | Revenues .... 2,000 | |
| | Retained Earnings ..... | 2,000 |

3-56. Using similar reasoning, write the journal entry that closes the $1,300 balance in the Expenses account to the Retained Earnings account.

| 8 | Retained Earnings .... 1,300 | |
| | Expenses .... | 1,300 |

3-57. Next, post these two entries to the ledger in Exhibit 5.

The accounts affected are:

Revenues

2,000	300
	800
	900

Expenses

200	*1,300*
500	
600	

Retained Earnings

(Dr.)	(Cr.)
1,300	*2,000*

9-22. If, in 2009, Chico Company received $300,000 cash from credit customers, Cash would increase and Accounts Receivable would decrease, as summarized in the following journal entry:

Dr. ——————— 300   Cash

     Cr. ——————— ——————— 300   Accounts Receivable

9-23. The above two entries have been posted to the accounts as shown below:

Cash			Accounts Receivable		
Beg. bal.	7		Beg. bal.	42	From customer 300
From customer	300		Sale	300	
End. bal.	307		End. bal.	42	

Revenues	
Sale	300

As these accounts show, when the balance in Accounts Receivable does not change, the increase in cash is [more than / less than / the same as] the sales revenue.   the same as

9-24. This is the case with all working capital accounts. If the beginning balance is the same as the ending balance, an adjustment from the accrual basis to the cash basis [is / is not] necessary when preparing the statement of cash flows.   is not

3-58. To get ready for preparing the financial statements, the balance in each asset, liability, and equity account is calculated. (Revenue and expense accounts have zero balances because of the closing process.) For the Cash account in Exhibit 5, the calculation is as follows:

Cash

(Dr.)	(Cr.)
10,000	2,000
5,000	
300	
800	
16,100	**2,000**
Balance **14,100**	

> **NOTE:** Each side is totaled. A single line is drawn above the total. A double line is drawn beneath the total. The difference between the two totals is entered beneath the double line.

Calculate the balance for each account in Exhibit 5.

(Details are not shown here. The amounts can be checked against the amounts in Frame 3-60.)

3-59. Journal entries *change* the balance in the account. The *calculation* of the balance does not change the balance. Therefore the calculation of a balance [does / does not] require a journal entry.

does not

3-60. The balance sheet is prepared from the balances in the asset, liability, and equity accounts. Complete the balance sheet for Evergreen Market, as of January 8, in Exhibit 6.

EVERGREEN MARKET
Balance Sheet as of January 8

Assets		Liabilities & Equity	
		Accounts	
Cash	$14,100	Payable	$ 2,000
Accounts		Note	
Receivable .	900	Payable	5,000
		Paid-in	
Inventory ...	2,700	Capital	10,000
		Retained	
		Earnings ...	700
Total		Total Liabilities	
Assets	$17,700	and Equity	$17,700

ADJUSTMENTS FOR CHANGES IN WORKING CAPITAL ACCOUNTS

9-18. Cash, accounts receivable, inventory, and similar items that will be converted into cash in the near future are c _____ assets.

current

Accounts payable, wages payable, and similar obligations that are due in the near future are c _____ liabilities. The difference between current assets and current liabilities is called **working capital.** Operating activities—such as making sales; purchasing materials for inventory; and incurring production, selling, and administrative expenses—are the principal causes of changes in working capital items. We shall analyze the asset and liability categories separately.

current

> **NOTE:** Although cash is, of course, an item of working capital, we exclude it here when we adjust for changes in working capital accounts because we want to analyze the impact of such changes on cash. Remember that the statement of cash flows *explains* the change in cash from one period to the next.

ADJUSTMENTS FOR CHANGES IN CURRENT ASSETS

9-19. If all revenues in 2009 were from cash sales, cash inflows [would / would not] be the same amount as revenues; that is, if sales revenues were $300,000, cash inflows would be $_____,000. However, in most companies, some sales are made to credit customers. These sales are first reported as the current asset, A _ _ _ _ _ _ _ _ R _ _ _ _ _ _ _ _ _ _ . The company will receive cash later on, when customers pay their bills.

would

300

Accounts
Receivable

9-20. In Chico Company, all sales were credit sales. If sales in 2009 were $300,000, Revenues would be $_____,000, and Accounts Receivable would increase by $_____,000 when these sales were made.

300

300

9-21. The journal entry summarizing the above transaction would be (omitting 000):

Dr. A _____ R _____   300

Cr. R _____   300

Accounts Receivable

Revenues

3-61. The income statement is prepared from information in the Retained Earnings account. Complete the income statement in Exhibit 6.

EVERGREEN MARKET
Income Statement
for the period January 2–8

Revenues	$2,000
Expenses	1,300
Net income	$ 700

3-62. After the closing process, the revenue and expense accounts have [debit / credit / zero] balances. These accounts are therefore **temporary** accounts. They are started over at the beginning of each period. The asset accounts have [debit / credit / zero] balances, and the liability and equity accounts have [debit / credit / zero] balances; these balances are carried forward to the next period. Income statement accounts are [temporary / permanent] accounts, and balance sheet accounts are [temporary / permanent] accounts.

zero

debit

credit

temporary

permanent

3-63. Most entities report individual items of revenues and expenses (such as salary expense, maintenance expense, insurance expense) on their income statement. In order to do this, they set up an account for each expense item. Thus, if the income statement reported 2 revenue items and 10 expense items, there would be at least _____ (how many?) revenue and expense accounts. We shall describe these accounts in later parts. The entries to them are made in exactly the same way as in the simple example given here.

12

3-64. Management needs more detailed information than is contained in the financial statements. For example, instead of one account, Accounts Receivable, it needs an account for each customer so that the amount owed by each customer is known. Therefore the ledger usually contains [the same number of / many more] accounts than there are items on the financial statements.

many more

> **NOTE:** Although you need to understand the bookkeeping process described in this part, you don't need to memorize the details. Our purpose is to show where the numbers in the financial statements come from. This helps you understand what the numbers mean.

9-14. If Depreciation expense was $4,000 higher than the amount reported in Exhibit 10, Net Income would be $4,000 [higher than / lower than / the same as] the amount reported. The $4,000 increase in Depreciation expense would offset exactly the $4,000 decrease in Net Income. Cash flow would be [higher than / lower than / the same as] the amount reported in Exhibit 11.

lower than

the same as

9-15. To reinforce this point, recall the journal entry that records Depreciation Expense:

Dr. D _____ E _____

    Cr. A _____ D _____

Depreciation Expense

  Accumulated Depreciation

The Cash account [was / was not] changed by this entry.

was not

9-16. To repeat, the cash for fixed assets was paid out when the fixed assets were purchased (or when borrowings made in connection with such a purchase were paid back). Cash [is / is not] affected by the depreciation charge; to do so would be double counting.

is not

> **NOTE:** Revenues and expenses that don't cause cash flows, such as amortization of intangible assets, write-off of losses, and other noncash expenses, also are added to net income to convert net income to cash flow from operating activities.

9-17. Thus, depreciation [is / is not] a source of cash. (This is a common misconception because of the role it plays on the statement of cash flows to adjust net income to a cash basis.)

is not

A NOTE ON COMPUTERS

Most entities use a computer to do their accounting. The computer makes debit and credit entries according to exactly the same rules as those we have described. In this program, we must show the journal entries manually because what goes on inside the computer is not visible. The computer has the following advantages over the manual system we use in this program:

- The computer is much faster.

- The computer does not make copying errors. For example, when the computer writes a check, the amount of the check is always the amount credited to the Cash account and debited to some other account. The amounts reported on the financial statement are the same as the balances in the accounts.

- The computer ensures that debit entries always equal credit entries. It will not accept an entry in which this equality does not exist.

- Once an amount has been recorded in the computer, it may be used for several purposes. For example, an entry to Accounts Receivable is used in calculating the total amount in the Accounts Receivable account, the accounts of individual customers, and the amount reported on the balance sheet.

- The computer does not make arithmetic errors.

- The computer may require that certain rules be followed. For example, the credit entry for a check is always to the Cash account.

- The computer has built-in safeguards that may help detect fraudulent or erroneous entries.

- In a company at several locations, an entry generated at one location can be transferred accurately to the central chart of accounts via the Internet. Companies have a chart of accounts that gives an account number for every possible transaction in the system. This can help to ensure the tracking of information if it is necessary.

However, if the initial input to the computer is made by a person, an error made by that person may not be detected. For example, if a check is supposed to be for $962 and the bookkeeper keys in $926, the computer may not detect the error. (Some input errors can be avoided by the use of automatic input devices, such as scanners that read bar codes.)

9-9. Net income is the difference between r __ __ __ __ __ __ es and e __ __ __ __ __ __ es. "Cash flow from operating activities" is the difference between **operating** cash inflows and **operating** cash outflows. To find the amount of cash flow from operating activities, we must make two types of adjustments to net income to convert it to a cash basis: (1) for depreciation and other expenses that will *never* require an outflow of c __ __ __ and (2) for changes in working capital accounts (accounts that are an integral part of daily operating activities).

revenues
expenses

cash

> **NOTE:** Recall that net income is added to beginning retained earnings to arrive at ending retained earnings. With no dividends, the change in the balance sheet account called retained earnings is simply net income. (Please review Frames 8-40 and 8-41 for this concept.)

ADJUSTMENT FOR DEPRECIATION EXPENSE

9-10. According to its balance sheet (Exhibit 10), Chico Company owned PPE, most of which it had acquired [prior to / in] the year 2009 at a cost of $__ __ __,000. The cash outflow for these assets occurred [prior to 2009 / in 2009].

prior to
108
prior to 2009

9-11. According to its income statement, Chico Company had a Depreciation expense of $__ __ __,000 in 2009. Depreciation recognizes a portion of the cost of fixed assets. The cash outflow for the assets on hand at the beginning of 2009 occurred in earlier years; this Depreciation expense therefore [was / was not] a cash outflow in 2009.

6

was not

9-12. Although depreciation expense is subtracted from revenue in arriving at net income, *it is not a cash outflow*. Net income is $6,000 less than it would have been with no depreciation expense. Therefore, Net Income is adjusted to a cash basis by [adding $6,000 to / subtracting $6,000 from] Net Income. Enter this adjustment in Exhibit 11. This completes our first adjustment to express net income on a cash basis.

adding $6,000 to

9-13. Suppose that Chico Company had decided to recognize Depreciation expense of $10,000, rather than $6,000, in 2009 but made no other changes in the accounts. The cash flow from operating activities would then be [higher than / lower than / the same as] the amount reported in Exhibit 11.

the same as

> **NOTE:** If you answered Frame 9-13 correctly, go to Frame 9-15.

Also, despite the built-in safeguards, the computer cannot detect certain types of fraudulent entries. As examples of multimillion dollar errors reported in the press demonstrate, there is no guarantee that errors do not exist. Therefore, there must be an audit function to check the possibility of fraud or error. We will introduce some of the safeguards that are in place to prevent fraud later in this book.

Although the computer may perform most of the bookkeeping functions, it cannot replace the accountant. The accountant specifies the rules to be followed in routine transactions, but, as we shall see, some transactions require judgment about the accounts affected and the amounts to be debited or credited. The accountant must tell the computer how to make these entries. If the accountant makes an incorrect decision, the accounts will be incorrect.

Most important is the fact that learning the financial accounting transactions and closing processes as you are doing here cannot be replaced by a computer. It is basic to the understanding of the underlying processes. Thus, it is also basic to analyzing the financial statements. Once you understand the mechanics behind and structure of the financial statements, using a computer to facilitate their completion makes sense.

KEY POINTS TO REMEMBER

- **Debit** refers to the left side of an account and **credit** to the right side.

- Increases in asset and expense accounts are debits.

- Increases in liability, equity, and revenue accounts are credits.

- Decreases are the opposite.

- For any transaction, debits must equal credits. For the whole set of accounts, debit balances must equal credit balances.

- Transactions are first recorded in a journal. Amounts are then posted to the accounts in a ledger.

- Revenue and expense accounts are temporary accounts. At the end of each accounting period, they are closed to Retained Earnings. They start over at the beginning of the next accounting period. The difference between the revenues of a period and the expenses of the period is the net income of the period. These revenues and expenses are reported on the income statement.

- Net income is the increase in retained earnings from operating performance during the period.

9-6. The indirect method uses balance sheet account *changes* to determine whether such changes had a positive or negative impact on c __ __ __ f __ __ __ __ . Since the balance sheet must always stay in balance, it is easy to determine the impact on c _____ by analyzing changes in each of the other accounts.

cash flow

cash

9-7. In preparing the statement of cash flows, we are interested in **changes** in the balance sheet accounts from one accounting period to another. The purpose of the statement of cash flows is to provide information about items that caused the c __ __ __ __ __ in cash from one balance sheet to another. This will help us to understand the **sources** and **uses** of cash during the accounting period.

change

9-8. Therefore, since the statement of cash flows must total the change in _____ for an accounting period, it must total to the difference in the Cash account from one _____ _____ (which financial statement?) to the next. We will show this reconciliation later.

cash

balance sheet

> **NOTE:** We next develop a statement of cash flows for Chico Company, using the indirect method and the balance sheet and income statement information in Exhibit 10.
>   We will work with the statement of cash flows in Exhibit 11. It consists of three sections. We will describe the first section, called "cash flow from operating activities," in some detail. We will describe the other two sections, called "cash flow from investing activities" and "cash flow from financing activities," together because the same principles apply to both. The principal purpose of this part is to show the relationship between the accrual accounting numbers and cash.

CASH FLOW FROM OPERATING ACTIVITIES—INDIRECT METHOD

> **NOTE:** The first section of the statement of cash flows reports how much cash was generated and/or used by the operating activities of the period—the day-to-day activities of the organization. To do this, we begin with net income and adjust this accrual amount for items that don't affect cash flow. We then make other adjustments to change net income from an accrual basis to a cash basis. This is somewhat complex, so we will review only the basics.

- Asset, liability, and equity accounts are permanent accounts. Their balances are carried forward to the next accounting period.

- Some revenues do not result in immediate cash inflows. Some expenses do not result in immediate cash outflows. Therefore, retained earnings are not the same as cash!

You have completed Part 3 of this program. If you think you understand the material in this part, you should now take Post-Test 3, which is found at the back of this text. If you are uncertain about your understanding, you should review Part 3.

The post-test will serve both to test your comprehension and to review the highlights of Part 3. After taking the post-test, you may find that you are unsure about certain points. You should review these points before going on to Part 4. Please review the answers to Post-Test 3, following the Post-Tests, at the back of this text.

9-3. Both the income statement and the statement of cash flows report flows during the period. The difference is that the income statement reports flows on the **accrual** basis; that is, inflows are measured as r _____ s and outflows are measured as e _____ s.   revenues expenses

By contrast, the statement of cash flows reports inflows and outflows of

c _____.   cash

> **NOTE:** The income statement focuses on *profitability.* The statement of cash flows focuses on *sources* and *uses* of cash.

9-4. For example, assume that an entity sold goods for $1,000 on May 1, and the customer paid $1,000 for these goods on June 1. Its cash inflow on May 1 would be [$0 / $1,000], and its revenue in May would $0

be [$0 / $1,000]. Its cash inflow on June 1 would be [$0 / $1,000], $1,000 $1,000

and its revenue in June would be [$0 / $1,000]. Its balance sheet at $0

the end of May would include this $1,000 as an asset, called

A _____ R _____.   Accounts Receivable

> **NOTE:** Therefore, an entity's revenues and expenses in a period do not necessarily match its cash receipts and disbursements in that period. This is one of the most important concepts to understand in learning financial accounting.

9-5. There are two acceptable methods of preparing the statement of cash flows. One is to summarize the inflows and outflows to the Cash account **directly;** it is therefore called the d __ __ __ __ __ method. Most   direct

companies, however, use the other method, which is called the

ind __ __ __ __ __ method.   indirect

> **NOTE:** Companies that use the indirect method report their cash flows *indirectly* by adjusting net income to remove the effects of accrual accounting. The indirect method is much more widely used because it shows the relationship between the income statement and the balance sheet and therefore aids in the analysis of these statements.

## Part 4

Revenues and Monetary Assets

Learning Objectives

In this part you will learn:

- The accounting period.
- What accrual accounting is.
- Three more of the nine basic accounting concepts:
    - The conservatism concept.
    - The materiality concept.
    - The realization concept.
- How revenue items are measured.
- How monetary assets are measured.
- The days' sales uncollected ratio.

4-1. In Part 3 we introduced the idea of **net income**, which is the difference between r _ _ _ _ _ _ _ and e _ _ _ _ _ _ _ _ .

revenues   expenses

4-2. Net income increases Retained Earnings. Retained Earnings is an item of [liabilities / equity] on the balance sheet. Any increase in Retained Earnings is also an increase in [liabilities / equity].

equity

equity

> **NOTE:** Net income results from the profitable operation of an entity. The amount of net income is one of the most important items of information that accounting reports. In this part we describe how the revenue portion of net income is measured.

## Part 9

Statement of Cash Flows

Learning Objectives

In this part you will learn:

- What a statement of cash flows is.
- How it differs from an income statement.
- The meaning of the term "cash flow from operations."
- The content of the other two sections, investing and financing activities.
- The relationship of depreciation to cash flow.
- Uses of the statement of cash flows.

9-1. A company must prepare three financial statements. We described two of them in earlier parts. The [balance sheet / income statement] reports the financial status of the company as of the end of each accounting period. The [balance sheet / income statement] reports financial performance during the period.

balance sheet

income statement

9-2. In this part, we describe the third required statement. It reports the **flow of cash** during the accounting period, and it is therefore called the statement of c __ __ __ __ f __ __ __ __ s.

cash flows

FISCAL YEAR

4-3. An income statement reports the amount of net income [at a moment in time / over a period of time]. The period of time covered by one income statement is called the **accounting period.**

over a period of time

4-4. For most entities, the official accounting period is one year, referred to as the **fiscal year.** However, financial statements, called **interim statements,** usually are prepared for shorter periods. In Part 3 you prepared an income statement for Evergreen Market for the period January 2 through January 8. This was an [annual / interim] statement, and the accounting period was one [week / month / year].

interim
week

4-5. Entities don't fire their employees and cease operations at the end of an accounting period. They continue from one accounting period to the next. The fact that accounting divides the stream of events into f _ _ _ _ _ _   y _ _ _ s makes the problem of measuring revenues and expenses in a fiscal year [an easy / the most difficult] problem in accounting.

fiscal years
the most difficult

ACCRUAL ACCOUNTING

4-6. On January 3, Evergreen Market borrowed $5,000 from a bank. Its cash therefore [increased / decreased / did not change]. A liability [increased / decreased / did not change].

increased
increased

4-7. Revenues are increases in equity. The receipt of $5,000 cash as a loan from the bank on January 3 [increased / decreased / did not change] Evergreen Market revenues and therefore [increased / decreased / did not change] equity.

did not change
did not change

4-8. On January 4, Evergreen Market purchased $2,000 of inventory, paying cash. This was an increase in one asset and a decrease in another asset. Since equity was unchanged, the payment of cash on January 4 [was / was not] associated with an expense.

was not

You have completed Part 8 of this program. If you think you understand the material in this part, you should now take Post-Test 8, which is found in the back of this text. If you are uncertain about your understanding, you should review Part 8.

The post-test will serve both to test your comprehension and to review the highlights of Part 8. After taking the post-test, you may find that you are unsure about certain points. You should review these points before going on to Part 9. Please review the answers to Post-Test 8, following the Post-Tests, at the back of this text.

4-9. On January 8, Evergreen Market sold merchandise for $900, and the customer agreed to pay $900 within 30 days. This transaction resulted in [an increase / a decrease / no change] in cash. Revenue was $_____. This revenue [was / was not] associated with a change in cash on January 8.

no change

$900   was not

4-10. Evidently revenues and expenses [are / are not] always accompanied, at the same time, by changes in cash. Moreover, changes in cash [are / are not] always coupled with corresponding changes in revenues or expenses.

are not

are not

4-11. Increases or decreases in cash are changes in an [equity / asset] account. Revenues or expenses are changes in an [equity / asset] account.

asset

equity

4-12. Net income is measured as the difference between [cash increases and cash decreases / revenues and expenses].

revenues and expenses

4-13. Net income measures the increase in e __ __ __ __ __ during an accounting period that was associated with earnings activities.

equity

4-14. Many individuals and some small businesses keep track only of cash receipts and cash payments. This type of accounting is called c __ __ __ accounting. If you keep a record of your bank deposits, the checks you write, and the balance in your bank account, you are doing __ __ __ __ accounting. Cash accounting [does / does not] measure changes in equity.

cash

cash   does not

KEY POINTS TO REMEMBER

- A company obtains its permanent capital from two sources: (1) debt (i.e., noncurrent liabilities) and (2) equity. It uses this capital to finance (1) working capital (i.e., current assets – current liabilities) and (2) noncurrent assets.

- Most debt capital is obtained by issuing bonds. Bonds obligate the company to pay interest and to repay the principal when it is due.

- Equity capital is obtained by (1) issuing shares of stock and (2) retaining earnings.

- The amount of capital obtained from preferred and common shareholders is the amount they paid in. The par, or stated, value of common stock is not an important number today, but it is still reported on the balance sheet.

- Cash dividends decrease the amount of equity capital. Stock dividends or stock splits do not affect the total equity.

- Retained earnings are total earnings (i.e., net income) since the entity began operations, less total dividends. (A net loss, of course, results in a decrease in retained earnings.)

- Although sometimes called "net worth," the amount of owners' equity does *not* show what the owners' interest is worth.

- In deciding on its permanent capital structure, a company attempts to strike the right balance between (1) risky but low-cost debt capital and (2) less risky but high-cost equity capital. For a given company this balance is indicated by its debt ratio.

- Many companies have subsidiaries. The economic entity is a family consisting of the parent and the subsidiaries (in which, by definition, it owns more than 50% of the stock). Consolidated financial statements are prepared for such an economic entity by combining their separate financial statements and eliminating transactions among members of the family.

- The consolidated balance sheet reports all the assets owned by the consolidated entity and all the claims of parties outside the family.

- The consolidated income statement reports only revenues from sales to outside parties and expenses resulting from costs incurred with outside parties. Intrafamily revenues and expenses are eliminated.

4-15. Most entities, however, account for revenues and expenses, as well as for cash receipts and cash payments. This type of accounting is called **accrual accounting.** Evidently, accrual accounting is [simpler / more complicated] than cash accounting, but accrual accounting [does / does not] measure changes in equity. The most difficult problems in accounting are problems of [cash / accrual] accounting.

more complicated
does

accrual

4-16. Because net income is the change in equity and measures the entity's financial performance, accrual accounting provides [more / less] information than cash accounting.

more

4-17. In order to measure the net income of a period, we must measure r __ __ __ __ __ __s and e __ __ __ __ __ __s of that period, and this requires the use of __ __ __ __ __ __ __ accounting.

revenues   expenses
accrual

CONSERVATISM CONCEPT

> **NOTE:** In this part, we describe the measurement of revenues. The measurement of expenses is described in later parts. First, we shall introduce three more accounting concepts: conservatism, materiality, and realization.

4-18. Suppose that in January, Sarah Young agreed to buy an automobile from Ace Auto Company; the automobile is to be delivered to Young in March. Because Ace Auto Company is in the business of selling automobiles, it [would / would not] be happy that Young has agreed to buy one.

would

4-19. Young agreed in January to buy an automobile for delivery in March. Although Young is [likely / unlikely] to take delivery in March, it is possible that she will change her mind. The sale of this automobile therefore is [absolutely certain / uncertain].

likely

uncertain

8-74. Palm Company owns 60% of the stock of Sand Company. This stock was reported on the balance sheet of Palm Company as an asset, Investment in Subsidiaries, at $60,000. The total equity of Sand Corporation is $100,000. On the consolidated balance sheet, the $60,000 asset would be eliminated, and because debits must equal credits, [$60,000 / $100,000] of Sand Company's consolidated equity also would be eliminated.

$60,000

8-75. Palm Company owns 60% of Sand Company's stock, which is a [majority / minority] of the stock. Other shareholders own the other 40% of Sand Company stock; they are [majority / minority] shareholders. They have an interest in the consolidated entity, and this interest is reported in the [assets / liabilities and equity] side of the consolidated balance sheet. It is labeled **minority interest.**

majority
minority

liabilities and equity

8-76. The consolidated income statement reports revenues from [all sales / sales to outside parties only] and expenses resulting from [all costs incurred / costs incurred with outside parties]. Intrafamily revenues and expenses are e __ __ __ __ __ __ __ __ __ __ d.

sales to outside parties only
costs incurred with outside parties

eliminated

8-77. The consolidated financial statements report on the entity called "Palm Company and Subsidiaries." This family of corporations [is / is not] an economic entity, but it [is / is not] a legal entity.

is
is not

8-78. Many corporations have subsidiaries. Since the consolidated financial statements give the best information about the economic entity, many published financial statements are c __ __ __ __ __ __ __ __ __ __ __ d financial statements.

consolidated

NOTE: In an entity with dozens of subsidiaries, some of which have their own subsidiaries, eliminating the intrafamily transactions is a complicated task. Only the general principles have been described here.

4-20. Young agreed in January to buy an automobile for delivery in March.

Because in January the sale of this automobile is uncertain, accounting [does / does not] recognize the revenue in January. If Jones does accept delivery in March, accounting recognizes r __ __ __ __ __ __ in March. This is a [conservative / risky] way to account for the transaction.

does not
revenue
conservative

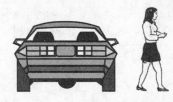

4-21. Increases in equity are recognized only when they are **reasonably certain.** To be conservative, decreases in equity should be recognized as soon as they probably occurred. Suppose an automobile was stolen from Ace Auto Company in January, and the company waits until March to decide that the automobile is gone for good. Conservatism requires that the decrease in equity be recognized when it is **reasonably possible**—that is, in [January / March].

January

4-22. The conservatism concept therefore has two parts:

1. Recognize **increases** in equity only when they are reasonably [certain / possible].

certain

2. Recognize **decreases** in equity as soon as they are reasonably [certain / possible].

possible

> **NOTE:** These are general ideas only. Specifics will be given in later parts of this program.

MATERIALITY CONCEPT

4-23. A brand new pencil is a(n) [asset / liability / equity] of the entity that owns it.

asset

4-24. Every time an employee writes with a pencil, part of the asset's value [increases / decreases], and the entity's equity also [increases / decreases].

decreases   decreases

8-70. In 2008, Palm Company had sales revenue of $1,000,000, Sea Company had sales revenue of $200,000, and Sand Company had sales revenue of $400,000. Palm Company sold $30,000 of products to Sea Company. All other sales were to outside customers. On the consolidated income statement, the amount of sales reported would be $_____.

$1,570,000
(Total sales = $1,000,000 + $200,000 + $400,000 = $1,600,000.
Intrafamily sales = $30,000.
Consolidated sales = $1,600,000 − $30,000 = $1,570,000.)

8-71. Intrafamily transactions are also eliminated from the consolidated balance sheet. For example, if Sand Company owed Palm Company $10,000, this amount would appear as Accounts [Receivable / Payable] on the balance sheet of Palm Company and as Accounts [Receivable / Payable] on the balance sheet of Sand Company. On the consolidated balance sheet, the Accounts Receivable and Accounts Payable would each be $10,000 [more / less] than the sum of these amounts on the balance sheets of each of the family members.

Receivable

Payable

less

8-72. The balance sheet of Palm Company reports as an asset the Sand Company and Sea Company stock that it owns. This asset [remains unchanged / must be eliminated] from the consolidated balance sheet. On the balance sheets of the subsidiaries, the corresponding amounts are reported as [noncurrent liabilities / equity], and these amounts are also eliminated on the consolidated balance sheet.

must be eliminated

equity

8-73. Palm Company owns 40% of Gray Company stock. This asset is listed on Palm Company's balance sheet at $100,000. This asset would *not* be eliminated from the consolidated balance sheet. Why not?

Because only companies in which the parent owns more than 50% are consolidated.

4-25. Would it be possible, theoretically, to find out each day the number of partly used pencils and to make a journal entry showing the amount of pencils that were used up and the corresponding "pencil expense" of that day? [Yes / No] Would it be practical? [Yes / No]

Yes   No

4-26. The accountant considers that the asset value of pencils was entirely used up at the time they were issued to the user. To do otherwise would be a waste of time. This solution is simple and [impractical / practical], but [more / less] exact than the theoretically correct treatment.

practical

less

4-27. The treatment of pencils is an example of the **materiality** concept. The materiality concept states that the accountant may disregard im__ __ __ __ __ __ __ __ events. When accountants consider the asset value of pencils to be entirely used up when they are issued to the user, they are applying the __ __ __ __ __ __ __ __ __ __ __ concept.

immaterial

materiality

> **NOTE:** Material transactions are those that make a difference in understanding an entity's financial affairs. Deciding which transactions are material is a matter of judgment. There are no mechanical rules.

4-28. The other side of the coin is that the financial statements must disclose all material facts. For example, if a large fraction of a company's inventory is found to be worthless, the m _____ concept requires that this fact be recorded in the accounts.

materiality

4-29. The materiality concept therefore has two parts: (1) [disregard / disclose] trivial (i.e., unimportant) matters, and (2) [disregard / disclose] all important matters.

disregard

disclose

CONSOLIDATED FINANCIAL STATEMENTS

8-65. A corporation that controls one or more other corporations is called the **parent,** and the controlled corporations are called **subsidiaries.**

Palm Company owns 100% of the stock of Sea Company, 60% of the stock of Sand Company, and 40% of the stock of Gray Company. The **parent** company is _____ _____. The subsidiaries are _____ _____ and _____ _____.

Palm Company

Sea Company   Sand Company

8-66. Since the management of the parent corporation, Palm Company, controls the activities of Sea Company and Sand Company, these three companies function as a single entity. The e __ __ __ __ __ concept requires that a set of financial statements be prepared for this family.

entity

8-67. Each corporation is a legal entity, with its own financial statements. The set of financial statements for the whole family brings together, or **consolidates,** these separate statements. The set for the whole family is therefore called a c __ __ __ __ __ __ __ __ __ __ __ d financial statement.

consolidated

8-68. For example, if Palm Company has $10,000 cash, Sea Company has $5,000 cash, and Sand Company has $4,000 cash, the whole family has $_____ cash, and this amount would be reported on the c_____ balance sheet.

$19,000

consolidated

8-69. An entity earns income by making sales to outside customers. It cannot earn income by dealing with itself. Corporations in the consolidated family may buy from and sell to one another. Transactions between members of the family [do / do not] earn income for the consolidated entity. The effect of these **intrafamily transactions,** therefore, must be eliminated from the consolidated statements.

do not

4-30. To review, the conservatism concept is this: recognize increases in equity only when they are r _ _ _ _ _ _ _ _ _ c _ _ _ _ _ _ , but recognize decreases as soon as they are r _ _ _ _ _ _ _ _ _ _ p _ _ _ _ _ _ _ _ . The materiality concept is this: [disregard / disclose] trivial matters, but [disregard / disclose] all important matters.

REALIZATION CONCEPT

4-31. Consider an entity that manufactures goods and then sells them. In accounting, the revenue from these goods is recognized at the time they are delivered to the customer, *not* at the time they are manufactured.

Evans Company manufactured an item in February, delivered it to a customer in March, and the customer paid for it in April. Revenue should be recognized in [February / March / April].

March

February	March	April
Goods manufactured	Goods delivered	Cash received

Revenue recognized

4-32. If a company sells services rather than goods, revenue is recognized at the time the services are [contracted for / delivered].

delivered

4-33. Goods (such as shoes) are *tangible* products. Services (such as repairing computers) are *intangible* products. Both goods and services are products. Thus, the general rule is that revenue from a product is recognized when the product is [manufactured / contracted for / delivered].

delivered

4-34. At the time of delivery, revenue is said to be realized. The realization concept is that revenue is recognized and recorded in the period in which it is r _ _ _ _ _ ed.

realized

DEBT RATIO

8-62. A common way of measuring the relative amount of debt and equity capital is the **debt ratio,** which is the ratio of debt capital to total permanent capital. Recall that **debt capital** is another name for [total / current / noncurrent] liabilities. Equity capital consists of total Paid-in Capital plus R _____ E _____.

noncurrent

Retained Earnings

8-63. Earlier you worked with the following permanent capital structure:

PASCALE COMPANY

Sources and Uses of Permanent Capital
as of December 31, 2008

Uses of Capital		Sources of Capital	
Working capital	$ 6,000	Noncurrent liabilities	$ 9,000
Noncurrent assets	20,000	Equity	17,000
Total uses	$26,000	Total sources	$26,000

Calculate the debt ratio for Pascale Company.

$$\frac{\text{Debt capital (noncurrent liabilities)}}{\text{Debt capital + equity capital}} = \frac{\boxed{\$\quad}}{\boxed{\$\quad}} = \boxed{\quad \%}^*$$

_____

* Calculate to nearest whole percentage

$\dfrac{\$\ 9,000}{\$26,000} = 35\%$

8-64. Most industrial companies have a debt ratio of less than 50%. Pascale Company [is / is not] in this category.

is

> **NOTE:** If one corporation owns more than 50% of the stock in another corporation, it can control the affairs of that corporation because it can outvote all other owners. Many businesses consist of a number of corporations that are legally separate entities but, because they are controlled by one corporation, are part of a single "family."

4-35. In January, Smith Company contracts to paint Joseph's house. The house is painted in February, and Joseph pays Smith Company in March. Smith Company should recognize revenue in _____ (what month?).

February

January	February	March
Services ordered	Services delivered	Cash received

Revenue recognized

4-36. Gordon Company manufactures some imitation carrots in May. In June it receives an order from Peter Rabbit, for one carrot. Gordon Company delivers the carrot in July. Peter Rabbit pays the bill in August and eats the carrot in September. Gordon Company would recognize revenue in _____, which is [before / after] the order was received and [before / after] the cash was received.

July   after

before

4-37. Revenue is realized when a *sale* is completed by the delivery of a product. Because of this, the word "sales" is often used along with revenue, as in the phrase "s _____ r _____."

sales revenue

4-38. A salesperson may say that he or she has "made a sale" when the order was written, even though the product is to be delivered at some future time. In accounting, writing a sales order [is / is not] a sale because the revenue has not yet been __ __ __ __ __ __ ed.

is not

realized

> **NOTE:** Revenue may be recognized (1) before, (2) during, or (3) after the period in which the cash from the sale is received. First, consider a case in which revenue is recognized in the same period as when the cash is received.

4-39. In January, Loren Company sold and delivered a motorcycle to Paul Owen, who paid $1,800 cash.

In this example, revenue is recognized in the [month before / same month as / month after] the related cash receipt.

same month as

8-59. A company runs the risk of going bankrupt if it has too high a proportion of [debt / equity] capital. A company pays an unnecessarily high cost for its permanent capital if it has too high a proportion of [debt / equity] capital.

debt
equity

8-60. A company that obtains a high proportion of its permanent capital from debt is said to be **highly leveraged.** If such a company does not get into financial difficulty, it will earn a high return for its equity investors because each dollar of debt capital takes the place of a [more / less] expensive dollar of equity capital.

more

8-61. However, highly leveraged companies are risky because the high proportion of debt capital and the associated requirement to pay interest [increases / decreases] the chance that the company will not be able to meet its obligations.

increases

> **NOTE:** In this introductory treatment, we focus on the basic differences between common stock and bonds. Some additional points are worth noting:
>
> 1. The interest on bonds is a tax-deductible expense to the corporation. If the annual interest expense on a 9% bond is $90,000, the corporation's taxable income is reduced by $90,000. At a tax rate of 40%, this means that the net cost to the corporation is only 60% of $90,000, or $54,000; the effective interest cost is 5.4%.
>
> 2. Preferred stock has risk and cost characteristics that are in between common stocks and bonds. Although dividends on preferred stock do not reduce a corporation's taxable income, many companies still use preferred stock as a source of capital.
>
> 3. In recent years, there has been a tremendous increase in the types of debt and equity securities. New financial instruments are structured with risk and cost characteristics designed to meet the needs of various types of investors. These concepts are beyond our introductory text.

4-40. In January, Loren Company sold another motorcycle for $3,800 and delivered it to Shannon Mills. Mills agreed to pay for the motorcycle in 30 days.

In this case revenue is recognized in the [month before / same month as / month after] the related cash receipt.

month before

4-41. When revenue is recognized before the related cash receipt, as in the preceding transaction, the revenue is accompanied by the right to collect the cash, which is an account receivable. Thus, the entry for the sale of the motorcycle on credit was:

Dr. _____ _____   3,800

    Cr. Sales _____   3,800

Dr. Accounts Receivable 3,800

    Cr. Revenue   3,800

4-42. When a customer pays an entity for a credit purchase, the entity records an increase in Cash and a corresponding decrease in Accounts Receivable. Thus, when Loren Company receives a check for $3,800 from Mills in February, Loren Company makes the following entry:

Dr. _____   3,800

    Cr. _____ _____ . . .   3,800

Dr. Cash 3,800

    Cr. Accounts Receivable   3,800

Revenue [was / was not] recognized in February.

was not

4-43. So far we have treated the cases in which

1. revenue is recognized *in the same period* as the associated cash receipt, and
2. revenue is recognized *before* the associated receipt of cash.

There remains the case in which

3. revenue is recognized _____ the associated receipt of cash.

after

8-54. Bonds are an obligation of the company that issues them, but stocks are not an obligation. Therefore, *investors* usually have more risk if they invest in a company's stock than if they invest in the bonds of the same company. They are not certain to get either dividends or repayment of their investment. Investors therefore demand a [higher / lower] return from an investment in stock than from an investment in bonds in the same company.

higher *(The tradeoff between risk and return is a more advanced concept. It is beyond the scope of this introductory text.)*

8-55. For example, if a company's bonds had an interest rate of 7%, investors would invest in its stock only if they expected that the return on stock would be [at least 7% / considerably more than 7%]. (The expected return on stock consists of both expected dividends and an expected increase in the market value of the stock.)

considerably more than 7%

8-56. Thus, from the viewpoint of the issuing company, stock, which is [debt / equity] capital, is a [more / less] expensive source of capital than bonds, which are [debt / equity] capital.

equity   more
debt

8-57. Circle the correct words in the following table, which shows the principal differences between debt capital and equity capital.

	Bonds (Debt)	Stock (Equity)		
Annual payments required	[Yes / No]	[Yes / No]	Yes	No
Principal payments required	[Yes / No]	[Yes / No]	Yes	No
Risk to the entity is	[High / Low]	[High / Low]	High	Low
But its cost is relatively	[High / Low]	[High / Low]	Low	High

8-58. In deciding on its permanent capital structure, a company must decide on the proper balance between debt capital, which has a relatively [high / low] risk and a relatively [high / low] cost, and equity capital, which has a relatively [high / low] risk and a relatively [high / low] cost.

high   low
low   high

4-44. When a customer pays an entity in advance of delivery of the product, the entity has an obligation to deliver the product. This obligation is a(n) [asset / liability / equity]. It is listed on the [left / right] side of the balance sheet with the title **Advances from Customers.**

liability   right

4-45. Thus, when an entity receives cash in advance of delivery, it records a debit to the Cash account and a corresponding credit to the liability account, Advances from Customers.

In March, King Company received $3,000 cash in advance from a firm to prepare an advertising brochure. Write the entry that King Company should make in March to record this transaction.

Dr. _____ 3,000

    Cr. _____ _____ _____ 3,000

Dr. Cash 3,000

    Cr. Advances from Customers   3,000

4-46. In March, King Company received $3,000 in advance from a firm to prepare an advertising brochure. It delivered the brochure in June. It therefore no longer had the liability, Advances from Customers. Write the entry that should be made in June.

Dr. _____ _____ _____ 3,000

    Cr. S _____ R _____ 3,000

Dr. Advances from Customers .. 3,000

    Cr. Sales Revenue 3,000

March	April	May	June
Cash received	Product made		Product delivered

Revenue recognized

8-49. A stock split has the same effect as a stock dividend. Cash [increases / decreases / is unchanged]. Retained Earnings [increases / decreases / is unchanged]. The market price per share [increases / decreases / is unchanged].

is unchanged
is unchanged
decreases

> **NOTE:** Although arithmetically a "two-for-one" stock split cuts the market price in half, in practice the decrease might be slightly less than this. The reason is that stocks with moderate stock prices tend to be regarded more favorably by investors than stocks with very high prices. This is generally the principal reason for making a stock split.

BALANCE BETWEEN DEBT AND EQUITY CAPITAL

8-50. A corporation obtains some capital from retained earnings. In addition, it obtains capital from the issuance of stock, which is [debt / equity] capital, and from the issuance of bonds, which is [debt / equity] capital.

equity
debt

8-51. A corporation has no fixed obligations to its common shareholders; that is, the company [must / need not] declare dividends each year, and [must / need not] repay the amount the shareholders have invested.

need not
need not

8-52. A company has two fixed obligations to its bondholders, however:

1. _____ ____ _____
2. _____ ____ _____

Payment of interest
Repayment of principal
   (See Frame 8-12.)

8-53. If the company fails to pay either the interest or the principal when due, the bondholders may force the company into bankruptcy.

Evidently bonds are a [less / more] risky method of raising capital by the corporation than stock; that is, debt capital is a [less / more] risky source of capital than equity capital.

more
more

4-47. A magazine publisher received a check for $50 in 2008 for a magazine subscription. The magazines will be delivered in 2009. Write the entry that the publisher should make in 2008.

Dr. _____ 50

Cr. _____ _____ _____ 50

Dr. Cash 50

Cr. Advances from Customers 50

NOTE: The terms "Deferred Revenue," "Precollected Revenue," and "Unearned Revenue" are sometimes used instead of "Advances from Customers." They are still liability accounts.

4-48. A publisher received $50 for a magazine subscription in 2008. In 2009, when the magazines are delivered, the publisher recognizes the $50 revenue and records a corresponding decrease in the liability account, Advances from Customers.

Write the names of the accounts and the amounts for the entry that should be made in 2009.

Dr. _____ _____ _____ ☐

Cr. _____ _____ . . . . . . ☐

Dr. Advances from Customers . . 50

Cr. Sales Revenue 50

4-49. The customer's advance may provide for revenue that will be earned over several future accounting periods. Suppose in 2008 a publisher received $80 for a magazine subscription, with the magazines to be delivered in 2009 and 2010. The entry for 2008 should be:

Dr. _____ . . . . ☐

Cr. _____ _____ _____ ☐

Dr. Cash 80

Cr. Advances from Customers 80

The amount of the liability at the end of 2008 would be [$80 / $40 / $20 / $0].

$80

DISTRIBUTIONS TO SHAREHOLDERS

8-45. Most corporations make an annual cash payment to their common shareholders. This is called a **dividend.** If Yellowstone Company declared and paid a dividend of $5 per share, and if it had 100,000 shares of common stock outstanding, the dividend would be $_____.

$500,000

The journal entry to record the effect of this distribution on Cash and Retained Earnings would be:

Dr. _____ _____ .... _____

Cr. _____ .... _____

Retained Earnings 500,000
    Cash   500,000

8-46. A company may distribute to shareholders a noncash asset, such as shares of stock in other companies it owns or even one of its products. The effect of this distribution is a [debit / credit] to Retained Earnings and an equal [debit / credit] to the asset account.

debit

credit

8-47. Yellowstone Company might declare a **stock dividend.** If it distributed one share of its own stock for each 10 shares of stock outstanding, shareholders would have more shares. No asset decreased, so, in order to maintain equality, equity would [increase / decrease / be unchanged].

be unchanged

8-48. Similarly, Yellowstone might send its shareholders additional shares equal to the number of shares they own, or even double or triple this number of shares. Yellowstone may do this because it believes a high market price per share has an undesirable influence in trading the stock. This is called a **stock split.** If Yellowstone's stock previously had a market price of $200 per share for its 100,000 shares, and it made a "two-for-one" stock split, the number of shares of stock outstanding would [increase / decrease / not change]. Cash would [increase / decrease / not change]. The market price per share would [increase / decrease / not change].

increase

not change

decrease

4-50. In 2008, a publisher received $80 for a magazine subscription, with the magazines to be delivered in 2009 and 2010. The entry for 2009 would be:

Dr. _____ _____ _____ ☐

    Cr. _____ _____ . . . . . . ☐

Dr. Advances from Customers . .   40

    Cr. Sales Revenue   40

At the end of 2009 [$80 / $40 / $20 / $0] would be reported as a liability on the balance sheet.

$40

4-51. In 2008, a publisher received $80 for a magazine subscription, with the magazines to be delivered in 2009 and 2010. The entry for 2010 would be:

Dr. _____ _____ _____   40

    Cr. _____ _____   40

Dr. Advances from Customers . .   40

    Cr. Sales Revenue   40

At the end of 2010 [$80 / $40 / $20 / $0] would be reported as a liability on the balance sheet.

$0

> **NOTE:** The effect of recording these transactions is to assign the total subscription of $80 to the years in which the magazine will be delivered—$40 to each year.

SERVICE REVENUE

4-52. Revenue is recognized in the period in which services are delivered. If a landlord receives cash from a tenant in January and in return permits the tenant to use an apartment in February, March, and April, the landlord recognizes revenue in [January / February / March / April].

February, March, April

8-40. The Retained Earnings account [decreases / increases] by the amount of net income each period and [decreases / increases] by the amount of dividends. Thus, if Retained Earnings are $100,000 at the start of a period during which a dividend of $20,000 is declared and during which net income is $30,000, Retained Earnings will be $_____ at the end of the period.

increases
decreases

$110,000
    (= $100,000 − $20,000 + $30,000)

8-41. Net income refers to the increase in equity [in one year / over the life of the corporation to date], whereas **retained earnings** refers to the net increases, after deduction of dividends, [in one year / over the life of the corporation to date].

in one year

over the life of the corporation to date

8-42. Retained earnings is one **source** of capital. It is reported on the [left / right] side of the balance sheet. The capital is in the form of assets, and assets are reported on the [left / right] side of the balance sheet.

right
left

> **NOTE:** Some people think that retained earnings are assets. Retained earnings are *not* assets. Remember that cash is an asset. Therefore, retained earnings are *not* cash. It is a common error to confuse retained earnings with available cash.

8-43. Equity is sometimes called "net worth." This term suggests that the amount of equity shows what the owners' claim on the assets is *worth*. Because the amounts reported on the assets side of the balance sheet [do / do not] represent the real worth of these assets, this suggestion is [approximately correct / dead wrong].

do not
dead wrong

8-44. The actual **worth** of a company's stock is what people will pay for it. This is the market price of the stock, which [does / does not] appear anywhere on the balance sheet.

does not

4-53. In January, a tenant paid the landlord $2,400 cash covering rent for February, March, and April. This type of revenue is called **rental revenue.** How much revenue would the landlord recognize each month, and how much liability would be reported at the end of each month?

	Rental Revenue for the month	Liability at the end of month
January	$	$
February	$	$
March	$	$
April	$	$

	Rental Revenue for the month	Liability at the end of month
January	$ 0	$2,400
February	$800	$1,600
March	$800	$ 800
April	$800	$ 0

4-54. When a bank lends money, it delivers a service; that is, the bank provides the borrower with the use of the money for a specified period of time. The bank earns revenue for the service it delivers during this period. This type of revenue is called **interest revenue.** In accordance with the realization concept, interest revenue is recognized in the period(s) [in which the interest is received / in which the borrower has the use of the money].

in which the borrower has the use of the money

> **NOTE:** The term "interest income" is sometimes used, but the amount actually is revenue, not income. Income is always a *difference* between revenue and expense.

4-55. Interest revenue is similar to rental revenue. Banks **deliver** a service when they "rent" money; landlords **deliver** a service when they rent apartments. In both cases, revenue is realized in the period(s) in which the service is d _ _ _ _ _ _ _ _ _ .

delivered

4-56. To summarize, accountants recognize revenue in the month *before* the related cash receipt by crediting Revenues and debiting a(n) [asset / liability / equity] account entitled A _ _ _ _ _ _ _ R _ _ _ _ _ _ _ _ _ _ .

asset

Accounts

Receivable

PREFERRED STOCK

8-34. Some corporations issue stock that gives its owners preferential treatment over the common shareholders. As the word "preferential" suggests, such stock is called p __ __ __ __ __ __ ed stock.

preferred

8-35. Usually preferred shareholders have a preferential claim over the common shareholders for the par value of their stock. Thus, if the corporation were liquidated, the owner of 500 shares of $100 preferred stock would have to receive $_____ before the common shareholders received anything.

$50,000 (= 500 × $100)

8-36. As you learned earlier, par value of common stock has [some / almost no] significance. Because preferred stock usually does have a preferential claim on assets equal to its par value, its par value has [some / almost no] significance.

almost no

some

8-37. Preferred shareholders usually have rights to a stated amount of dividends. Stillwater Corporation has issued $100,000 of 9% preferred stock. No dividend can be paid to common shareholders until the preferred shareholders have received their full dividend of 9% of $100,000, amounting to $_____ per year.

$9,000

RETAINED EARNINGS AND DIVIDENDS

8-38. The net income of a period increases e __ __ __ __ __ __ . The directors may vote to distribute money to the shareholders in the form of **dividends.** Dividends decrease e __ __ __ __ __ __ .

equity

equity

8-39. Earnings is another name for "net income." If earnings are not distributed as dividends, they are **retained** in the corporation. This amount is reported on the balance sheet as R __ __ __ __ __ __ __ __ E __ __ __ __ __ __ __ s.

Retained
Earnings

4-57. Accountants recognize revenue in the month *after* the related cash receipt by debiting Cash and crediting a(n) [asset / liability / equity] account when the cash is received. Revenue is recognized when the product is d_ _ _ _ _ _ _ _ _ in accordance with the r _ _ _ _ _ _ _ _ _ _ _ concept.

liability

delivered

realization

> **NOTE:** There are exceptions to the principle that revenue is recognized when a product is delivered. They involve certain types of installment sales, certain long-term contracts, and a few other special situations. They are outside the scope of this introductory treatment.

AMOUNT OF REVENUE

> **NOTE:** The realization concept describes when revenue is recognized. The conservatism concept governs both *when* and *how much* revenue is recognized. In the following frames, you will apply the conservatism concept.

4-58. Loren Company sold a motorcycle to Bryan Harder for $3,000 on credit, but Harder never paid the $3,000. Since Loren Company's assets decreased by one motorcycle but there was no actual increase in another asset, Loren Company's equity actually [increased / stayed the same / decreased] as a result of this transaction. Loren Company [did / did not] realize revenue from this transaction.

decreased

did not

4-59. Obviously, if Loren Company knew in advance that Harder would not pay for the motorcycle, Loren would not have delivered it. Although Loren [would / would not] knowingly sell a motorcycle to someone who is not going to pay, if some customers do not pay, there is a **bad debt.** Loren [must / need not] take this possibility into account in measuring its income. It does this by estimating the amount of revenue that it is **reasonably certain** to receive from all its sales during the accounting period.

would not

must

4-60. Recognizing only the amount of revenue that is reasonably certain to be received is required by the [conservatism / materiality / realization] concept.

conservatism

8-29. The balance sheet amount for common stock is the amount for the number of shares of stock outstanding.

Adatto Company has authorized 100,000 shares of stock. It has issued 60,000 shares, for which it received the stated value of $10 per share. As of December 31, 2008, it has bought back 10,000 shares, paying $10 per share. These shares are its treasury stock. The balance sheet amount for common stock is $_____.

$500,000 [= (60,000 × $10) − (10,000 × $10)]

8-30. Shareholders may sell their stock to other investors. Such sales [do / do not] affect the balance sheet of the corporation. This is an example of the __ __ __ __ __ __ concept.

do not

entity

8-31. When shareholders sell their stock to other investors, the price at which the sale takes place is determined in the **marketplace.** The value at which a stock is sold in such a transaction is called the [market / par / stated] value.

market

8-32. The market value of a company's stock has no necessary relation to its par value, its stated value, or the amount of paid-in capital. If the par value of a certain stock is $1, the market value [will be $1 / can be any value].

can be any value

If the stated value of another stock is $10, the market value [will be $10 / can be any value].

can be any value

If paid-in capital is $12 per share, the market value [will be $12 / can be any value].

can be any value

8-33. The amount reported as total equity equals total assets less total liabilities. On the balance sheet, this is not likely to equal the total market value of all stock outstanding. Evidently accounting [does / does not] report the market value of the shareholders' equity.

does not

4-61. In 2008, Loren Company sold $500,000 of motorcycles to customers, all on credit. It estimated that 2% of these credit sales would never be collected; that is, they would become **bad debts.** Its estimate of bad debts for 2008 was $_____, and its increase in equity in 2008 was therefore only $_____.

$10,000 (= .02 × $500,000)

$490,000 (= $500,000 − $10,000)

4-62. Loren Company recorded each sale as revenue at the time the motorcycles were delivered. In order to measure its increase in equity properly, it must [increase / decrease] the total amount of the change in equity by $_____.

decrease

$10,000

4-63. After this decrease, the amount recognized as revenue is $_____. This is the amount that is [possible / reasonably certain] to be realized. This is in accordance with the [conservatism / materiality] concept.

$490,000   reasonably certain

conservatism

4-64. Since the Accounts Receivable account includes amounts from customers who probably will never pay their bills, it overstates the real asset value. Thus, if the Loren Company decreases its equity by $10,000, it must also [increase / decrease] its Accounts Receivable account by $10,000. Otherwise, the equality of Assets = Liabilities + Equity will not be maintained.

decrease

4-65. However, accountants usually can't decrease the Accounts Receivable account directly because they don't know *which* customers will not pay their bills. Therefore, accountants usually set up a separate account, called **Allowance for Doubtful Accounts.** They record the estimated amount of bad debts as an increase in this account. Accounts Receivable, like all asset accounts, has a [debit / credit] balance. Allowance for Doubtful Accounts, which is subtracted from Accounts Receivable, therefore must have the opposite balance; that is, a [debit / credit] balance.

debit

credit

8-25. If Jones's payment of $10,000 was the only equity transaction, this section of the Marple Company balance sheet would appear as follows:

Common stock . . . . $_____		$ 1,000
Additional paid-in capital . . . . _____		9,000
	_____	
Total paid-in capital . . . . $_____		$10,000

8-26. Not all stocks have a par value. For these **no-par-value stocks,** the directors **state** a value. This value, called the s _____d value, is usually set close to the amount that the corporation actually receives from the issuance of the stock. The difference between this amount and cash received is A_____ P____ - ___ C_____, just as in the case of par-value stock. Below is an example of a stock "without par value." Note the upper right corner of the certificate.

stated

Additional Paid-in
Capital

8-27. When a corporation is formed, its directors vote to **authorize** a certain number of shares of stock and generally to **issue** some of this authorized stock to investors. Thus, at any given time the amount of stock authorized is usually [larger than / the same as / smaller than] the amount issued.

larger than

8-28. A corporation may buy back some of the stock that it had previously issued. Such stock is called **treasury stock.** The **outstanding stock** consists of the issued stock less the treasury stock.

If a company issues 100,000 shares and buys back 15,000 shares, its treasury stock is _____ shares, and its outstanding stock is _____ shares.

15,000

85,000 (=100,000 − 15,000)

4-66. Although this decrease in equity theoretically resulted from the overstatement of revenue, accountants usually record it as an account called **Bad Debt Expense.** The amount recorded as Bad Debt Expense would be $_____. An increase in expense has the same effect on equity as a(n) [decrease / increase] in revenue.

$10,000

decrease

4-67. The entry to record Loren Company's estimate that Bad Debt Expense should be increased by $10,000 and an Allowance for Doubtful Accounts of $10,000 should be established is:

Dr. _____ _____ _____ 10,000

    Cr. _____ _____

           _____ _____ 10,000

Dr. Bad Debt Expense 10,000

    Cr. Allowance for

         Doubtful Accounts   10,000

4-68. On December 31, 2008, Loren Company had $125,000 of Accounts Receivable before subtracting the Allowance for Doubtful Accounts. Fill in the amounts that would be reported on Loren Company's December 31, 2008, balance sheet.

Accounts Receivable, gross . . . . $ _____

Less Allowance for Doubtful Accounts . . . . . . – _____

Accounts Receivable, net . . . . $ _____

$125,000

10,000
_____

$115,000

COMMON STOCK

8-23. Some stock is issued with a specific amount printed on the face of each certificate. This amount is called the **par value.** In the stock certificate shown below, for example, the par value is $_____$.

$1.00
(See text just below the owner's namebox.)

NOTE: Strangely, the par value of stock has almost no significance. It is a holdover from the days when shareholders were liable if they purchased stock for less than its par value. In order to avoid this liability, stock today is almost always issued for much more than its par value. Nevertheless, the par value of stock continues to be reported on the balance sheet, often accompanied by a notation.

8-24. The amount that the shareholders paid the corporation in exchange for their stock is **paid-in capital.** The difference between par value and the total paid-in capital is called **additional paid-in capital.**

Jones paid $10,000 cash to Marple Company and received 1,000 shares of its $1 par-value common stock. Complete the journal entry that Marple Company would make for this transaction.

Dr. Cash . . . . _____

    Cr. Common stock . . . . _____

    Cr. Additional paid-in capital . . . . _____

10,000

1,000 (at par value)

9,000

4-69. Sometime in 2009, Loren Company recognizes that it is never going to collect the $3,000 owed by Harder. It therefore *writes off* the bad debt. It does this by decreasing Accounts Receivable and also decreasing Allowance for Doubtful Accounts. Write the entry for this transaction.

Dr. _____ _____

_____ _____ 3,000

Cr. _____ _____ 3,000

Dr. Allowance for

   Doubtful Accounts 3,000

   Cr. Accounts Receivable 3,000

4-70. Loren Company's equity in 2008 was reduced by the estimated bad debts on sales made in 2008, but its equity in 2009 [was / was not] affected by this write-off of a bad debt.

was not
(*Since equity was decreased in 2008, it should not be decreased again for the same motorcycle.*)

4-71. In the above entry, the gross Accounts Receivable was reduced by $3,000 and the Allowance for Doubtful Accounts was also reduced by $3,000. Therefore, the write-off [increased / decreased / had no effect on] the "Accounts Receivable, Net" item on the balance sheet.

had no effect on

MONETARY ASSETS

4-72. Monetary assets are cash and promises by an outside party to pay the entity a specified amount of money. Which of the following assets are monetary assets?

A. Inventory	D. Buildings
B. Accounts receivable	E. Equipment
C. Notes receivable	F. Bonds owned by the entity

B, C, and F

4-73. As with accounts receivable, other monetary assets are usually reported on the balance sheet at the amounts that are r _____ c _____ to be received. By contrast, nonmonetary assets, such as buildings and equipment, are reported at their c _____ . This is in accordance with the asset-measurement concept.

reasonably

certain

cost

8-19. A **partnership** is an unincorporated business owned by two or more persons jointly. If there are only a few partners, the equity of each would be shown separately.

John Black and Henry Brown are equal partners in a laundry business. On December 31, 2008, the equity in the business totaled $100,000. The equity might be reported on that date as follows:

John Black, Capital	$ 50,000
Henry Brown, Capital	50,000
Total equity	$100,000

_____ _____, Capital $_____

_____ _____, Capital _____

_____

Total equity $_____

8-20. Equity in a partnership consists of capital paid in by owners plus earnings retained in the business. Thus the item "John Black, Capital, $50,000" means (circle the correct answer):

A. John Black contributed $50,000 cash to the entity.

B. The entity owes John Black $50,000.

C. John Black's ownership interest in the assets is $50,000.

C

Not A: We don't know the amount of the original contribution.

Not B: Unlike its bondholders, the entity does not "owe" its owners.

8-21. Owners of a **corporation** are called **shareholders** because they hold shares of the corporation's stock. The equity section of a corporation's balance sheet is therefore labeled s __ __ __ __ __ __ __ __ __ __ __ e __ __ __ __ y.

shareholder

equity

8-22. There are two types of shareholders: **common shareholders** and **preferred shareholders.** The stock held by the former is called _____ stock, and that held by the latter is called _____ stock. We shall first describe accounting for common stock.

common

preferred

NOTE: Most organizations are proprietorships, partnerships, or corporations. Other forms, not described here, include limited partnerships, trusts, and S Corporations. Special rules apply to equity transactions and/or tax accounting in these organizations.

DAYS' SALES UNCOLLECTED

4-74. In Part 1 we described the current ratio, which is:

$$\frac{\text{Current A\_\_ \_\_ \_\_ \_\_ \_\_ s}}{\text{Current L\_\_ \_\_ \_\_ \_\_ \_\_ \_\_ \_\_ \_\_ \_\_ \_\_ s}}$$

$$\frac{\text{Current Assets}}{\text{Current Liabilities}}$$

4-75. Another useful ratio is days' sales uncollected. This is the number of days of sales that are reported in Accounts Receivable at the end of the accounting period. Sales per day are total credit sales for the year divided by 365. The formula is:

$$\text{Days' Sales Uncollected} = \frac{\boxed{\text{A} \qquad} \boxed{\text{R} \qquad}}{\text{Credit sales} \div 365}$$

$$\frac{\text{Accounts Receivable}}{\text{Credit sales} \div 365}$$

4-76. Calculate the days' sales uncollected ratio for Pierce Company from the following data:

Accounts receivable, December 31, 2008 . . . . $50,000

Credit sales for the year 2008 . . . . $365,000

$$\text{Days' Sales Uncollected} = \frac{\boxed{\$ \qquad}}{\boxed{\$ \qquad} \div 365} = \boxed{\qquad} \text{ days}$$

$$\frac{\$50,000}{\$365,000 \div 365} = 50 \text{ days}$$

4-77. The days' sales uncollected ratio indicates whether customers are paying their bills when they are due. If Pierce Company expects customers to pay within 30 days from the date of the sale, the ratio of 50 days indicates that customers [are / are not] paying on time.

are not

NOTE: This is only a rough indication; it assumes that sales are made evenly throughout the year, which is not the case with seasonal sales.

8-16. Some companies obtain funds by issuing an instrument that is backed by other instruments. For example, a bank may issue an instrument that promises to pay interest from a portfolio of mortgages it holds. The return on such an instrument is derived from the underlying mortgages, and the instrument is therefore called a d __ __ __ __ __ __ ive.

derivative

> **NOTE:** Derivatives may be backed by a complicated set of promises. Therefore, measuring the value of a derivative and accounting for this value may be extremely complicated. Accounting for derivatives is described in advanced texts.

TYPES OF EQUITY CAPITAL

8-17. As noted in earlier parts, there are two sources of equity capital:

1. Amounts paid in by equity investors, who are the entity's owners. This amount is called [Paid-in Capital / Retained Earnings].

Paid-in Capital

2. Amounts generated by the profitable operation of the entity. This amount is called [Paid-in Capital / Retained Earnings].

Retained Earnings

8-18. Some entities do not report these two sources separately. An unincorporated business owned by a single person is called a **proprietorship.** The equity item in a proprietorship is often reported by giving the proprietor's name, followed by the word "Capital."

Penny Smith is the proprietor of Smith Market. Smith Market has total equity of $10,000. Show how the owner's equity item would look by filling in the blanks.

Penny Smith, _____ .... $_____

Capital $10,000

KEY POINTS TO REMEMBER

- The official accounting period is called the fiscal year, but financial statements can be prepared for shorter periods. They are called interim statements.

- Accrual accounting measures revenues and expenses during an accounting period and the difference between them, which is net income. Accrual accounting is more complicated, but more useful, than accounting only for cash receipts and cash payments.

- The conservatism concept: Recognize increases in equity when they are reasonably certain, but recognize decreases as soon as they are reasonably possible.

- The materiality concept: Disregard trivial matters, but disclose all important matters.

- The realization concept: Revenue is usually recognized when goods and services are delivered.

- If revenue is recognized before the cash receipt, an asset, Accounts Receivable, is debited (increased). If cash is received before revenue is recognized, a liability, Advances from Customers, is credited (increased). The liability is debited (decreased) in the period(s) in which revenue is recognized.

- The equity and accounts receivable balances in a period are reduced by estimated bad debt losses. A Bad Debt Expense account is used to record the decrease in equity. When specific bad debts are later discovered, Accounts Receivable is reduced, but revenue is unaffected.

- The days' sales uncollected ratio is

$$\frac{\text{Accounts Receivable}}{\text{Credit Sales} \div 365}$$

It indicates whether customers are paying their bills on time.

You have completed Part 4 of this program. If you think you understand the material in this part, you should now take Post-Test 4, which is found at the back of this text. If you are uncertain about your understanding, you should review Part 4.

The post-test will serve both to test your comprehension and to review the highlights of Part 4. After taking the post-test, you may find that you are unsure about certain points. You should review these points before going on to Part 5. Please review the answers to Post-Test 4, following the Post-Tests, at the back of this text.

8-12. When an entity issues bonds, it assumes two obligations: (1) to repay the face amount, the **principal,** on the due date, and (2) to pay **interest,** often, but not always, at semiannual intervals (i.e., twice a year). The obligation to pay the principal is usually a [current / noncurrent] liability. The liability for interest that has been earned but is unpaid is a [current / noncurrent] liability.

noncurrent

current

8-13. Interest on bonds is an expense and should be recognized in the accounting period to which the interest applies. Thus, if in January 2009 an entity makes a semiannual interest payment of $3,000 to cover the last six months of 2008, this interest expense should be recognized in 20 ___ ___ . This is required by the m ___ ___ ___ ___ ___ ___ g concept.

2008   matching

8-14. The $3,000 of unpaid interest that was an expense in 2008 is recorded in 2008 by the following entry:

Dr. I _____ E _____   3,000

    Cr. I _____ P _____   3,000

Interest Expense

    Interest Payable

8-15. In 2009, when this interest was paid to the bondholders, the following entry would be made:

Dr. _____ _____   3,000

    Cr. _____   3,000

Interest Payable 3,000

    Cash   3,000

As the above entries indicate, on the balance sheet, at any given time, the liability for the principal payment is the total face value of the bond, but the interest liability is the [amount of interest expense incurred but unpaid / total amount of interest].

amount of interest expense incurred but unpaid

## Part 5

Expense Measurement; The Income Statement

Learning Objectives

In this part you will learn:

- The difference between "expense" and "expenditure."
- How the expenses of a period are measured.
- The last of the nine basic accounting concepts:
    - The matching concept.
- The meaning of items reported on an income statement.
- Methods of analyzing an income statement.

5-1. In Part 4 you learned that the revenues recognized in an accounting period were not necessarily associated with the cash receipts in that period. If $1,000 of goods were delivered to a customer in August, and the customer paid cash for these goods in September, revenue would be recognized in [August / September].

August

5-2. Revenues are [increases / decreases] in equity during an accounting period. Expenses are [increases / decreases] in equity during an accounting period. Just as revenues in a period are not necessarily the same as cash receipts in that period, the expenses of a period [are / are not] necessarily the same as the cash payments in that period.

increases

decreases

are not

8-8. A common source of debt capital is the issuance of **bonds.** A bond is a written promise to pay someone who lends money to the entity. Since a bond usually is a noncurrent liability, the payments are due [within one year / sometime after one year].

sometime after one year

8-9. The total amount that must be repaid is specified on the face of a bond and is termed the **face amount.**

If Green Company issues 10-year bonds whose face amounts total $100,000, Green Company has a liability, Bonds Payable, of $_____.

$100,000

> **NOTE:** If the entity does not receive cash equal to the face amount of the bonds in connection with their issuance, there are accounting complications not discussed in this introductory program.

8-10. Suppose that Green Company receives $100,000 cash from the issuance of bonds that have a face amount of $100,000. Write the journal entry necessary to record the effect of this transaction on the Cash and Bonds Payable accounts.

Dr. _____ .... _____

Cr. _____ _____ .... _____

Cash 100,000

Bonds Payable 100,000

8-11. When they are issued, the bonds are [current / noncurrent] liabilities. However, as time passes and the due date becomes less than one year, a bond becomes a [current / noncurrent] liability. In 2008, a bond that is due on January 1, 2010, would be a [current / noncurrent] liability. In 2009, the same bond would be a [current / noncurrent] liability.

noncurrent

current

noncurrent

current

EXPENSE AND EXPENDITURE

5-3. When an entity acquires goods or services, it makes an **expenditure.** In August, Juarez Shop purchased goods for its inventory at a cost of $1,000, paying cash; it had an e _____ of $1,000 in August. It would record this transaction with the following journal entry:

Dr. I _____	1,000	
Cr. C _____		1,000

expenditure

Inventory 1,000

   Cash 1,000

5-4. If in August, Juarez Shop purchased $2,000 of goods for inventory, agreeing to pay in 30 days, it had an e _____ of $2,000 in August. Accounts Payable, which is a liability account, increased. Juarez would record this transaction with the following journal entry:

Dr. I _____	2,000	
Cr. A _____ P _____ ..		2,000

expenditure

Inventory 2,000

   Accounts Payable 2,000

5-5. Thus, an expenditure results either in a decrease in the asset C _____ or an increase in a l _____, such as Accounts Payable.

Cash   liability

> **NOTE:** Occasionally an expenditure results in a decrease in an asset other than cash. For example, when an old automobile is traded in for a new automobile, part of the expenditure is the decrease in the asset, Automobiles.

5-6. Juarez Shop had e _____ s of $3,000 in August for the purchase of goods for inventory. If $500 of these goods were sold in August, there was an **expense** in August of $500. The remaining $2,500 of goods are still in inventory at the end of August; they therefore are an **asset.** Thus, the expenditures of a period are either _____ of the period or _____ at the end of the period.

expenditures

expenses   assets

SOURCES OF CAPITAL

8-5. To highlight how working capital and the noncurrent assets were financed, we can rearrange the items on the balance sheet as follows:

PASCALE COMPANY

Sources and Uses of Permanent Capital
as of December 31, 2008

Uses of Capital		Sources of Capital	
[ ]	$ 6,000	Noncurrent liabilities	$ 9,000
Noncurrent assets	20,000	Equity	17,000
Total uses	$26,000	Total sources	$26,000

Fill in the box above.

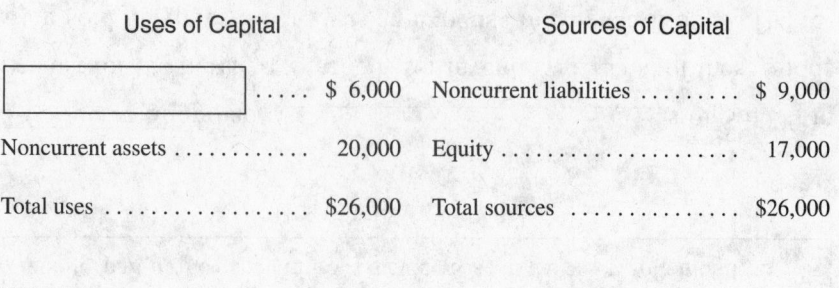

Working capital

8-6. The right-hand side of the balance sheet given above shows the sources of capital used to finance the working capital and the noncurrent assets. Collectively, these sources are called **permanent capital.** As the balance sheet indicates, there are two sources of permanent capital:

(1) N _ _ _ _ _ _ _ _ _ _ t l _ _ _ _ _ _ _ _ _ _ _ _ _ s, and

(2) E _ _ _ _ _ y. The total of these two sources is $_____,
and they are used to finance assets that also total $_____.

> **NOTE:** In this part we describe the two types of permanent capital and how they are recorded in the accounts. Although these items are often called "capital," they are more accurately labeled "sources of capital."

Noncurrent liabilities

Equity $26,000

$26,000

DEBT CAPITAL

8-7. Although most liabilities are debts, the term **debt capital** refers only to noncurrent liabilities. Debt capital therefore refers to liabilities that come due [within one year / sometime after one year].

sometime after one year

5-7. Juarez Shop sold the remaining $2,500 of goods in September. In September it had an [expenditure / expense] of $2,500, but it did not have any [expenditure / expense] for these goods in September.

expense
expenditure

5-8. In August, Juarez Shop paid an employee $2,000 cash for services rendered in August. It had both an _____ and an _____ of $2,000 for labor services in August.

expense
expenditure
  (*either order*)

5-9. When an asset is used up or consumed in the operations of the business, an expense is incurred. Thus, an asset gives rise to an [expenditure / expense] when it is acquired, and to an [expenditure / expense] when it is consumed.

expenditure
expense

5-10. Suppose that Madison Company purchased a supply of fuel oil in 2008, paying $10,000 cash. No fuel oil was consumed in 2008. In 2009, $8,000 of fuel oil was consumed, and in 2010, $2,000 was consumed. There was an expenditure in _____ (when?), and there were expenses in _____ (when?).

2008
2009 and 2010

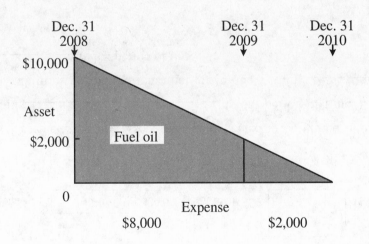

5-11. Between the time of their purchase and the time of their consumption, the resources of a business are assets. Thus, when fuel oil is purchased, there is an expenditure. The fuel oil is an _____ until consumed. When consumed, it becomes an _____.

asset
expense

PASCALE COMPANY

Balance Sheet as of December 31, 2008

[ ]			[ ]	and	[ ]	Assets Liabilities and Equity
Current	[ ]	$10,000	Current	[ ]	$ 4,000	Assets Liabilities
Noncurrent	[ ]	20,000	Noncurrent	[ ]	9,000	Assets Liabilities
			Paid-in Capital		7,000	
			Retained Earnings		10,000	
Total	[ ]	$30,000	Total	[ ]	$30,000	Assets Liabilities and Equity

8-2. Current assets are assets that are expected to be turned into cash within _____ _____ (what period of time?). Current liabilities are obligations that come due within _____ _____ (what period of time?).

one year

one
year

8-3. For Pascale Company, we can say that $4,000 of the $10,000 in current assets was financed by the c __ __ __ __ __ __ __ liabilities. The remaining $6,000 of current assets and the $20,000 of noncurrent assets were financed by the $9,000 of _____ _____ plus the $17,000 of _____ .

current

noncurrent liabilities

equity

8-4. That part of the current assets not financed by the current liabilities is called **working capital.** Working capital is therefore the difference between c _____ a _____ and c _____ l _____ . In the example given above, working capital is:

$_____ − $_____ = $_____ .

current assets   current
liabilities

$10,000 − $4,000 = $6,000

5-12. Madison Company purchased a two-year supply of fuel oil in 2008, paying $10,000. None of it was consumed in 2008, $8,000 was consumed during 2009, and $2,000 was consumed in 2010. The balance sheet item for the asset Fuel Oil Inventory will show the following amounts:

As of December 31, 2008	$	$10,000
As of December 31, 2009	$	$ 2,000
As of December 31, 2010	$	$ 0

5-13. Madison Company purchased a two-year supply of fuel oil in 2008, paying $10,000. None was consumed in 2008, $8,000 was consumed in 2009, and $2,000 was consumed in 2010. The item Fuel Oil Expense on the income statements will be as follows:

For the year 2008	$	$ 0
For the year 2009	$	$8,000
For the year 2010	$	$2,000

5-14. Over the life of a business, most expenditures [will / will not] become expenses, but in a single accounting period, expenses [are / are not] necessarily the same as expenditures.

will

are not

UNEXPIRED AND EXPIRED COSTS

5-15. Expenditures result in costs. When inventory or other assets are acquired, they are recorded at their acquisition c __ __ __ . Expenses are the c __ __ __ of the resources used up in an accounting period.

cost

cost

5-16. Costs that are used up or consumed in a period are e __ __ __ __ __ __ __ s. Costs that are represented by resources on hand at the end of the period are a __ __ __ __ s.

expenses

assets

## Part 8

Liabilities and Equity

Learning Objectives

In this part, you will learn:

* The nature of working capital.
* Types of permanent capital: debt and equity.
* How to account for debt capital.
* Accounting for equity capital in proprietorships, partnerships, and corporations:
    * Paid-in capital: common and preferred stock.
    * Retained earnings and dividends.
* The debt / equity ratio.
* The nature of consolidated financial statements.

WORKING CAPITAL

8-1. In earlier parts you learned that the balance sheet has two sides with equal totals. Fill in the two missing names in the boxes in the simplified balance sheet given on the following page.

5-17. Costs that have been consumed are gone; they have **expired.** Costs of resources still on hand are **unexpired.** You will find it useful to think of expenses as [expired / unexpired] costs and assets as [expired / unexpired] costs.

expired   unexpired

5-18. Madison Company purchased $10,000 of fuel oil in 2008, consumed $8,000 of it in 2009, and consumed $2,000 of it in 2010. At the end of 2008, the total expenditure of $10,000 was an [asset / expense] because none of the cost had expired. In 2009, $8,000 of the cost expired, and $8,000 was therefore an [asset / expense] in 2009. At the end of 2009, $2,000 was an unexpired cost and therefore an [asset / expense]. The remaining $2,000 expired in 2010, so it was an [asset / expense] in 2010.

asset

expense

asset

expense

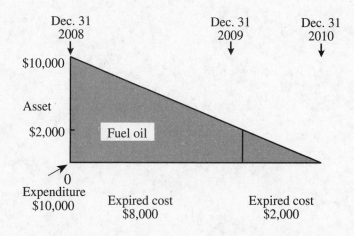

MATCHING CONCEPT

5-19. An important task of the accountant is to measure the net income of an accounting period. Net income is the difference between r _ _ _ _ _ _ _ _ s and e _ _ _ _ _ _ _ _ s of the period. Expenses are [expired / cash] costs.

revenues   expenses

expired

5-20. As you learned in Part 4, the concept governing the recognition of revenues of a period is the r _ _ _ _ _ _ _ _ _ _ _ concept; revenue is recognized in the period in which goods or services are d _ _ _ _ _ _ _ ed.

realization

delivered

The post-test will serve both to test your comprehension and to review the highlights of Part 7. After taking the post-test, you may find that you are unsure about certain points. You should review these points before going on to Part 8. Please review the answers to Post-Test 7, following the Post-Tests, at the back of this book.

5-21. The concept governing the recognition of expenses of a period is the **matching** concept. It is that **costs associated with the revenues of a period are** [cash payments / expenses] **of that period.**

expenses

5-22. To illustrate, consider an automobile that Michel Company, an automobile dealer, purchased for $15,000 in March and sold (i.e., delivered) for $18,000 in May. At the end of March, the automobile was in the Michel Company inventory, so its cost was [expired / unexpired]. At the end of April, its cost was [expired / unexpired].

unexpired
unexpired

5-23. Michel Company purchased an automobile for $15,000 in March and sold it for $18,000 in May.

In May, Michel Company recognizes $18,000 of _____ from the sale of this automobile. It must m __ __ __ __ the $15,000 of cost with the revenue from the sale of the same automobile. Thus, its expense in May is $15,000. The $18,000 of revenue and the $15,000 of expense relate to the same automobile. The expense **matches** the revenue.

revenue
match

> **NOTE:** Accounting concepts require that expenses must be matched to revenues in the accounting period.

OTHER ASSETS THAT WILL BECOME EXPENSES

5-24. When products are delivered, their costs are matched with revenues in the period in which the sale takes place. These costs become expenses of that period. This is one application of the m __ __ __ __ __ __ __ concept. Other costs associated with activities of the current period are also expenses, even though they are not directly related to the products delivered in the period.

matching

5-25. If expenditures were made in an earlier period, the unexpired costs are a __ __ __ __ s until the period in which the expense is recognized. We shall consider several examples. The first is an intangible asset.

assets

KEY POINTS TO REMEMBER

- When acquired, a property, plant and equipment (PPE) asset is recorded at its cost, including installation and other costs of making the asset ready for its intended use.

- Land has an unlimited life and is rarely depreciated.

- PPE assets are depreciated over their service life. Each year, a fraction of their cost is debited to Depreciation Expense and credited to Accumulated Depreciation.

- Depreciation Expense is an estimate. We do not know how long the service life will be, nor the asset's residual value.

- The book value of a PPE asset is the difference between its cost and its accumulated depreciation. When book value reaches zero or the residual value, no more depreciation expense is recorded.

- Book value does *not* report what the asset is worth.

- When an asset is sold, the difference between the sale price and book value is a gain or loss and is so reported on the income statement.

- In financial accounting, depreciation is calculated either by an accelerated method or by the straight-line method.

- In the units-of-production method, the annual depreciation expense is calculated by multiplying the number of service units produced in that year by a unit cost. This unit cost is found by dividing the asset's depreciable cost by the number of service units estimated to be produced over the asset's total life.

- In the straight-line method, the annual depreciation expense is calculated by multiplying the asset's depreciable cost by a constant percentage. This percentage is found by dividing 1 by the number of years in the asset's estimated service life.

- Accelerated depreciation is often used for income tax purposes because it decreases the amount of taxable income in the early years.

- Taxable income may differ from pretax income reported on the income statement. If so, the difference between the tax expense and the amount of tax actually paid is a balance sheet item, Deferred Income Taxes.

- Depletion is the process of writing off wasting assets, and amortization is the process of writing off intangible assets. The accounting for both processes is similar to depreciation, except that the credit is made directly to the asset account.

You have completed Part 7 of this program. If you think you understand the material in this part, you should now take Post-Test 7, which is found at the back of this text. If you are uncertain about your understanding, you should review Part 7.

5-26. A **tangible asset** has physical substance; an **intangible asset** does not have physical substance. Buildings, equipment, and inventories of goods are [tangible / intangible] assets. The protection provided by an insurance policy is a(n) [tangible / intangible] asset.

tangible
intangible

5-27. The general name for intangible assets that will become expenses in a future period is **prepaid expenses.** The asset account may identify the particular type of prepaid expense. Thus, the name of the asset account that shows the cost incurred for insurance protection in future periods is P _____ Insurance.

Prepaid

5-28. Michel Company purchased a two-year insurance policy on December 31, 2008, for $2,000.

The effect of this expenditure is a decrease in Cash and an increase in the asset Prepaid Insurance. Record the journal entry for this transaction.

Dr. _____ _____ 2,000

Cr. _____ 2,000

Prepaid Insurance 2,000

Cash 2,000

5-29. Michel Company purchased a two-year insurance policy on December 31, 2008, for $2,000.

During 2009 Michel Company used up half of this insurance protection, thereby incurring $1,000 of insurance expense. The effect on the accounts in 2009 is a decrease in the asset Prepaid Insurance and an increase in Insurance Expense. Record the journal entry for 2009.

Dr. _____ _____ . . . . . . _____

Cr. _____ _____ . . . . . . _____

Insurance Expense 1,000

Prepaid Insurance 1,000

On December 31, 2009, the balance in the asset account, Prepaid Insurance, was $_____.

$1,000

INTANGIBLE ASSETS

7-67. In accordance with the asset-measurement concept, intangible items such as goodwill, trademarks, and patents are not treated as assets unless [their fair value can be determined / they have been acquired at a measurable cost].

they have been acquired at a measurable cost

7-68. When intangibles are recognized as assets, their cost is written off over their service life. For example, patents have a maximum life of approximately 17 years. In no case can the life of an intangible asset exceed 40 years. The process is called **amortization.** Amortization, therefore, means . . . .

writing off the cost of intangible assets.

7-69. Company A reports $1,000,000 of trademarks on its balance sheet, but Company B reports no such item. Which statement is more likely to be correct?

1. Company A has more valuable trademarks than Company B, *or*
2. Company A has purchased trademarks, but Company B has not.

2

> **NOTE:** The Accounting treatment of trademarks is similar to that of goodwill.

7-70. Three terms that refer to the writing off of an asset's cost are:

A. Depr __ __ __ __ tion, which refers to _____ (what type of?) assets.

Depreciation   PPE

B. Dep __ __ tion, which refers to _____ (what type of?) assets.

Depletion   wasting

C. Amor __ __ __ __ tion, which refers to _____ (what type of?) assets.

Amortization   intangible

> **NOTE:** Although we have used the word **amortization** just for intangible assets, it is sometimes used as a general term for expensing the cost of all assets; that is, some people call **depreciation** and **depletion** special cases of amortization.

5-30. Michel Company purchased a two-year insurance policy on December 31, 2008, for $2,000.

During 2010 Michel Company received the remaining $1,000 of insurance protection. Make the journal entry for 2010.

Dr. _____ _____ . . . . _____

    Cr. _____ _____ . . . . . . _____

Insurance Expense 1,000

    Prepaid Insurance   1,000

On December 31, 2010, the amount of insurance protection has completely expired. The balance in the Prepaid Insurance account on that date therefore was $_____.

$0

> **NOTE:** If you were uncertain about the responses to these frames, refer back to Frames 5-10 through 5-13.

5-31. Similarly, if Cameron Company made an advance payment of $1,800 to its landlord on January 31 for two months' rent, its asset account P__ __ __ __ __ __ Rent would have a balance of $_____ on January 31, a balance of $_____ on February 28, and a balance of $_____ on March 31. Its rent expense would be $_____ in February and $_____ in March.

Prepaid

$1,800 $900

$0

$900 $900

5-32. Buildings and equipment also benefit future periods. They are assets like Prepaid Insurance and Prepaid Rent, except that they usually have a longer life and therefore benefit [more / fewer] future periods. The amount reported as an asset on the balance sheet is the [expired / unexpired] cost as of the date of the balance sheet.

more

unexpired

5-33. Also, as with insurance and rent, the amount of building and equipment cost that is reported as an expense in each period is the amount of [expired / unexpired] cost in that period.

expired

7-61. The book value of a PPE asset represents [what the asset can be sold for / that portion of the cost not yet expensed]. Therefore, the statement "book value reports what the asset is worth" is [correct / incorrect].

that portion of the cost not yet expensed

incorrect
(This is a very common error.)

DEPLETION

7-62. Natural resources such as coal, oil, and other minerals are called **wasting assets.** Of the following, circle those that are wasting assets.

building	natural gas	freight car
iron ore mine	cash	oil well

natural gas

iron ore mine   oil well
(Technically, the iron ore and the oil are the wasting assets.)

7-63. When the supply of oil in a well or coal in a mine is reduced, the asset is said to be **depleted.** This word, when used as the noun "dep __ __ __ ion," is the name for the process of writing off the cost of these w __ __ __ __ __ __ assets.

depletion

wasting

7-64. The [depletion / depreciation] of a wasting asset is similar to the [depletion / depreciation] of a PPE asset. However, in accounting for **depletion,** the asset account is reduced directly. Therefore, an accumulated depletion account [is / is not] ordinarily used.

depletion

depreciation

is not

7-65. Depletion is usually calculated by multiplying the quantity of the resource used in a period by a unit cost. If in 2008 Hill Company purchased a coal mine for $3,000,000 and estimated that the mine contained 1,000,000 tons of coal, it would use a unit cost of $_____ per ton.

$3 (= $3,000,000 ÷ 1,000,000 tons)

7-66. In 2009, Hill Company mined 100,000 tons of coal. The cost of this coal was estimated to be $3 per ton. The depletion expense in 2009 was $_____. How will the coal mine asset appear on the balance sheet for December 31, 2009?

$300,000 (= $3 × 100,000)

Coal mine . . . . $ [   ]

$2,700,000 (= $3,000,000 – $300,000)

5-34. The expired cost for buildings and equipment is called **depreciation expense.** If Michel Company bought a machine for $5,000 and expected it to provide service for five years, the amount of expired cost in each year probably would be 1/5 of $5,000. In each of the five years d _ _ _ _ _ _ _ _ _ _ _ _ _ _ e _ _ _ _ _ _ _ would be reported as $_____. Accounting for depreciation is discussed in more detail in Part 7.

depreciation expense

$1,000

EXPENSES THAT CREATE LIABILITIES

> **NOTE:** We have described expenditures that first were assets and then became expenses as the costs expired. We now describe expenses for which the related expenditures are liabilities.

5-35. Amounts earned by the employees of Stockman Company for services performed in 2008 are e _ _ _ _ _ _ _ _ s of 2008. If Stockman paid its employees one week after the week they worked, the amounts earned in the last week of 2008 would be a cash disbursement in _____ (what year?).

expenses

2009

5-36. Employees of Stockman Company earned $10,000 in the last week of 2008, for which they were paid in 2009. The $10,000 was [an expense / an expenditure / both an expense and an expenditure] in 2008.

both an expense and an expenditure

On December 31, 2008, Stockman Company owed its employees $10,000. It would report a l _ _ _ _ _ _ _ _ _ y of $10,000 on its December 31, 2008, balance sheet.

liability

	Dec.	31	
	2008		2009
	Employees earn $10,000		Employees paid $10,000
Expenditure	Yes		No
Expense	Yes		No
Cash paid	No		Yes

Liability
$10,000

7-56. The difference between book value and the amount actually realized from a sale of a plant asset is called a **gain** (or **loss**) **on disposition of PPE.** For example, if an asset whose book value is $10,000 is sold for $12,000, $_____ would be the [gain / loss] on disposition of PPE and would be so reported on the income statement.

$2,000 (= $12,000 − $10,000)

gain

7-57. When the asset is sold, its cost and its accumulated depreciation are removed from the accounts. For an asset that cost $40,000, had accumulated depreciation of $30,000, and sold for $12,000, the journal entry would be:

Cash	12,000	
Accumulated Depreciation		30,000
PPE		40,000
Gain on disposition of plant		2,000

> **NOTE:** The above journal entry removes any trace of the assets from the balance sheet and records the amount greater than the book value as a gain.

SIGNIFICANCE OF DEPRECIATION

7-58. The purpose of depreciation is to [show the decline in an asset's value / write off a fair share of the cost of the asset in each year in which it provides service].

write off a fair share of the cost of the asset in each year in which it provides service

7-59. Actually, an asset may be as valuable at the end of a year as at the beginning. Depreciation expense for a given year [represents / does not represent] a decrease in the asset's real value or usefulness during the year.

does not represent

7-60. Remember that in accounting for a PPE asset, original cost is [known / an estimate], service life is [known / an estimate], and residual value is [known / an estimate].

known   an estimate

an estimate

5-37. Liabilities for expenses incurred but not yet paid for are called **accrued liabilities.** Account titles may describe the nature of the liability, in this case A __ __ __ __ __ __ Salaries.

Accrued

5-38. In the last week of 2008, Stockman Company had a salary expense of $10,000, which was not paid to its employees. Write the journal entry for this transaction.

Dr. _____ _____ .... _____

Cr. _____ _____ ...   _____

Salary Expense 10,000

Accrued Salaries 10,000

> **NOTE:** Employees are not paid the total amount that they earn. Part of their salary is withheld by the employer, who pays it to the federal government for income taxes. Amounts are also deducted for social security taxes and for other reasons. We shall disregard these complications and assume that total earnings are paid in cash to the employees.

5-39. In January 2009, Stockman Company employees were paid the $10,000 owed them for work done in 2008. This payment decreases the liability Accrued Salaries. The journal entry for this transaction is:

Dr. _____ _____ .... _____

Cr. _____ .... _____

Accrued Salaries 10,000

Cash 10,000

FRINGE BENEFITS

5-40. Many companies agree to pay employees a pension when they retire. Employees earn the right to their pension benefits when they work. Therefore, if an employee earns a $2,000 pension benefit in 2008 because he or she worked in 2008, the $2,000 is an expense in [2008 / when he or she retires]. It is a liability in [2008 / when he or she retires]. The liability is called **Accrued Pensions.**

2008

2008

7-52. Refer to the following diagram:

	12/31/2008	12/31/2009	12/31/2010

Book value $4,000 — Accumulated depreciation $1,000

$3,000 — $2,000

$2,000 — $3,000

etc

Depreciation expense → $1,000 $1,000 $1,000

Show how the asset would be reported on the company's balance sheet at the end of 2010.

_____ .... | $ |

Less _____ _____ . | |

_____ _____ .... | |

PPE $5,000

Less accumulated depreciation 3,000

Book value 2,000

7-53. After the cost of an asset has been completely written off as depreciation expense, no more depreciation is recorded, even though the asset continues to be used. In the example given above, the book value at the end of 2012 is zero. If the asset continued to be used in 2013, depreciation expense in 2013 would be _____.

zero

7-54. To calculate the book value of an asset, you must subtract the _____ _____ from the original _____. Book value [does / does not] report the fair value of the asset.

accumulated depreciation   cost

does not

SALE OF A PPE ASSET

7-55. The calculation of book value depends on estimates of service life and residual value. Because the actual residual value probably differs from these estimates, the amount realized from the sale of a PPE asset will probably be [equal to / different from] its book value.

different from

5-41. Melissa Best earned a pension benefit of $2,000 in 2008. She had earned similar benefits in earlier years. The journal entry for this transaction is:

Dr. Pension Expense 2,000

Cr. _____ _____ 2,000   Accrued Pensions

5-42. Melissa Best retired on December 31, 2008. She will be paid a pension of $10,000 in 2009. The journal entry for the 2009 payment is:

Dr. _____ _____ 10,000   Accrued Pensions

Cr. Cash 10,000

> **NOTE:** Many companies transfer amounts earned for pensions to an insurance company or bank, which makes the actual payments. The effect on the company's financial position is nevertheless the same as that illustrated in the above journal entries.

5-43. Many companies agree to pay for health care or other benefits to retired employees. These fringe benefits are called **Other Post Employment Benefits,** abbreviated to the initials __ __ __ __ .   OPEB

5-44. OPEB are accounted for in the same way as pensions; that is, the expense is incurred [in the years in which the employee earns the right to them / when the benefits are paid]. The liability is incurred [in the years in which the employee earns the right to them / when the benefits are paid]. When the benefit is paid, there [is / is not] an expense.

in the years in which the employee earns the right to them

in the years in which the employee earns the right to them
is not

7-49. The balance sheet for December 31, 2009, would include the following items.

PPE .... $ [ ]	PPE $10,000
Less _____ _____ .... [ ]	Less accumulated depreciation 5,000
Book value .... $ [ ]	Book value .... $ 5,000

The income statement for 2009 would include an item:

Depreciation expense .... $ [   ] $1,000

7-50. Each year, the write-off of $1,000 of the cost of the asset is recorded with the following journal entry:

Dr. _____ _____ .... _____   Depreciation Expense 1,000

Cr. _____ _____ .... _____   Accumulated Depreciation 1,000

7-51. The table below shows the original cost, annual depreciation expense, accumulated depreciation (at year end), and book value (at year end) for a PPE asset with an original cost of $5,000, a service life of five years, and zero residual value. Complete the amounts for 2012.

Year	Original Cost	Depreciation Expense	Accumulated Depreciation	Book Value
2008	$5,000	$1,000	$1,000	$4,000
2009	5,000	1,000	2,000	3,000
2010	5,000	1,000	3,000	2,000
2011	5,000	1,000	4,000	1,000
2012	5,000	[ ]	[ ]	[ ]

1,000   5,000   0

What is the total amount charged as depreciation expense during the service life of the asset? $_____. $5,000

RENT EXPENSE

5-45. Stockman Company will pay its December rent of $5,000 in January. In December 2008, it records the Rent Expense of December and the related liability, Accrued Rent, by the following journal entry:

Dr. _____ _____ .... _____

    Cr. _____ _____ ...... _____

Dr. Rent Expense 5,000

    Cr. Accrued Rent   5,000

5-46. In January 2009, Stockman Company paid $5,000 to its landlord for the December 2008 rent. The journal entry in January is:

Dr. _____ _____ .... _____

    Cr. _____ .... _____

Accrued Rent 5,000

    Cash   5,000

5-47. Earlier we saw that if rent is paid *prior* to the period in which the expense was incurred, the amount is first debited to Prepaid Rent, which is a(n) [asset / liability] account. As the previous frame indicates, if rent is paid *after* the period in which the expense was incurred, the credit is made to Accrued Rent, which is a(n) [asset / liability] account.

asset

liability

5-48. Prepaid Expenses are turned into expenses by a debit to the [asset / expense] account and a credit to the [asset / expense] account. Accrued Liabilities are discharged by a debit to . . . [Cash / Accrued Liabilities] and a credit to [Cash / Accrued Liabilities].

expense
asset
Accrued Liabilities
Cash

5-49. Of course, many items of expense are paid for in cash during the accounting period. Salaries of $90,000 earned in 2008 and paid in cash in 2008 is recorded in the following entry.

Dr. _____ _____ .... _____

    Cr. _____ .... _____

Dr. Salary Expense 90,000

    Cr. Cash   90,000

7-46. On the balance sheet, the balance in the Accumulated Depreciation account is shown as a deduction from the original cost of the asset, and the remaining amount is called **book value.** For example, the listing:

Property, Plant and Equipment	$10,000
Less accumulated depreciation	4,000
Book value	$ 6,000

shows that the PPE originally cost $_____, that $_____ of its original cost has so far been recognized as depreciation expense, and that $_____ of book value remains to be depreciated in future years. (Part of the book value may be the estimated residual value.)

$10,000 $4,000

$6,000

7-47. If the depreciation expense on this machine was $1,000 per year, we know from the above that depreciation expense has been taken for _____ (how many?) years and that it will be taken for _____ (how many?) more years in the future, assuming zero residual value.

four

six

7-48. Suppose that the ledger showed the following account balances on January 1, 2009, and that annual depreciation expense was $1,000. Enter the amounts for depreciation in 2009.

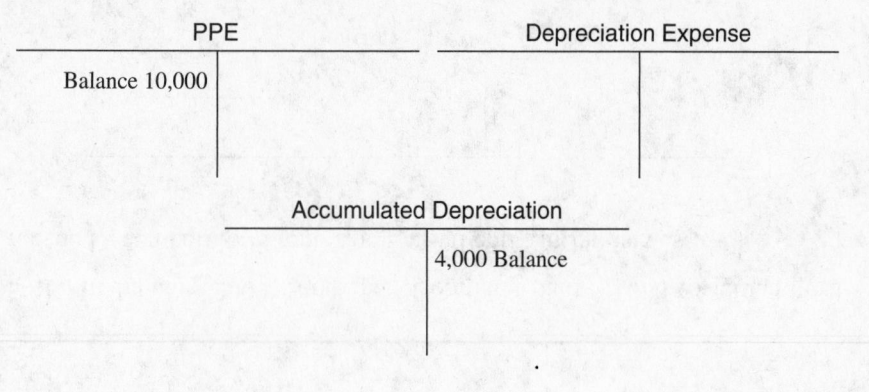

PPE		Depreciation Expense
Balance 10,000		

Accumulated Depreciation
4,000 Balance

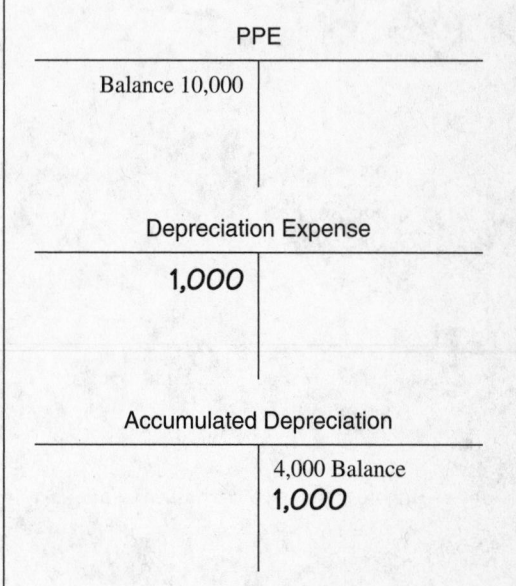

PPE	
Balance 10,000	

Depreciation Expense
1,000

Accumulated Depreciation
4,000 Balance
1,000

LOSSES

5-50. Assets provide benefits to future periods. Suppose Michel Company owned an uninsured machine that was destroyed by fire in 2008. The machine [will / will not] benefit future periods. The asset amount carried for the machine therefore expired in 2008, and this amount is recorded as an [expense / expenditure] in 2008.

will not

expense

5-51. Thus, although an asset does not provide benefits during a period, it is an expense of that period if its cost has expired for any reason. Such expenses are called **losses.** A loss is recorded as an expense [in the period in which the loss occurs / over the periods that the asset was supposed to benefit].

in the period in which the loss occurs

5-52. A loss is recorded as an expense if it is **reasonably possible** that the loss occurred, even though it is not certain. Thus, if a customer sues Michel Company in 2008, and if it seems reasonably possible that Michel Company will lose the lawsuit, the estimated loss is recorded as an expense [in 2008 / when the lawsuit is settled]. This is in accordance with the concept that requires expenses to be recognized when they are reasonably possible, which is the c _ _ _ _ _ _ _ _ _ _ _ m concept.

in 2008

conservatism

SUMMARY OF MATCHING CONCEPT

5-53. Three types of costs are expenses of the current period. First, there are the costs of the goods and services that are **delivered** in the current period and whose r _ _ _ _ _ _ _ _ are recognized in that period.

revenues

> **NOTE:** The period in which revenues are recognized is determined first, according to the principles described in Part 4. Then the associated costs are matched with those revenues. Costs are matched against revenues, not vice versa.

7-41. Similarly, if a company purchased a three-year insurance policy in advance for $9,000 on December 31, 2008, the following journal entry would be made to record Insurance Expense in 2009.

Dr. _____ _____ . . . . _____

    Cr. _____ _____ . . . .   _____

Insurance Expense	3,000	
Prepaid Expense		3,000
(*or* Prepaid Insurance)		

7-42. In accounting for depreciation, the procedure is similar. First, we recognize the appropriate amount of expense for the period. In this case the title of the expense account is D_____ Expense.

Depreciation

7-43. Next, we must recognize an equal [decrease / increase] in the amount of the asset. However, accountants prefer to show the original cost of PPE assets on the balance sheet at all times. Therefore, decreases in the amount of a PPE asset [are / are not] shown as a direct reduction in the asset amount.

decrease

are not

7-44. Instead, decreases in the asset amount of a PPE asset because of depreciation expense are accumulated in a separate account called **Accumulated Depreciation.**

A decrease in an asset is always a [debit / credit]. Accumulated Depreciation is a decrease in an asset, and therefore has a [Dr. / Cr.] balance. (Accumulated Depreciation is called a *contra-asset* account.)

credit

Cr.

7-45. Suppose $1,000 of depreciation expense is recognized for a given year. What is the journal entry?

Dr. D_____ E_____ . . . . . . _____

    Cr. A_____ D_____   _____

Depreciation Expense	1,000	
Accumulated Depreciation ..		1,000

5-54. Second, there are costs that are **associated with activities of the period.** The expenditures for these costs were made either in the current period or in an earlier period. If made in an earlier period, these amounts are a _____ on the balance sheet as of the beginning of the current period.

assets

5-55. Third, there are **losses** that are recognized in the current period. These may recognize a reasonably possible decrease in a(n) [asset / liability] because of fire, theft, or other reasons. Or, they may recognize a reasonably possible increase in a(n) [asset / liability] arising from events occurring in the period, such as a lawsuit.

asset

liability

5-56. The cash payments associated with any of these expenses may have been made in a prior period or in the current period, or they may be made in a future period, when the [assets / liabilities] are paid.

liabilities

5-57. The balance sheet at the beginning of a period reports assets obtained as a result of e __ __ __ __ __ __ __ __ __ __ s made in earlier periods. Part of these asset amounts will expire and therefore will be e __ __ __ __ __ __ s of the current period. The remainder will be carried forward to future periods and will be reported as a __ __ __ __ __ on the balance sheet at the end of the current period.

expenditures

expenses

assets

NOTE: The next set of frames is an extended example of the use of the matching and realization concepts. If you now are comfortable with these concepts, skip to Frame 5-67. If you want additional practice, proceed with Frame 5-58.

7-38. There are many ways of calculating accelerated depreciation amounts. The following table shows one of them. The asset has a depreciable cost of $15,000 and a service life of five years. Enter the amounts for straight-line depreciation and show whether accelerated depreciation is larger or smaller in each of the five years.

Year	Accelerated Depreciation	Straight-line Depreciation	Accelerated is		
1	$ 5,000	$_____	larger/smaller	$3,000	larger
2	4,000	_____	larger/smaller	3,000	larger
3	3,000	3,000	same	3,000	same
4	2,000	_____	larger/smaller	3,000	smaller
5	1,000	_____	larger/smaller	3,000	smaller
Total	$15,000	$ 15,000			

Accelerated depreciation is used principally in calculating taxable income. Taxable income and accounting income are not always the same, and hence the income tax paid and the income tax expense may be different. The difference becomes a liability account on the balance sheet called Deferred Income Taxes. This concept is beyond the scope of the introductory material in this text.

> **NOTE:** It is neither illegal nor against accounting principles to record depreciation in several different ways.

ACCOUNTING FOR DEPRECIATION

7-39. In Part 5 we described how certain types of assets were converted into expenses with the passage of time. When this occurs, there is a [Dr. / Cr.] entry to the asset account, which shows the [decrease / increase] in the amount of the asset, and there is an equal [Dr. / Cr.] to the expense account.

Cr.

decrease

Dr.

7-40. For example, if an entity had a fuel oil asset of $2,000 at the beginning of March and used $500 of fuel oil during March, the entity will recognize $_____ of fuel oil expense for March, and it will also recognize an equal decrease of $_____ in the fuel oil asset. On the balance sheet of March 31, the fuel oil asset will be reported at $_____.

$500

$500

$1,500 (= $2,000 − $500)

AN EXAMPLE OF MATCHING

> **NOTE:** Homes, Inc., is a company that buys and sells houses. Exhibit 7 describes some of its transactions during May, June, and July. These events relate to the sale of two houses, House A and House B. We will measure the net income for Homes, Inc., for the month of June.

5-58. Delivery of the deed to a house is delivery of the ownership of the house. Exhibit 7 states that for House A this happened in _____ (what month?); therefore, revenue from the sale of House A is recognized in _____ (what month?).

June
June

5-59. The amount of revenue for House A is measured by two transactions. List these below and find the revenue for House A.

Date	Transaction*	Amount
May 2	_____ _____	$
June 5	_____	
	Revenue from House A	$

*Write a brief description of the transaction.

Date	Transaction	Amount
May 2	Down payment	$ 16,000
June 5	Payment	144,000
	Revenue from House A	$160,000

5-60. Now consider the costs that are associated with the total revenue from the sale of House A, $160,000, in June. One of these costs was the cost of House A, which was $_____.

$140,000

5-61. Two of the cash payments related specifically to the sale of House A. What were these cash decreases?

Date	Transaction	Amount
May ____	_____	$
July ____	_____	
	Total	$

Date	Transaction	Amount
May 15	Commission	$ 800
July 2	Commission	7,200
	Total	$8,000

7-34. Complete the following table.

If the estimated life of an asset is:	The straight-line depreciation rate is:	
2 years	%	50%
3 years	%	33-1/3%
4 years	%	25%
5 years	20%	

7-35. In the straight-line method, the amount of **depreciation expense** for a given year is found by multiplying the depreciable cost by the depreciation rate. Thus, if the depreciable cost is $9,000 and the depreciation rate is 20%, the amount of depreciation expense each year will be $_____.

$1,800 (= $9,000 × 0.20)

ACCELERATED DEPRECIATION

7-36. If you want an automobile to go faster, you press down on the accelerator. **Accelerated depreciation** writes off the cost of an asset [faster / slower] than straight-line depreciation.

faster

7-37. In accelerated depreciation, more depreciation expense is reported in the early years of the asset's service life and therefore [more / less] in the later years. The total amount of depreciation expense is the same as in the straight-line method.

less

5-62. The **matching** concept requires that the costs associated with the revenues of a period be recognized as expenses of that period. Therefore, the two commissions associated with House A, totaling $_____, should be recognized as expenses in _____ (what month?), even though they were not paid in that month.

$8,000   June

5-63. In accordance with the realization concept, the $24,000 down payment received on House B in June [was / was not] revenue in June. It will be revenue in _____ (what month?). Because Homes, Inc., has an obligation to deliver the house, the $24,000 is a(n) [asset / liability] on the balance sheet at the end of June.

was not

July

liability

5-64. The matching concept says that general costs of operations during any period are expenses of that period. Thus the $4,000 general costs of operations in June are expenses in _____ (what month?).

June

5-65. Refer to Frames 5-59 through 5-64 and complete the income statement for Homes, Inc., for the month of June, applying the realization concept and the matching concept.

HOMES, INC.

Income Statement for June

Sales Revenue	$	$160,000 (= $16,000 + $144,000)
Expenses:		
Cost of House A	$	$140,000
Commission Expense		$8,000 (= $800 + $7,200)
General Expense		4,000
Total Expense		152,000
Net Income	$	$8,000

STRAIGHT-LINE DEPRECIATION

7-31. The depreciation of a plant asset with a cost of $10,000, no residual value, and a five-year life, may be graphed as follows:

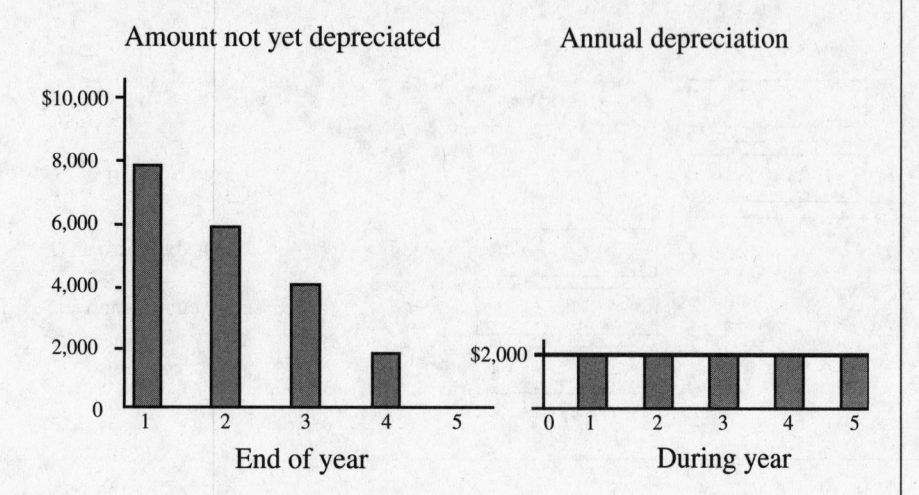

The line showing annual depreciation expense as a function of time is [straight / vertical].

straight

7-32. Because of this, charging off an equal fraction of the asset cost each year is called the s __ __ __ __ __ __ __ - line method of depreciation. Most companies use this method.

straight

7-33. The percentage of cost charged off each year is called the depreciation rate. In the straight-line method, we obtain the rate by finding:

$$\frac{1}{\text{number of years of service life}}$$

For example, if an asset is to be depreciated over five years, the d _____ r _____ is _____ %.

depreciation rate   20% (1/5)

5-66. According to Exhibit 7, cash transactions in June were:

June	Event	Cash Increases	Cash Decreases
2	Down payment on House B	$ 24,000	
5	Final payment on House A	144,000	
30	Commission on House B		$1,200
	General expenses for June		4,000

In June, Cash increased by a net amount of $_____. This increase [was approximately the same as / had no relation to] the $8,000 net income for June.

Homes, Inc.
INCOME STATEMENT, JUNE

Revenue	
May payment—A	$ 16,000
June payment—A	144,000
Total Revenue	160,000
Expenses	
Cost of house	140,000
May Commission—A	800
June Commission—A	7,200
June Expenses	4,000
Total expenses	152,000
Net Income	$ 8,000

$162,800 (= $168,000 – 5,200)

had no relation to

THE INCOME STATEMENT

5-67. The equity section of a balance sheet shows the two sources of equity capital: (1) the capital supplied by equity investors (i.e., proprietors, partners, shareholders), which is called Paid-in C _ _ _ _ _ _ _ , and (2) that portion of the earnings resulting from profitable operations that have been retained in the entity, which is called R _ _ _ _ _ _ _ _ _ E _ _ _ _ _ _ _ _ _ .

Capital

Retained Earnings

5-68. The amount added to Retained Earnings as a result of profitable operations during a period is the **income** of the period. An i _ _ _ _ _ _ statement explains how this income was earned.

income

> **NOTE:** The income statement is also called a profit and loss, or earnings, statement. The term "bottom line" refers to the difference between revenues and expenses.

7-28. The difference between the cost of a plant asset and its residual value is called the **depreciable cost.** Thus, if an automobile purchased for $30,000 is expected to have a five-year life and to have a residual value of $5,000 at the end of that life, $30,000 is the original _____ and $25,000 is the _____ _____ .

cost (or gross cost)

depreciable cost

7-29. Here is a list of factors that are relevant to the depreciation of an asset:

1. original cost
2. residual value
3. service life

Which factors are used in arriving at the depreciable cost? . . . .   1 and 2

The amount of depreciation expense in a given year? . . . .   1, 2, and 3

Which factors are estimates? . . . .   2 and 3

NOTE: There are many methods of calculating the amount that is to be recorded as depreciation expense in each year of the estimated service life. In the following sections we describe three of them:

1. Units-of-production depreciation
2. Straight-line depreciation
3. Accelerated depreciation

UNITS-OF-PRODUCTION DEPRECIATION

7-30. In the units-of-production method, a cost per unit of production is calculated, and depreciation expense for a year is found by multiplying this unit cost by the number of units that the asset produced in that year.

Grady Company purchased a truck in 2008 for $44,000. It estimated that the truck would provide services for 100,000 miles and would have a residual value of $4,000.

Its depreciable cost was $_____ .

$40,000 (= $44,000 − $4,000)

Its estimated cost per mile was $_____ .

$0.40 (= $40,000 ÷ 100,000)

In 2009, the truck was driven 15,000 miles. Its depreciation expense in 2009 was $_____ .

$6,000 (= $0.40 × $15,000)

5-69. There is no standard format for an income statement. The lower portion of Exhibit 8 shows one common format. The first item on this income statement is _____ _____, which is the amount of products (i.e., goods and services) _____ during the period.

Sales Revenue

delivered to customers, or sold

5-70. The item on the second line is labeled _____ _____ _____. It reports the cost of the goods or services whose revenue is reported on the first line. This is an example of the _____ concept.

Cost of

Sales

matching

5-71. The difference between sales and cost of sales is called _____ _____ in Exhibit 8. Write an equation, using the terms **cost of sales, sales revenue,** and **gross margin.**

Gross Margin

_____ = _____ − _____

gross margin = sales revenue − cost of sales

5-72. Exhibit 8 shows that _____ _____ are subtracted from Gross margin, giving the item _____ _____ _____.

operating expenses

Income

before Taxes

5-73. In accordance with the m __ __ __ __ __ __ __ concept, these expenses include costs related to the c __ __ __ __ __ __ __ period and costs that do not benefit f __ __ __ __ __ periods (i.e., losses).

matching

current

future

5-74. The next item on Exhibit 8, _____ _____ _____ _____, is shown separately because it is an especially important expense. These taxes relate to the income tax payable on the current period's income, not the income tax paid in that period.

Provision for

Income Taxes

5-75. The final item (the bottom line) on an income statement is called _____ _____ (or **Net Loss,** if expenses were larger than revenues).

Net Income

7-23. To summarize:

1. Depreciation is the process of converting the cost of an asset into expense over its service life.

2. This process recognizes that an asset gradually loses its usefulness.

3. An asset can lose its usefulness for either of two reasons:

   a. ....   it wears out

   b. ....   it becomes obsolete

4. The asset's service life is the [longer / shorter] of these two   shorter
   causes.

7-24. In the summary above, no mention was made of market value. Depreciation [is / is not] related to changes in the market value of an   is not
asset. This is consistent with the _____ - _____   asset-measurement
concept.

7-25. In some cases, an entity expects to be able to sell the plant asset at the end of its service life. The amount that it expects to sell it for is called its **residual value.** If an entity buys a truck for $60,000 and expects to sell it for $10,000 five years later, the estimated residual value is $10,000
$_____.

7-26. In most cases, an entity expects that a plant asset will be worthless at the end of its service life. If so, its residual value is _____   zero
(how much?).

> **NOTE:** Residual value, as such, does not appear in the accounts. It is merely an estimated number used to calculate depreciation.

7-27. Suppose a restaurant oven that cost $22,000 is expected to have a residual value of $2,000 at the end of its 10-year life. In this case, the total amount of depreciation that should be recorded during the service life of the asset is only $_____. The depreciation expense for $20,000
each of the 10 years would be $_____. $2,000 (= 1/10 × $20,000)

Total cost ($22,000) / Depreciable cost ($20,000) / Residual value $2,000

5-76. To arrive at net income, **dividends** [are / are not] subtracted from revenues. Dividends [are / are not] an expense. Dividends are a distribution of earnings to shareholders.

are not

are not

5-77. Revenues are defined as [increases / decreases] in the _____ _____ item on the balance sheet. Expenses are [increases / decreases] in that item. Net income is the difference between _____ and _____.

increases

Retained Earnings

decreases

revenues   expenses

5-78. Because income is always supposed to be the *difference* between sales revenue and expenses, a term such as "sales income" [is / is not] a misleading term. However, it is sometimes used.

is

A PACKAGE OF ACCOUNTING REPORTS

5-79. An income statement is a summary of R _____ E _____ that have been generated during a fiscal year.

Retained

Earnings

5-80. A(n) _____ _____ (what accounting report?) reports certain changes in retained earnings that have taken place between two _____ _____ (what accounting reports?).

income statement

balance sheets

5-81. Thus, a useful accounting "report package" consists of a(n) _____ _____ at the beginning of the accounting period, a(n) _____ _____ for the period, and a(n) _____ _____ at the end of the period.

balance sheet

income statement

balance sheet

5-82. Exhibit 8 shows a financial report package consisting of an income statement and two balance sheets. Exhibit 8 shows that Retained Earnings on December 31, 2008, was $_____.

$11,908,000

7-17. When a machine or other item of plant is acquired, we [know / do not know] how long it actually will be of service. Therefore, we [can know with certainty / must estimate] its service life.

do not know

must estimate

7-18. Since some portion of a plant asset is used up during each year of its service life, a portion of the cost of the asset is treated as a(n) [revenue / expense] in each year. For example, suppose a machine is purchased at a cost of $50,000. It has an estimated service life of five years and will be worthless then. It would be reasonable to charge _____ (what fraction?), or $_____ as expense in each of the five years.

expense

1/5 $10,000 (= 1/5 × $50,000)

7-19. The portion of the cost of a plant asset that is recognized as an expense during each year of its estimated service life is called **depreciation.** The $10,000 recorded as an expense during each one of the five years of service life of the machine that cost $50,000 is called the _____ expense for that year.

depreciation

7-20. A plant asset can become useless for either of two reasons: (1) it may wear out physically, or (2) it may become obsolete (i.e., no longer useful). The latter reason is called **obsolescence.** Loss of usefulness because of the development of improved equipment, changes in style, or other causes not related to the physical condition of the asset are examples of _____.

obsolescence

7-21. The **service life** of an asset considers both physical wear and obsolescence. The service life is the shorter of the two periods. Thus an asset with an estimated physical life of 10 years that is estimated to become obsolete in five years has an estimated service life of [5 / 10] years.

5

7-22. Since depreciation considers obsolescence, it is [correct / not correct] to regard depreciation and obsolescence as two different things.

not correct

5-83. During 2009, profitable operations resulted in Net Income of $_____, which increased Retained Earnings by this amount. (Net income is the **bottom line** on the income statement.)

$6,122,000

5-84. Retained Earnings decreased by $4,390,000, representing a distribution to the shareholders in the form of _____.

dividends

5-85. As a result, the total Retained Earnings on December 31, 2009, was $_____.

$13,640,000 (= $11,908,000 + $6,122,000 − $4,390,000)

5-86. Remember that dividends are [an expense / a distribution of earnings to owners]. Dividends are *not.* [an expense / a distribution of earnings to owners].

a distribution of earnings to owners

an expense

> **NOTE:** The "package" of required financial reports also includes a Statement of cash flows. This statement is described in Part 9.

INCOME STATEMENT PERCENTAGES

5-87. In an analysis of a business's performance, **percentages** of certain income statement items are usually calculated. The base, or denominator (i.e., 100%), is **sales revenue.** One percentage is the **gross margin percentage;** it is found by dividing G __ __ __ __ M __ __ __ __ __ __ by S __ __ __ __ __ R __ __ __ __ __ __ __ .

Gross Margin

Sales Revenue

5-88. Calculate the gross margin percentage for Garsden Company in 2009.

Gross margin $ [   ]

_____ = _____ = [   ] %*

Sales revenue $ [   ]

$23,251
────── = 31%
$75,478

_____
*Show the nearest percent.

7-12. Even though the entity does not own the item, a capital lease is treated like other plant assets. A capital lease is an exception to the general rule that assets are property or property rights that are ___ ___ ___ ___ ___ by the entity.

owned

> **NOTE:** Special rules apply to accounting for capital leases. They are beyond the scope of this introductory treatment.

DEPRECIATION

7-13. Except in rare cases, land retains its usefulness indefinitely. Land therefore continues to be reported on the balance sheet at its acquisition cost, in accordance with the _____ - _____ concept. This is because land is a [monetary / nonmonetary] asset.

asset-measurement
nonmonetary

If Hanover Hospital purchased a plot of land in 1993 at a cost of $100,000, it would have been reported at $_____ on the December 31, 1993, balance sheet. If Hanover Hospital still owned the land in 2009, and its market value then was $300,000, it would be reported on the December 31, 2009, balance sheet at [$100,000 / $300,000].

$100,000

$100,000

7-14. Unlike land, plant assets eventually become useless. They have a(n) [limited / unlimited] life.

limited

7-15. Plant assets will become completely useless at some future time. At that time, the item is no longer an asset. Usually this process occurs gradually; that is, a portion of the asset is used up in each year of its life, until finally it is scrapped or sold and therefore is no longer ___ ___ ___ ful to the entity. At that time, it [is / is not] an asset.

useful
is not

7-16. The period of time over which a plant asset is estimated to be of **service** to the company is called its s ___ ___ ___ ___ ___ ___ life.

service

5-89. An even more important percentage is the **net income percentage.** Calculate it for Garsden Company.

Net income $\dfrac{\text{Net income} \quad \boxed{\$ \qquad}}{\text{Sales revenue} \quad \boxed{\$ \qquad}} = \boxed{\qquad} \%^*$

_____

*Show the nearest percent.

$$\frac{\$\ 6{,}122}{\$75{,}478} = 8\%$$

> **NOTE:** The net income percentage varies widely among companies. In some industries the percentages are readily available.

REVIEW OF BASIC CONCEPTS

> The nine basic concepts described in this program are listed in the following frames, together with some guides that will refresh your memory of their meaning. Complete the meaning of each concept. (These concepts are not stated as such in accounting literature, but most accountants would agree that they are the basic underpinnings of accounting.)

5-90. Dual-aspect concept: _____ = _____ + _____.

Assets = Liabilities + Equity (*See frames 1-16 to 1-22.*)

5-91. Money-measurement concept: Accounting reports only facts that can be expressed _____.

in monetary amounts (*If you have the general idea, fine. Your words need not be exactly like those given here.*) (*See frames 1-27 to 1-33.*)

5-92. Entity concept: Accounts are kept for an _____ as distinguished from the p _ _ _ _ _ _ associated with that entity.

entity

persons (*See frames 1-34 to 1-39.*)

5-93. The accounting concept that assumes that an entity will continue to operate indefinitely and that it is not about to be sold is the g _ _ _ _ _ -c _ _ _ _ _ _ _ concept.

going-concern (*See frames 1-40 to 1-43.*)

7-8. If an entity constructs a machine or a building with its own personnel, all costs incurred in construction are included in the asset amount.

Madrona Company built a new building for its own use. It spent $800,000 in materials, $3,200,000 in salaries to workers directly engaged in the building's construction, $1,200,000 to purchase services, and $600,000 in overhead costs related to the building. This building should be recorded in the accounts at its cost, $_____.

$5,800,000 (= $800,000 + $3,200,000 + $1,200,000 + $600,000)

CAPITAL LEASES

7-9. Most assets are *owned* by the entity. When an entity leases (i.e., rents) a building, a machine, or other tangible item, the item is owned by someone else (the **lessor**); the entity [does / does not] own it. In other words, most leased items [are / are not] assets of the entity that leases them (the **lessee**).

does not

are not

7-10. However, if an entity leases an item for a long period of time, it has as much control over the use of that item as if it owned it. A lease for a long time—almost the whole life of the asset—is called a **capital lease.** Because the entity controls the item for almost its whole life, a c _ _ _ _ _ _ _ l _ _ _ _ _ is recorded as an asset.

capital lease

7-11. The amount recorded for a capital lease is the amount the entity would have paid if it had purchased the item rather than leased it. If an entity leased a machine for 10 years, agreeing to pay $10,000 per year, and if the purchase price of this machine was $70,000, this c _ _ _ _ _ _ _ l _ _ _ _ _ would be recorded as an asset at an amount of [$70,000 / $100,000], as in this entry:

capital lease
$70,000

Capital Lease . . . . _____

70,000

     Lease Obligation . . . . _____

70,000

5-94. Asset-measurement concept: Accounting focuses on the f __ __ __ v __ __ __ __ __ of monetary assets; nonmonetary assets are reported at an amount based on c __ __ __ .

fair value

cost *(See frames 1-44 to 1-57.)*

5-95. Conservatism concept: Revenues are recognized when they are reasonably c __ __ __ __ __ __ __ . Expenses are recognized when they are reasonably p __ __ __ __ __ __ __ __ .

certain

possible *(See frames 4-18 to 4-22.)*

5-96. Materiality concept: Disregard _____ matters.

immaterial (or insignificant)

Disclose _____ matters.

all important *(See frames 4-23 to 4-30.)*

5-97. Realization concept: Revenues are recognized when goods or services are _____ .

delivered *(See frames 4-31 to 4-51.)*

5-98. The **mat __ __ __ __ __** **concept** states that the expenses of a period are costs associated with the revenues or activities of the period.

matching *(See frames 5-19 to 5-23.)*

KEY POINTS TO REMEMBER

- Expenditures are made when goods or services are acquired. If these goods or services are used up during the current period, they are expenses of the period. If not used up, they are assets at the end of that period. These assets will become expenses in future periods as they are used up.

- Some expenditures result in liabilities that will be paid in future periods. An example is accrued salaries.

- Expenses are expired costs. Assets are unexpired costs.

- Matching concept: Costs associated with the revenues or activities of a period are expenses of the period.

- Expenses of a period are (1) cost of the products (i.e., goods and services) that were delivered to customers during the period; (2) other expenditures that benefit operations of the period; and (3) losses, that is, decreases in assets from fire, theft, and other unusual reasons, and increases in liabilities from unusual events, such as lawsuits.

7-3. On the balance sheet, tangible noncurrent assets are often labeled **fixed assets,** or **property, plant,** and **equipment.** Equipment is a [current / noncurrent] and [tangible / intangible] asset.

noncurrent

tangible

7-4. For brevity, we shall use the term **PPE** (property, plant, and equipment) for all tangible noncurrent assets except land. Thus, buildings, equipment, and furniture are items of ___ ___ ___ . These assets are expected to be useful for longer than _____ _____ .

PPE

one year

ACCOUNTING FOR ACQUISITIONS

7-5. When an item of PPE is acquired, it is recorded in the accounts at its _____ (what value?). This is because it is a [monetary / nonmonetary] asset.

cost   nonmonetary

7-6. The cost of an asset includes all costs incurred to make the asset ready for its intended use.

Bird Corporation paid $100,000 for a plot of land. It also paid $3,000 as a broker's fee, $1,200 for legal fees, and $10,000 to tear down the existing structures in order to make the land ready for a new building. The land should be recorded in the accounts at an amount of $_____ .

$114,200 (= $100,000 + $3,000 + $1,200 + $10,000)

(Note: Some accountants charge the $10,000 as a cost of the new building.)

7-7. Transportation and installation costs are usually included as part of equipment cost.

Cascade Bank purchased a computer system for $40,000. The bank also paid $200 in freight charges and $2,000 in installation charges. This equipment should be recorded in the accounts at its cost, $_____ .

$42,200 (= $40,000 + $200 + $2,000)

- The income statement summarizes revenues and expenses of the period. Its "bottom line," or net income, shows the increase in equity resulting from activities during the period.

- Dividends are a distribution of earnings to shareholders. Dividends are not expenses.

- Retained Earnings at the beginning of the period + Net Income − Dividends = Retained Earnings at the end of the period.

- Percentages are calculated for various income statement items, especially gross margin and net income, taking sales revenue as 100%.

You have completed Part 5 of this program. If you think you understand the material in this part, you should now take Post-Test 5, which is found at the back of this text. If you are uncertain about your understanding, you should review Part 5.

The post-test will serve both to test your comprehension and to review the highlights of Part 5. After taking the post-test, you may find that you are unsure about certain points. You should review these points before going on to Part 6. Please review the answers to Post-Test 5, following the Post-Tests, at the back of this text.

## Part 7

Noncurrent Assets and Depreciation

Learning Objectives

In this part you will learn:

• How plant assets are recorded in the accounts.

• The meaning and significance of straight-line and accelerated depreciation.

• How depreciation is recorded.

• The meaning of depletion and how it is recorded.

• How intangible assets are recorded.

NONCURRENT ASSETS

7-1. Earlier, you learned that current assets are cash or items likely to be converted to cash within one _____ (what time period?). Evidently, **noncurrent** assets are expected to be of use to the entity for longer than _____ _____.

year

one year

7-2. Tangible assets are assets that can be touched. Intangible assets are assets that have no physical substance (other than pieces of paper) but give the entity valuable rights. Which of the following are tangible assets?

Current Assets	Noncurrent Assets
1. Accounts receivable	5. Land
2. Notes receivable	6. Goodwill
3. Inventory	7. Buildings
4. Prepaid rent	8. Investment in another entity

3, 5, and 7 (*Although a note receivable is shown by a paper that can be touched, the asset is the sum of money that is promised. This is an intangible asset.*)

## Part 6

Inventories and Cost of Sales

Learning Objectives

In this part you will learn:

- How the cost of sales is calculated.
- Methods of arriving at inventory amounts.
- When inventory amounts on the balance sheet are reduced.
- How inventory is measured in a manufacturing company.
- The distinction between product costs and period costs.
- How overhead rates are calculated.

FINDING COST OF SALES

6-1. In the income statement in Part 5, the first item subtracted from sales revenue was called **Cost of Sales.** It is the cost of the same products whose revenues are included in the sales amount. This is an example of the m _ _ _ _ _ _ _ _ concept. (Some businesses call this item **Cost of Goods Sold.**) In most businesses the cost of sales is the [smallest / largest] item of expense, amounting to as much as 85% of sales revenues in a profitable supermarket and 60% to 70% in a profitable manufacturing company.

matching

largest

- If the fair value (i.e., market value) of items in inventory decreases below their cost, the inventory is written down to fair value.

- The cost of goods produced in a manufacturing company is the sum of their direct materials cost, direct labor cost, and production overhead cost.

- Period costs are costs that are charged as expenses in the period in which the costs were incurred. Product costs become Cost of Sales in the period in which the products are sold, which may be later than the period in which the products were manufactured.

- Overhead is charged to products by means of an overhead rate, such as a rate per direct labor dollar.

- The inventory turnover ratio shows how many times the inventory turned over during a year.

You have now completed Part 6 of this program. If you think you have understood the material in this part, you should now take Post-Test 6, which is found at the back of this text. If you are uncertain about your understanding, you should review Part 6.

The post-test will serve both to test your comprehension and to review the highlights of Part 6. After taking the post-test, you may find that you are unsure about certain points. You should review these points before going on to Part 7. Please review the answers to Post-Test 6, following the Post-Tests, at the back of this text.

6-2. In some entities, matching cost of sales and sales revenue is easy. For example, an automobile dealer keeps a record of the cost of each automobile in its inventory. If the dealer sold two automobiles during a given month, one for $36,000 that had cost $32,000, and the other for $20,000 that had cost $15,000, sales revenue for the period would be recorded as $_____ and cost of sales as $_____. This is the **specific identification** method.

$56,000 (= $36,000 + $20,000)

$47,000 (= $32,000 + $15,000)

6-3. A dealer sold an automobile costing $32,000 for $36,000 cash. Write the journal entry that records the effect of this transaction solely on the Sales Revenue and Cash accounts:

Dr. _____ . . . . _____

    Cr. _____ _____ . . . _____

Cash 36,000

    Sales Revenue 36,000

6-4. A dealer sold an automobile costing $32,000 for $36,000 cash. Write the journal entry that records the effect of this transaction solely on the Inventory and Cost of Sales accounts:

Dr. _____ ____ _____ . . . . _____

    Cr. _____ . . . . _____

Cost of Sales 32,000

    Inventory 32,000

6-5. A dealer that sells televisions might keep a record of its inventory of each type of television, something like the following:

Item: Television #602, Cost $200 each

Date	Receipts		Shipments to Customers		On Hand	
	Quantity	Cost	Quantity	Cost	Quantity	Cost
May 1					4	800
6			1	200	3	600
10	10	2,000			13	2,600
13			6	1,200	7	1,400
31			2	400	5	1,000
Totals	10	2,000	9	1,800	5	1,000

6-66. Cost of sales for 2008 was $1,000,000. Inventory on December 31, 2008, was $200,000. Calculate the inventory turnover ratio to determine how many times the inventory turned over in 2008.

$$\frac{\boxed{}}{\boxed{}} = \frac{\boxed{\$}}{\boxed{\$}} = \boxed{} \text{ times}$$

$$\frac{\text{Cost of sales}}{\text{Inventory}} = \frac{\$1,000,000}{\$200,000} = 5 \text{ times}$$

6-67. Slow-moving inventory ties up capital and increases the risk that the goods will become obsolete. Thus, an inventory turnover of five times is generally [better / worse] than an inventory turnover of four times. However, if inventory is too small, orders from customers may not be filled promptly, which can result in lost sales revenue. This would reduce [cash receipts / income / both cash and income].

better

both cash and income

6-68. Look back at the calculation of the inventory turnover ratio. The turnover ratio can be increased either by selling [more / less] goods with the same level of inventory or by having [more / less] inventory for the same amount of sales volume.

more

less

KEY POINTS TO REMEMBER

- If an entity has no record of the cost of the specific items that were sold during a period, it deduces Cost of Sales by (1) adding purchases to the beginning inventory, which gives the goods available for sale, and (2) subtracting the cost of the ending Inventory.

- In doing this, the entity must make an assumption about which items were sold.

- The first-in, first-out (FIFO) method assumes that the oldest items are the first to be sold.

- The last-in, first-out (LIFO) method assumes that the most recently purchased items are the first to be sold. In periods of rising prices, it results in a higher Cost of Sales and hence a lower taxable income than the FIFO method.

- The average-cost method charges both Cost of Sales and the ending Inventory at the average cost of the goods available for sale.

- The inventory method that a company selects **does not necessarily reflect the physical flow of its goods.**

This is called a **perpetual inventory** record. "Receipts" are [increases / decreases] in inventory, and "Shipments to Customers" are [increases / decreases] in inventory.

increases

decreases

6-6. Information in the perpetual inventory records corresponds to that in the Inventory account. From the previous frame, we see that the beginning balance for Television #602 in the Inventory account on May 1 was $_____. There were receipts during May of $_____, which added to Inventory; these were [Dr. / Cr.] to the Inventory account. Shipments during May decreased inventory by $_____, which were [Dr. / Cr.] to the Inventory account. This decrease in inventory was Cost of Sales in May, which was $_____.

$800 $2,000

Dr.

$1,800

Cr.

$1,800

6-7. Using the *totals* in the perpetual inventory record, enter the inventory transactions for May in the T-accounts given below. (The inventory purchases were on credit.)

Inventory	Accounts Payable
Beg. bal. 800	

Cost of Sales

Inventory

Beg. bal. 800	
2,000	**1,800**

Accounts Payable

	2,000

Cost of Sales

1,800	

> *Refer back to Frame 6-6 if you are uncertain. Remember that debits must equal credits.*

6-62. If a certain pair of shoes required $20 of direct material cost, $15 of direct labor cost, and overhead at a cost of $1.20 per dollar of direct labor, its total cost would be $_____. The Inventory cost of these shoes would be $_____. When they were sold, the Cost of Sales of these shoes would be $_____.

$53 = \$20 + \$15 + (\$15 \times 1.2)$

$53

$53

6-63. Although $53 is reported as the "actual" cost of this pair of shoes, it cannot represent the actual overhead cost. By definition, it [is / is not] possible to determine the actual indirect cost of a product. The overhead rate does charge products with what is believed to be a *fair share* of their cost. For this reason, the process of *allocating* overhead costs to products is more complex than the scope of this book.

is not

> **NOTE:** There are several other methods of assigning overhead costs to products. One of these, called activity-based costing, assigns indirect or overhead costs on the basis of relative activities. This process looks at the *cost drivers* associated with overhead activities. Activity-based costing is useful for analyzing the often complex processes of manufacturing or service delivery.

INVENTORY TURNOVER

6-64. In earlier parts we described ratios and percentages that are useful in analyzing financial statements. Find the gross margin percentage from the following facts:

$$\frac{\$\ 600{,}000}{\$1{,}500{,}000} = \underline{\hspace{1cm}} \% \text{ Gross margin}$$

$$\frac{\text{Gross margin}}{\text{Sales (or Sales revenue)}} = 40\% \text{ Gross margin}$$

6-65. A useful ratio for analyzing inventory is the **inventory turnover ratio.** This ratio shows how many times the inventory turned over during a year. It is found by dividing Cost of Sales for a period by I _____ at the end of the period (or by the average inventory during the period).

Inventory

6-8. Televisions that cost $1,800 were sold in May for $2,500. Complete the following partial income statement, assuming these were the only items sold.

Income Statement
May

Sales revenue	$
Cost of sales	
Gross margin	$

Income Statement
May

Sales revenue	$2,500
Cost of sales	1,800
Gross margin	$ 700

FINDING COST OF SALES BY DEDUCTION

6-9. If an entity has a p _____ inventory, as illustrated above, finding cost of sales in a month is easy. We shall next show how to deduce cost of sales in a business that does not have this record. This method is the process of **deduction.**

perpetual

6-10. Many stores, such as hardware stores, carry so many relatively low-value items that keeping a perpetual inventory record for each separate item is not practical. When the salesperson rings up a sale on the cash register, a record is made of the [cost of sales / sales revenue] but not the [cost of sales / sales revenue].

sales revenue

cost of sales

> **NOTE:** With computers, many more companies use the perpetual inventory method. The cash register (point-of-sale terminal) then records both sales revenue and the cost of sales.

6-11. If a hardware store does not keep a record of the cost of each item in inventory, it [can arrive at cost of sales directly / must deduce cost of sales by an indirect method].

must deduce cost of sales by an indirect method

6-12. Items in a hardware store's **beginning inventory** on January 1, 2008 [are / are not] available for sale during 2008. Additional items **purchased** and placed on the shelves during 2008 [are / are not] available for sale during 2008.

are

are

6-57. This entry included only $400,000 of overhead costs, although $480,000 of overhead costs were actually incurred in the year 2009. The Cost of Sales amount [was / was not] the same as the amount of cost actually incurred in the year 2009.

was not

6-58. [Period / Product] costs reduce income in the period in which the costs were incurred. [Period / Product] costs reduce income in the period in which the product is sold, which often is a later period.

Period
Product

OVERHEAD RATES

6-59. By definition, **direct material** and **direct labor** costs can be traced *directly* to the products for which they were incurred; the cost accounting system does this. However, production overhead, which is an **indirect** cost, cannot be so traced. The cost of heating a shoe factory [can / cannot] be traced directly to the cost of manufacturing each pair of shoes made in the factory. Assigning these indirect costs to products requires the use of an **overhead rate.**

cannot

6-60. The overhead rate is a rate per direct labor dollar, per direct labor hour, per machine hour, or some other measure of volume. If Marcos Shoe Company expected to incur $480,000 of production overhead costs in the year 2009, and it expected that direct labor costs in the year 2009 would be $400,000, it would establish an overhead rate of $_____ per direct labor dollar.

$1.20 (480,000/400,000)

6-61. This overhead rate would be used to calculate the overhead cost of each pair of shoes worked on. If an actual pair of shoes required $10 of direct labor cost, its overhead cost would be recorded as $_____.

$12

6-13. Therefore, the **goods available for sale** in a period are the sum of the b _____ inventory plus the p _____ during the period.

beginning   purchases

6-14. On January 1, 2008, Madison Hardware had an inventory that cost $200,000. During 2008 it purchased $600,000 of additional merchandise. The cost of goods **available for sale** in 2008 was $_____.

$800,000 (= $200,000 + $600,000)

6-15. Accountants *assume* that goods available for sale during a period either are in inventory at the end of the period or were sold. Thus, if goods costing $800,000 were available for sale during 2008 and goods costing $300,000 were in inventory on December 31, 2008, cost of sales in 2008 is **assumed** to be $_____.

$500,000 (= $800,000 − $300,000)

6-16. At the end of each accounting period, all goods currently on hand are counted. This process is called **taking a physical inventory.** Since its purpose is to find the cost of the goods that were sold, each item is reported at its [cost / selling price].

cost

6-17. In order to determine the ending inventory of one period and the beginning inventory of the next period, how many physical inventories must be taken? _____

One (*The ending inventory on December 31, 2008 is also the beginning inventory on January 1, 2009*)

> **NOTE:** Entities that use the perpetual inventory method count physical inventory at least annually. This inventory may reveal that the actual ending inventory is lower than is indicated in the perpetual inventory records because of theft, errors in record keeping, or items that have been discarded. If so, the ending inventory is reduced by a credit entry. The offsetting debit entry is to an expense account, Loss on Inventory.

6-53. The process of assigning production costs to products is called **cost accounting.** The assignment of costs to various services in banks, schools, hotels, and all types of service organizations also involves c _ _ _ _ a _ _ _ _ _ _ _ _ _ _ _ _ . We shall describe some of its major aspects.

cost accounting

PRODUCT COSTS AND PERIOD COSTS

6-54. Costs are divided into two categories; they are treated differently for **purposes of accounting:**

1. **product costs**—those that are associated with the production of products, and
2. **period costs**—those that are associated with the sales and general activities of the accounting period.

For example, the cost of heating the offices of the sales department would be considered a [product / period] cost. The cost of heating the production plant itself would be a [product / period] cost.

period

product

6-55. Overhead costs that are classified as product costs are added to direct labor costs and direct material costs to find the total cost that is added to the Inventory account. If Marcos Shoe Company incurred $480,000 of production overhead costs in the year 2009, these costs would be added to inventory by this journal entry:

Dr. _____ 480,000

    Cr. Various overhead accounts 480,000

Inventory

6-56. Costs are moved from Inventory to Cost of Sales when the products are sold. If in the year 2009 Marcos Shoe Company sold shoes with direct material and labor costs of $1,000,000 and overhead costs of $400,000, the entry would be:

Dr. Cost of Sales .... _____

    Cr. _____ .... _____

.... 1,400,000

Inventory 1,400,000

6-18. In the deduction method, goods not in inventory are assumed to have been sold. Sometimes goods are stolen, damaged, or spoiled. Therefore, the assumption that goods not in the closing inventory were sold [is / is not] necessarily valid. However, steps are taken to discover and record this **shrinkage.**

is not

6-19. To summarize, many entities [do / do not] keep track of individual items in inventory. They find their cost of sales by the process of **deduction.** This requires a [perpetual / physical] inventory. An automobile dealership finds its cost of sales directly from its [perpetual / physical] inventory records.

do not

physical
perpetual

6-20. Entities that must calculate cost of sales do so by subtracting the ending inventory from the total goods available, as in the following table:

	Cost ($000 omitted)
Beginning inventory	$ 200
Purchases	600
Total goods available	[ ]
Ending inventory	300
Cost of sales	[ ]

	Cost ($000 omitted)
Beginning inventory	$ 200
Purchases	600
Total goods available	800
Ending inventory	300
Cost of sales	500

6-21. The same situation is shown in the following diagram. Fill in the boxes.

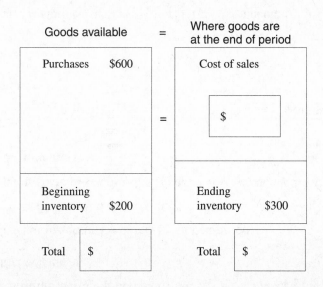

$500

$800 $800

6-49. In a **manufacturing** company, the cost of a finished product consists of three elements:

1. cost of materials used directly in that product;
2. cost of labor used directly on that product;
3. a fair share of overhead, or general costs associated with the production process.

Circle one word in each of 1, 2, and 3 above that best summarizes the whole phrase.

materials

labor

overhead

6-50. Some materials, such as oil for lubricating machinery, are not used directly in a product. The materials that are used *directly* in the product are called d __ __ __ __ __ materials. Similarly, the labor used directly to make the product is called _____ labor.

direct

direct

6-51. Production overhead consists of all other production costs, that is, costs that are not d_____ m_____ or d_____ l_____.

direct materials

direct labor

> **NOTE:** In some manufacturing companies, computers and automated machine tools replace workers, so direct labor cost is relatively small. These companies combine labor costs and production overhead costs into a single item called **Other Production Costs.**

6-52. The three elements of production cost—**direct labor, direct materials,** and **overhead**—are added together to determine the total cost of the finished product. Until the product is sold, this amount is held in the Inventory account. When the product is sold, this amount becomes Cost of Sales. Thus, if a product requires $5 of direct labor, $7 of direct materials, and $3 of overhead, the product will be costed at $_____ as long as it is in the Inventory account. When it is sold, C __ __ __ of S __ __ __ __ will be $_____.

$15 (= $5 + $7 + $3)

Cost

Sales $15

INVENTORY VALUATION: ASSUMPTIONS

> **NOTE:** In the preceding frames, we assumed that all units of a given item, such as all Televisions #602, were purchased at the same time. Actually, the cost of goods purchased at different times may differ. For example, because inflation leads to increases in cost, the cost of goods purchased recently may be higher than the cost of the same goods purchased some time ago. In the following frames, we describe the three principal methods of finding cost of sales and ending inventory in such a situation.

6-22. Complete the following table, filling in all empty boxes.

	Quantity	Unit Cost	Total Cost
Beginning inventory, April 1	400	$1.00	$
Purchases, April 6	300	1.00	
Purchases, April 20	300	1.00	
Total goods available		1.00	
Ending inventory, April 30	600	1.00	
Cost of sales, April			

Quantity	Unit Cost	Total Cost
400	$1.00	$ 400
300	1.00	300
300	1.00	300
1,000	1.00	1,000
600	1.00	600
400	1.00	400

6-23. Lewis Fuel Company deals in fuel oil. Its inventory and purchases during April are shown in the top section of Exhibit 9. Fill in the two empty boxes in the column titled "Units."

Total goods available   1,000
Cost of sales, April   400

6-24. The "Unit Cost" column of Exhibit 9 shows that fuel oil entered the inventory at [identical / different] unit costs during April.

different

6-25. In Exhibit 9 fill in the first four boxes in the column headed "Total Cost."

Units	Unit Cost	Total Cost
400	$1.00	$ 400
300	1.10	330
300	1.20	360
1,000		1,090

6-44. In "writing down" inventory, the Inventory account is [debited / credited], and Cost of Sales is [debited / credited].

credited
debited

6-45. If inventory is written down by $20, what would the appropriate journal entry be?

Dr. _____ _____ _____   20

   Cr. _____   20

Cost of Sales   20

   Inventory   20

INVENTORY IN A MANUFACTURING COMPANY

6-46. Retail stores, wholesalers, and distributors are [merchandising / manufacturing] companies. A company that makes shoes is a [merchandising / manufacturing] company.

merchandising
manufacturing

6-47. A company that sells finished goods that it purchased from other vendors is a [merchandising / manufacturing] company. A company that converts raw materials into finished goods and then sells these goods is a [merchandising / manufacturing] company.

merchandising

manufacturing

6-48. A merchandising company buys its goods in salable form; it receives an invoice showing the cost for each item. The costs on these invoices are the amounts used to record the additions to inventory. A manufacturing company adds value to the raw material it buys; it must include these **conversion costs** in its inventory and in its cost of sales.

Measuring inventory and cost of sales is therefore more complicated in a [merchandising / manufacturing] company.

manufacturing

6-26. The problem now is this: What unit cost should we assign to the ending inventory? There are three choices: (1) we could assume that the older fuel oil was sold, leaving the [older / newer] fuel oil in inventory; (2) we could assume that the newer fuel oil was sold, leaving the [older / newer] fuel in inventory; or (3) we could assume that a mixture of old and new oil was sold. Because the fuel oil has been mixed together in the storage tank, we [have / do not have] a record of the cost of the specific quantities of fuel oil actually sold during the month. Therefore the solution [is / is not] clearcut.

newer

older

do not have

is not

FIRST-IN, FIRST-OUT (FIFO) METHOD

6-27. In this situation, many companies make the **f**irst-**i**n, **f**irst-**o**ut (**FIFO**) assumption, *for financial accounting purposes only.* They assume that the goods that came into the inventory [first / last] are the [first / last] to move out.

first

first

6-28. If you applied the FIFO method to the data of Exhibit 9, you would assume that the [newer / older] fuel oil was sold during the month and that the [newer / older] fuel oil remains in the ending inventory.

older

newer

6-29. The FIFO method assumes that the older units were sold during the period; therefore, the ending inventory of 600 units of fuel oil is assumed to be the most recently purchased fuel oil, namely, the 300 units purchased on April _____ at $_____ per unit and the 300 units purchased on April _____ at $_____ per unit.

20    $1.20

10    $1.10

6-30. In the "FIFO Method" section of Exhibit 9, enter these amounts and calculate the ending inventory.

Ending inventory

	300 units @ $1.20 =	$360
	300 units @ $1.10 =	330
Total	600 units	$690

6-39. In calculating income taxes, cost of sales is one of the items subtracted from revenue in order to find taxable income.

Assume that the revenue of Lewis Fuel Company was $1,000. Disregarding other expenses, if cost of sales was $470 (as in LIFO), LIFO taxable income would be $_____. If cost of sales was $400 (as in FIFO), FIFO taxable income would be $_____.

$530

$600

6-40. As can be seen from the above, the higher the cost of sales, the [lower / higher] the taxable income. The lower the taxable income, the [lower / higher] will be the income tax based on that income.

lower

lower

6-41. Companies usually prefer to pay as low an income tax as they legally can. Therefore, they prefer the method that results in the [lower / higher] cost of sales. If prices are rising, this is usually the [FIFO / LIFO] method.

higher

LIFO

NOTE: Any of the methods described above is permitted in calculating taxable income in the United States. However, a company cannot switch back and forth between methods from one year to the next. In many countries, the LIFO method is not permitted. The method chosen by a company must be disclosed in the financial statements.

INVENTORY VALUATION: ADJUSTMENT TO MARKET

6-42. We have assumed so far that inventory is recorded at its cost. Suppose, however, that the fair value (i.e., market value) of the inventory falls below its original cost. The conservatism concept requires that we reduce the inventory account to the [higher / lower] amount.

lower

6-43. For this reason, if the fair value of an item of inventory at the end of an accounting period is lower than its original cost, the item is "written down" to its f _____ v _____. For example, if an item whose original cost was $100 and whose current fair value is $80, its inventory amount should be written down by $_____. (This is an exception to the general rule that nonmonetary assets are reported at cost.)

fair value

$20 (= $100 − $80)

6-31. Earlier, you found the amount of goods available for sale to be $1,090. Enter this amount in your calculation, and subtract the ending inventory of $690 from it. The difference is the FIFO c _____ of s _____, which is $_____.

cost

sales $400

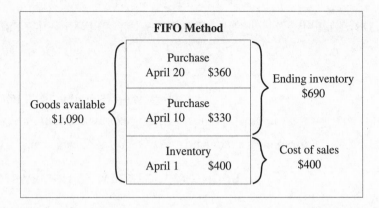

LAST-IN, FIRST-OUT (LIFO) METHOD

6-32. The FIFO method assumes that the oldest units—that is, those F _____ I _____ — were the first to be sold; that is, that they were the F _____ O _____. The **LIFO** method assumes the opposite, namely, that the [oldest / newest] units, which were the last in, were the first to be sold; that is, that they were [last out / first out]; hence the name **last-in, first-out.**

First In

First Out

newest

first out

6-33. Because the LIFO method assumes that the last units purchased were the first ones to be sold, the ending inventory is assumed to consist of any remaining units in beginning inventory, plus the earliest units purchased. In Exhibit 9, the ending inventory was 600 units, and in the LIFO method these 600 units are assumed to be the _____ (how many?) units in beginning inventory plus _____ (how many?) of the 300 units purchased on April _____.

400

200

April 10

6-34. In the LIFO section in Exhibit 9, enter the amount available for sale, $1,090; calculate the ending inventory; and subtract to find the cost of sales.

Goods available	$1,090
Ending inventory:	

400 units @ $1.00 = $400	
200 units @ $1.10 = 220	
Total 600 units	620
Cost of sales	$ 470

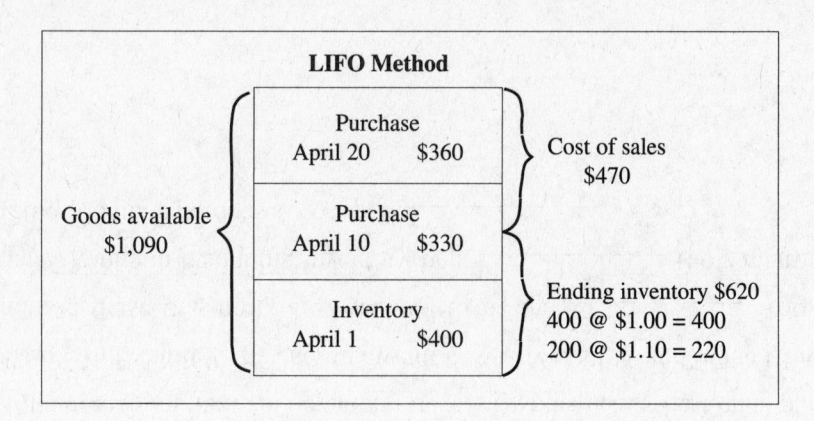

LIFO Method

Goods available $1,090 {
- Purchase April 20 $360
- Purchase April 10 $330
- Inventory April 1 $400

} Cost of sales $470

Ending inventory $620
400 @ $1.00 = 400
200 @ $1.10 = 220

AVERAGE-COST METHOD

6-35. The third method is the **average-cost** method. It calculates the cost of both the ending inventory and the cost of sales at the average cost per unit of the goods available. In Exhibit 9, the number of units available in April was _____, and the total cost of these goods was $_____, so the average cost per unit was $_____.

1,000

$1,090 $1.09 (= $1,090 ÷ 1,000)

6-36. Using the average cost of $1.09 per unit, complete the average-cost section of Exhibit 9.

$\frac{\$1,090}{1,000}$ = $1.09 cost per unit

Ending inventory: 600 units @ $1.09 = $654
Cost of sales: 400 units @ $1.09 = $436

COMPARISON OF INVENTORY METHODS

6-37. Most businesses try to sell their oldest goods first, so the goods that were first out are likely to be the goods [first in / last in]. The [FIFO / LIFO] method reflects this practice.

first in   FIFO

6-38. From Exhibit 9, we see that cost of sales under FIFO was $_____, and under LIFO it was $_____. Cost of sales was [lower / higher] under LIFO. In most companies, during periods of rising prices (i.e., inflation) this same relationship holds.

$400 $470

higher

Exhibits
Post-Tests and Mini Cases
Answers to Post-Tests and Mini Cases
Glossary

EXHIBIT 1

GARSDEN COMPANY

Balance Sheet
as of December 31, 2009
($000 omitted)

ASSETS		LIABILITIES AND EQUITY	
CURRENT ASSETS		**CURRENT LIABILITIES**	
Cash...	$ 1,449	Accounts Payable..............................	$ 5,602
Marketable Securities	246	Bank Loan Payable	1,000
Accounts Receivable, net...................	9,944	Accrued Liabilities.............................	876
Inventories..	10,623	Estimated Tax Liability......................	1,541
Prepaid Expenses	389	Current Portion of Long-term Debt...	500
Total Current Assets	22,651	Total Current Liabilities	9,519
NONCURRENT ASSETS		**NONCURRENT LIABILITIES**	
Property, Plant, Equipment, at cost ...	$26,946	Long-term Debt, less current portion	2,000
Accumulated Depreciation	−13,534	Deferred Income Taxes...................	824
Property, Plant, Equipment, net	13,412		
Investments	1,110	Total Liabilities...............................	12,343
Patents and Trademarks	403		
Goodwill	663	**EQUITY**	
		Common Stock	1,000
		Additional Paid-in Capital	11,256
		Total Paid-in Capital.......................	12,256
		Retained Earnings	13,640
		Total Equity	25,896
TOTAL ASSETS.................................	$38,239	TOTAL LIABILITIES AND EQUITY	$38,239

EXHIBIT 2

EVERGREEN MARKET

	Assets		Liabilities and Equity	
January 2. Evergreen Market received $10,000 from Steve Smith and banked the money.	Cash	$10,000	Smith, Capital	$10,000
		$10,000		$10,000
January 3. Evergreen Market borrowed $5,000 from a bank, giving a note therefor.	Cash	$15,000	Note Payable	$ 5,000
			Smith, Capital	10,000
		$15,000		$15,000
January 4. Evergreen Market purchased inventory costing $2,000, paying cash for it.	Cash	$13,000	Note Payable	$ 5,000
	Inventory	2,000	Smith, Capital	10,000
		$15,000		$15,000
January 5. Evergreen Market sold merchandise for $300 cash that cost $200.	Cash	$13,300	Note Payable	$ 5,000
	Inventory	1,800	Smith, Capital	10,000
			Retained Earnings	100
		$15,100		$15,100
January 6. Evergreen Market purchased and received merchandise for $2,000, agreeing to pay within 30 days.	Cash	$13,300	Accounts Payable	$ 2,000
	Inventory	3,800	Note Payable	5,000
			Smith, Capital	10,000
			Retained Earnings	100
		$17,100		$17,100
January 7. Merchandise costing $500 was sold for $800, which was received in cash.	Cash	$14,100	Accounts Payable	$ 2,000
	Inventory	3,300	Note Payable	5,000
			Smith, Capital	10,000
			Retained Earnings	400
		$17,400		$17,400
January 8. Merchandise costing $600 was sold for $900, the customer agreeing to pay $900 within 30 days.	Cash	$14,100	Accounts Payable	$ 2,000
	Accounts Receivable	900	Note Payable	5,000
	Inventory	2,700	Smith, Capital	10,000
			Retained Earnings	700
		$17,700		$17,700

EXHIBIT 3

ACCOUNTS FOR GREEN COMPANY

Assets	Liabilities and Equity

Cash

	(Dr.)	(Cr.)
Beg. bal.	1,000	

Accounts Receivable

	(Dr.)	(Cr.)
Beg. bal.	3,000	

Inventory

	(Dr.)	(Cr.)
Beg. bal.	4,000	

Other Assets

	(Dr.)	(Cr.)
Beg. bal.	10,000	

Accounts Payable

(Dr.)	(Cr.)	
	2,000	Beg. bal.

Paid-in Capital

(Dr.)	(Cr.)	
	7,000	Beg. bal.

Retained Earnings

(Dr.)	(Cr.)	
	9,000	Beg. bal.

EXHIBIT 4

EVERGREEN MARKET
JOURNAL

2009		Accounts		Dr.	Cr.
Jan.	2	Cash	√	10,000	
		Paid-in Capital	√		10,000
	3	Cash	√	5,000	
		Notes Payable	√		5,000
	4	Inventory	√	2,000	
		Cash	√		2,000
	5	Cash	√	300	
		Revenues	√		300
	5	Expenses	√	200	
		Inventory	√		200
	6	Inventory	√	2,000	
		Accounts Payable	√		2,000
	7	Cash	√	800	
		Revenues	√		800
	7	Expenses	√	500	
		Inventory	√		500
	8				
	8				

(continued on next page)

EXHIBIT 4 (continued)

EVERGREEN MARKET
JOURNAL

20__		Transactions		Dr.	Cr.

EXHIBIT 5

EVERGREEN MARKET LEDGER

Cash			Accounts Payable		Revenues	
10,000	2,000			2,000		300
5,000						800
300						
800						

Accounts Receivable		Note Payable		Expenses	
			5,000	200	
				500	

Inventory		Paid-in Capital		Retained Earnings	
2,000	200		10,000		
2,000	500				

EXHIBIT 6 FINANCIAL STATEMENTS

EVERGREEN MARKET
Balance Sheet as of January 8

Assets

Cash $14,100

Accounts Receivable ....

Inventory ....

Total Assets .... $

Liabilities and Equity

Accounts Payable..................... $

Note Payable ....

Paid-in Capital........................

Retained Earnings ....

Total Liabilities and Equity...... $

Income Statement
for the period January 2–8

Revenues .... $

Expenses..................................

Net Income.............................. $

EXHIBIT 7

TRANSACTIONS OF HOMES, INC.

Date	Event	Effects on Cash
May 2	Able agrees to buy House A from Homes, Inc., and makes a $16,000 down payment.	increase $16,000
May 15	Homes, Inc., pays $800 commission to the salesperson who sold House A (5% of cash received).	decrease $800
May	Homes, Inc., general expenses for May were $4,400 (assume for simplicity these were paid in cash in May).	decrease $4,400
June 2	Baker agrees to buy House B and makes a $24,000 down payment.	increase $24,000
June 5	Able completes the purchase of House A, paying $144,000 cash. Homes, Inc., delivers the deed to Able thereby delivering ownership of the house. (House A cost Homes, Inc., $140,000.)	increase $144,000
June 30	Homes, Inc., pays $1,200 commission to the salesperson who sold House B.	decrease $1,200
June	Homes, Inc., general expenses for June were $4,000.	decrease $4,000
July 2	Homes, Inc., pays $7,200 additional commission to the salesperson who sold House A.	decrease $7,200
July 3	Baker completes the purchase of House B, paying $216,000 cash. Homes, Inc., delivers the deed to Baker, thereby delivering ownership of the house. (House B cost Homes, Inc., $200,000.)	increase $216,000
July 30	Homes, Inc., pays $10,800 commission to the salesperson who sold House B.	decrease $10,800
July	Homes, Inc., general expenses for July were $4,800.	decrease $4,800

EXHIBIT 8

A "PACKAGE" OF ACCOUNTING REPORTS
($000 omitted)

GARSDEN COMPANY

Condensed Balance Sheet
as of December 31, 2008

Assets

Current Assets	$23,024
Buildings and Equipment	14,100
Other Assets	1,662
Total Assets	$38,786

Liabilities and Equity

Liabilities	$14,622
Equity:	
Paid-in Capital	12,256
Retained Earnings	11,908
Total Liabilities and Equity	$38,786

Condensed Balance Sheet
as of December 31, 2009

Assets

Current Assets	$22,651
Buildings and Equipment	13,412
Other Assets	2,176
Total Assets	$38,239

Liabilities and Equity

Liabilities	$12,343
Equity:	
Paid-in Capital	12,256
Retained Earnings	13,640
Total Liabilities and Equity	$38,239

Income Statement
for the Year 2009

Sales Revenue	$75,478
Less Cost of Sales	52,227
Gross Margin	23,251
Less Operating Expenses	10,785
Income before Taxes	12,466
Provision for Income Taxes	6,344
Net Income	$ 6,122

Statement of Retained Earnings

Retained Earnings, 12/31/08	$11,908
Add Net Income, 2009	6,122
	18,030
Less Dividends	4,390
Retained Earnings, 12/31/09	$13,640

EXHIBIT 9

LEWIS FUEL COMPANY

	Units	Unit Cost	Total Cost
Beginning inventory, April 1	400	1.00	
Purchase, April 10	300	1.10	
Purchase, April 20	300	1.20	
Total goods available			
Ending inventory, April 30	600		
Cost of sales, April			

FIFO Method

Goods Available .... $_____

Ending inventory:

_____ units @ $_____ = $_____

_____ units @ $_____ = _____

Total 600 units..................................... _____

   Cost of sales .... _____

LIFO Method

Goods Available .... $_____

Ending inventory:

_____ units @ $_____ = $_____

_____ units @ $_____ = _____

Total 600 units..................................... _____

   Cost of sales .... _____

Average-Cost Method

Average cost of $_____

               _____ = _____ cost per unit

_____

Goods available $1,090

   Ending inventory 600 units @ $ _____ = _____

   Cost of sales   400 units @ $ _____ = _____

EXHIBIT 10

CHICO COMPANY
Balance Sheets
($000 Omitted)

Assets

	As of December 31			
		2009		2008
Current Assets				
Cash		$ 20		$ 7
Accounts Receivable		40		42
Inventory		60		56
Prepaid Expenses		20		20
Total Current Assets		140		125
Noncurrent Assets				
Land		$ 30		$ 30
PPE, at cost	$120		$108	
Less Accumulated Depreciation	70	50	64	44
Goodwill and Patents		10		10
Total Assets		230		209

Liabilities and Equity

		2009		2008
Current Liabilities				
Accounts Payable		$ 30		$ 33
Accrued Wages		10		6
Income Taxes Payable		20		20
Total Current Liabilities		60		59
Noncurrent Liabilities				
Mortgage Bonds Payable		$ 40		$ 34
Total Liabilities		100		93
Shareholder Equity				
Paid-in Capital (4,800 shares outstanding)		$ 60		$ 60
Retained Earnings		$ 70		56
Total Shareholder Equity		130		116
Total Liabilities and Equity		230		209

Income Statement, 2009
($000 Omitted)

		Percentage
Sales Revenue	$300	100.0
Less Cost of Sales	− 180	60.0
Gross Margin	120	40.0
Less Depreciation Expense	− 6	2.0
Other Expenses	− 72	24.0
Earnings before Interest and Taxes	42	14.0
Interest Expense	− 5	1.7
Earnings before Income Tax	37	12.3
Provision for Income Taxes	− 13	4.3
Net Income	24	8.0
Less Dividends	− 10	
Addition to Equity	14	

EXHIBIT 11

CHICO COMPANY
Statement of Cash Flows, 2009

Cash Flow from Operating Activities

Net income .... $ 24

Adjustments required to reconcile net income to cash flows:

Depreciation expense .... $.....

Decrease in accounts receivable ....

Increase in inventory .... (.....)

Decrease in accounts payable .... (.....)

Increase in accrued wages ....

    Total adjustments to net income ....

    Total cash flow from operating expenses ....

Cash Flow from Investing Activities

Purchase of property, plant, and equipment .... (.....)

Cash Flow from Financing Activities

Issuance of long-term debt ....

Dividends paid[*] .... (.....)   (.....)

Net increase or decrease in cash and cash equivalents .... $.....

Cash balance, beginning of period .... $.....

Cash balance, end of period .... $.....

Note: Parentheses indicate decreases in cash.

[*](See Note after Frame 9-56.)

EXHIBIT 12

REPORT OF INDEPENDENT AUDITORS

The Board of Directors and Shareholders
Chico Company

We have audited the accompanying balance sheets of Chico Company as of December 31, 2009 and 2008, and the related statements of income and cash flows for each of the three years in the period ended December 31, 2009. These financial statements are the responsibility of the company's management. Our responsibility is to express an opinion on these financial statements based on our audits.

We conducted our audits in accordance with generally accepted auditing standards. Those standards require that we plan and perform the audit to obtain reasonable assurance about whether the financial statements are free of material misstatement. An audit includes examining, on a test basis, evidence supporting the amounts and disclosures in the financial statements. An audit also includes assessing the accounting principles used and significant estimates made by management, as well as evaluating the overall financial statement presentation. We believe that our audits provide a reasonable basis for our opinion.

In our opinion, the financial statements referred to above present fairly, in all material respects, the financial position of Chico Company at December 31, 2009 and 2008, and the results of its operations and its cash flows for each of the three years in the period ended December 31, 2009, in conformity with generally accepted accounting principles.

Clark and Lewis

Seattle, Washington
February 21, 2010

EXHIBIT 13

CHICO COMPANY
Factors Affecting Return on Equity
(Year 2009, $000 Omitted)

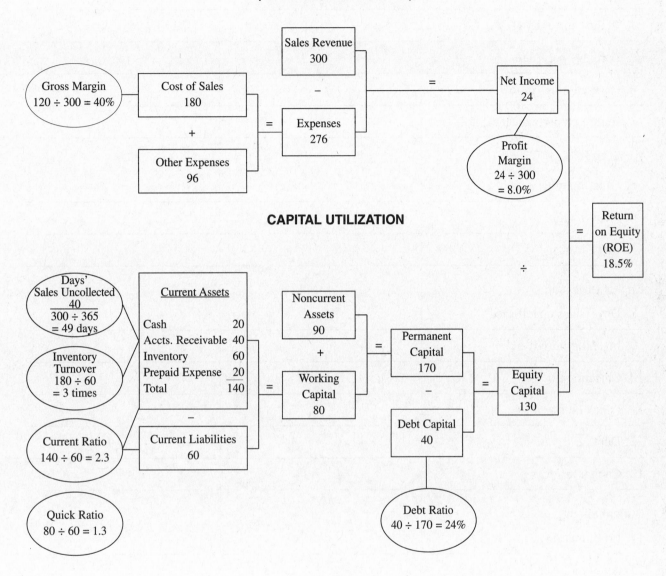

CAPITAL UTILIZATION

EXHIBIT 14

SOME COMMON RATIOS

Overall Performance	Numerator	Denominator
1. Return on equity (ROE)		
2. Earnings per share		
3. Price-earnings ratio		
4. Return on permanent capital		
Profitability		
5. Gross margin %		
6. Profit margin %		
7. EBIT margin %		
Capital Utilization		
8. Days' sales uncollected		
9. Inventory turnover		
10. Current ratio		
11. Quick ratio		
12. Debt ratio		
13. Capital turnover		
DuPont Identity		
14. Profit margin		
15. Asset turnover		
16. Equity multiplier		

EXHIBIT 15a

MERCER COMMUNITY SERVICES
Statements of Financial Position
($000 Omitted)

Assets

	As of June 30	
	2009	2008
Assets:		
Cash and Cash Equivalents	$ 38	$ 230
Accounts Receivable	1,065	835
Inventories	200	350
Prepaid Expenses	105	150
Contributions Receivable	1,512	1,350
Land, Buildings, and Equipment	33,313	33,725
Long-term Investments	109,035	101,750
Total Assets	$145,268	$138,390

Liabilities and Net Assets

Liabilities and Net Assets:		
Accounts Payable	$ 1,285	$ 525
Refundable Advances		325
Grants Payable	438	650
Notes Payable		570
Long-term Debt	2,750	3,250
Total Liabilities	4,473	5,320
Net Assets:		
Unrestricted	57,614	51,835
Temporarily Restricted	12,171	12,735
Permanently Restricted	71,010	68,500
Total Net Assets	140,795	133,070
Total Liabilities and Net Assets	$145,268	$138,390

EXHIBIT 15b

MERCER COMMUNITY SERVICES
Statement of Activities
($000 Omitted)
Year Ended June 30, 2009

	Unrestricted	Temporarily Restricted	Permanently Restricted	Total
Revenues, gains, and other support:				
Contributions	$4,320	$4,055	$140	$8,515
Fees	2,700			2,700
Income on long-term investments	2,800	1,290	60	4,150
Other investment income	425			425
Net realized and unrealized gains on				
long-term investments	4,114	1,476	2,310	7,900
Other	75			75
Net assets released from restrictions:				
Satisfaction of program restrictions	5,995	(5,995)		
Expiration of time restrictions	1,375	(1,375)		
Total revenue, gains, and other support	21,804	(549)	2,510	23,765
Expenses and losses:				
Program X	6,550			
Program Y	4,270			
Program Z	2,880			
Administration	1,250			
Fundraising	1,075			
Other losses		15		30
Total expenses	16,025	15		16,040
Change in net assets:	5,779	(564)	2,510	7,725
Net assets at beginning of year	51,835	12,735	68,500	133,070
Net assets at end of year	57,614	12,171	71,010	140,795

Post-Tests

Please note, all Post-Test Answers follow the Post-Test section.

POST-TEST 1

1. Give the accounting name for the following terms:

   (a) Things of value owned

      by an entity   _____.

   (b) Money   _____.

   (c) Claims of creditors   _____.

   (d) Claims of investors   _____.

2. List the two types of sources of funds; list first the type having the stronger claim on an entity's assets:

   Stronger claim _____

   Lesser claim   _____

3. A balance sheet reports the status of an entity [at a point in time / over a period of time].

4. Give the fundamental accounting equation:

   _____ = _____ + _____

5. The above equation is consistent with what concept?

_____–_____ _____

6. The money-measurement concept states that accounting reports only facts that can be expressed in

_____ _____.

7. A balance sheet does not report all the facts about a business. What concept limits the amount or type of information that can be reported? _____-

_____ _____

8. Brown Company has $10,000 cash. Fred Foy, its sole owner, withdraws $100 for his own use. Fred Foy is [better off / worse off / no better or worse off] than he was before. Brown Company now has [the same amount of / less] cash. The fact that this event affects Fred Foy differently than it affects Brown Company is an illustration of the _____ concept.

9. The entity concept states that accounts are kept for _____ as distinguished from the _____ who own those entities.

10. On December 31, 2008, Lewis Corporation has $12,000 cash on hand and in the bank. It owns other things of value, totaling $25,000. Its only debt is a bank loan of $10,000. Prepare a balance sheet for Lewis Corporation as of December 31, 2008, using the form below:

                 _____ _____

          _____ _____ as of _____ _____ 2008

          _____   _____ and _____

_____ ....$_____   _____ ....$_____

Other _____ ...._____   _____ ...._____

       _____ ....$_____   _____ ....$_____

11. The going-concern concept is: Accounting assumes that an _____ will continue to operate _____ .

12. The asset-measurement concept is: If reliable information is available, accounting focuses on the _____ _____ of assets. Nonmonetary assets are reported at their original _____ .

13. An item can be reported as an asset if it passes three of the following tests. Select "yes" for these and "no" for the others.

    (a) Item is valuable. [yes / no]

    (b) Item is located in a building owned by the entity. [yes / no]

    (c) Item is used by the entity. [yes / no]

    (d) The entity has ordered the item. [yes / no]

    (e) Item was acquired at a measurable cost. [yes / no]

    (f) Item is owned or controlled by the entity. [yes / no]

14. Goodwill is a favorable name or reputation _____ by the entity.

15. An asset is classified as "current" if it is cash or is expected to be converted into cash in the near future, usually within _____ _____ [what time period?].

16. A liability is classified as "current" if it becomes due in the near future, usually within _____ _____ [what time period?].

> **NOTE:** Please see Exhibit 1 for hints on the following questions.

17. Marketable securities are [current / noncurrent] assets. Property, plant, and equipment (PPE) are [current / noncurrent] assets.

18. Answer True or False:

Shoes in a manufacturing company are considered inventory ....[T / F]

The building in which the shoes are manufactured is considered inventory ....[T / F]

19. An insurance policy paid in advance of the time period covered is an example of a prepaid expense. Prepaid expenses are usually _____ _____ .

20. A building, an item of equipment, and an automobile may all be examples of _____ _____ .

21. Parker Company operates a furniture store. On December 31, 2008, it had 30 desks that it was holding for sale. These would be reported as _____ . The desk that is used by the president of Parker Company would be reported as a _____ _____ .

22. Indicate whether the following statements about the balance sheet of a corporation are true or false:

    (a) Assets list all the valuable things owned by the entity...............................[T / F]

    (b) The amount reported for the paid-in-capital item is approximately the fair value of the stock ....[T / F]

    (c) The amount reported for total equity is approximately the fair value of the corporation's stock...............................[T / F]

    (d) Total equities (also called "net worth") show approximately what the entity is worth ....[T / F]

    (e) Retained earnings is the amount of cash retained in the entity ....[T / F]

Lighter Light Solutions—Part 1

Bill turned on his computer as he thought about the meeting scheduled in the morning. Eight months after his business, Lighter Light Solutions (LLS), had released the Lighter Light—a tiny flashlight that recharges continually in a car's cigarette lighter—sales were brisk and business looked bright. However, cash flows were uncertain and inventory arrangements were fluctuating.

With an office, a warehouse, and the use of a factory (without formal ownership) in China and with warehouses and sales representatives in the Pacific Northwest, Bill needed to formalize his international business arrangements. This meant meeting with an international banker. However, before this meeting could happen Bill needed to pull together eight months' worth of information.

Which of the following items belong on Lighter Light Solution's balance sheet?

Which of the following items do not belong on the balance sheet, but represent important financial information that should be highlighted in the meeting with the international banker?

1. Records of inventory being held in Bill's Seattle warehouse, the China warehouse, and with the company's sales force
2. Information about the strengths and weaknesses of the sales force
3. Information about apartment rentals in China for Bill's use when he is there
4. The amounts that Bill and his business partner Matt initially invested in the business
5. The profit Bill expects to earn in future sales of Lighter Lights
6. The amount that LLS has available on its business credit card for employee travel
7. Information about office rentals in China
8. The cost of the car LLS purchased six months ago
9. The costs involved in making a single Lighter Light
10. Projected sales during the coming year
11. The amount of cash LLS has in the bank
12. The amount of loans taken out by LLS but not yet paid back
13. Information about other businesses that would be potential competitors with LLS

Pizza Box Mulch I—Part 1

Mike kicked an empty pizza box into the corner as he walked through the dorm lounge. Then he sighed, turned around, and picked it up. While it pained him to do so, Mike carried the greasy box to the dorm kitchen and placed it in the garbage.

An avid environmentalist, Mike was appalled at the towers of pizza boxes he saw discarded week after week. During his freshman year Mike had started a campaign to advocate that College City Recycling allow dorm residents to recycle the cardboard boxes, but he had been told that the greasy leftover cheese gummed up the utility's machines. During his sophomore year Mike had tried an educational campaign that urged residents to tear out and recycle the clean parts of the boxes, but his emails had been ignored and the greasy boxes still hovered near the trash.

It was now junior year and Mike knew that time was running out. He stared at the pizza boxes and the garbage can. And then, picking up the boxes, Mike walked to his room and began sketching out a business plan for Mike's Pizza Box Mulch.

Mike decided to put the $500 he had in his checking account into the new business. Since his advertising would happen via emails, all Mike needed to get started would be a machine to turn the pizza boxes into mulch. Through his friends in the mechanical engineering department Mike was able to have one made for $300. He started scouting out the best locations to find discarded pizza boxes.

Mike's roommate was studying accounting. He looked at the pizza boxes and he looked at Mike. "If you're going to start a business let's do it right," he said. "How about we set you up with a beginning balance sheet?"

Lidija Perez—Part 1

Lidija Perez lives in a small rural community in Nicaragua. When Lidija learns that a local lending organization will be offering loans to the women in her community, she decides to start a business raising pigs from her home. Lidija knows that on Fridays the families in her community have extra cash, so she plans to use the meat from the pigs to make various foods that she can sell on payday.

Lidija also knows that she can feed the pigs from table scraps and the parts of corn plants that are not normally consumed. She therefore will not have to buy feed. Together with her children, Lidija will be able to gather the firewood she needs for her business from the surrounding area. She already has pots and knives so she doesn't plan on buying any tools at the start of her business.

As a condition for taking out the loan Lidija begins attending a series of trainings. One of the things that she learns in the trainings is the importance of keeping careful financial records. In order to take out her loan Lidija needs to prepare an initial balance sheet.

Using the following information please help Lidija prepare a balance sheet effective as of the end of the day on her first day of business. The initial loan is for the equivalent of $150. Part of the loan agreement is that Lidija must also contribute $20 of her own funds. Since the loan is being offered through the work of a nonprofit organization, no interest is due during the first year.

Lidija knows a farmer who has a sow that just delivered a litter of pigs. The farmer has already agreed to sell Lidija five pigs at a price of $25 each, so the day Lidija receives her loan she immediately buys her pigs and starts her business. After buying the pigs Lidija puts the rest of her cash in a book and tucks it away until she has a better idea how she will use it.

What would Lidija's balance sheet look like at this point in her adventure?

1. On January 2, Rose Brown started the Brown Company. In January, Brown Company did the following things:

(a) It received $5,000 cash from Rose Brown as its capital.

(b) It borrowed $10,000 from a bank, giving a note therefor.

(c) It purchased $4,000 of inventory for cash.

(d) It sold $2,000 of its inventory for $6,000 to a customer, who paid $3,500 cash and agreed to pay $2,500 within 30 days.

(e) It purchased an auto for $7,000. It paid $2,000 down and gave a note to the automobile dealer for the remaining $5,000.

(f) Brown withdrew $1,000 cash for her personal use.

(g) Brown was offered $10,000 for her equity in the business, but she refused the offer.

On a separate piece of paper, prepare a rough draft of a balance sheet for Brown Company as of the close of business January 31, and an income statement for January.

BROWN COMPANY

Balance Sheet as of _____ _____

_____   _____ and _____

_____ ....$_____   _____ _____ ....$_____

_____ _____ ...._____   _____-_____ ...._____

_____ ...._____   _____ _____ ...._____

_____ ...._____   _____

Total...$_____   Total..$_____

BROWN COMPANY

Income Statement for _____

_____ ....$_____

_____ ....$_____

Income...$_____

2. Brown Company's income was $4,000, but its Retained Earnings was only $3,000. Reread the first frame and choose the item (a–g) that explains the difference.

No]. This is an illustration of the _____-_____ concept. Nonmonetary assets are reported at their _____ rather than their worth or _____ _____.

3. Rose Brown claims that the inventory as of January 31 is worth $6,000, as shown by the fact that inventory costing $2,000 was actually sold for $6,000. Would you change the balance sheet? [Yes /

4. Fox Company sold $1,000 of goods on credit to Golden Company. This would be recorded as an account [receivable / payable] of Fox Company and as an account [receivable / payable] of Golden Company.

Pizza Box Mulch II—Part 2

"I knew a green business could be a success!"

During the first year of business, Mike was able to find a steady stream of pizza boxes and then as spring turned into summer he discovered there were numerous clients in the area who needed mulch for their gardens. Even the college he attended started using his mulch. Mike decided to take out a loan and have a second, bigger machine made. Whenever friends came to his dorm room they often found themselves running pizza boxes through the machines.

Now it was graduation and not only was Mike about to walk up to receive his diploma, but he was also looking at some nice numbers. That is, some nice and confusing numbers.

"How is it that we had a $1070 surplus this year but that doesn't show up anywhere on the balance sheet?" Mike asked his roommate the accounting major. "How can I have $2070 in something called *retained earnings,* but only $1620 in the bank? And what about that $500 I put in? These numbers look good, but they don't really make sense!"

Can you answer Mike's questions?

Balance Sheet as of June 2009

Assets		Liabilities	
Cash	$1,620	Loan	$500
Accounts Receivable	750		
Machine #1	300	**Equity**	
Machine #2	400		
		Paid-in Capital	500
		Retained Earnings	2,070
	$3,070	....	$3,070

Income Statement June 2008–2009

Revenues	$4,570
Expenses	–3,500
Profit	$1,070

Lidija Perez—Part 2

Six months after starting her business Lidija stares at a notebook filled with names and numbers. She has been working hard and business has been brisk, and yet the $45 she had at the end of her first day of business is now completely gone and she is about to slaughter her last pig. Lidija isn't quite sure what happened, but she knows that most of the problem is in the long list of people who have not yet paid.

Lidija hopes that she might be able to take out a second loan, but she knows that before she can approach the loan officer she is going to need to go through her records and bring her balance sheet up to date.

Lidija waited four months before slaughtering her first pig, so that it could be of good size and have plenty of meat. She thought that her family would be able to live during this time from what her husband would earn during the fishing season. However within two months he needed money for gas for the boat, and Lidija lent him $10 from the cash she had left. She is still waiting for repayment, but she knows he doesn't have the money so she isn't asking for it. And then when school started Lidija needed to buy shoes for her daughter, and that was another $8.

When Lidija did kill her first pig she was excited when she thought about the money that she would earn. But then after a long day of slaughtering, cooking, and walking door-to-door she found that most of her neighbors wanted to buy on credit. "I'll pay you next week," they said. Without refrigeration Lidija decided she had to sell her product, even though at the end of the day she only had the equivalent of $10 in cash and the beginning of her list of unpaid accounts. Totaling the numbers that night Lidija found that her neighbors owed her $35.

The next week Lidija killed another pig, gaining $5 in cash and another $30 from neighbors who didn't pay her. Lidija decided it was time to start repaying her loan so she took $25 of the money she had earned to the loan officer.

However, when Lidija killed her third pig suddenly it seemed like no one had money. She wasn't sure what had happened, but all she could do was sell $25 worth of meat, and all of that on credit. That night her children ate well, but Lidija was worried.

Lidija knew that she needed to buy more pigs if her business was going to continue. Her mother offered her a piglet for $20 and Lidija decided to go ahead and buy it with the last of her cash ($17) and a promise to pay $3 more.

Lidija then killed her fourth pig. She was able to earn another $50—$20 in cash and $30 in promises—but it was time to make another $25 payment on her loan. Lidija took the $20 she had to the loan officer, knowing that she was going to hear a lecture about the risks of selling on credit.

What does Lidija's balance sheet look like after she makes the $20 payment to the loan officer? What advice would you give Lidija as she thinks about the future of her business?

POST-TEST 3

1. On March 5, Kay Company purchased $6,000 of inventory, paying cash. Prepare a journal entry for this transaction below.

Journal

Transactions	Dr.	Cr.
___ ___	_____	_____
	_____	_____

2. On March 10, Kay Company made a $15,000 sale to a customer who paid $6,000 cash and agreed to pay the other $9,000 in 30 days. The merchandise sold had cost $8,000. Prepare a journal entry for the sale below.

Journal

Transactions	Dr.	Cr.
___ ___ ___		
___ ___ ___		
	_____	_____

3. On March 10, Kay Company made a sale for $15,000 for merchandise that had cost $8,000. Prepare a journal entry to record the cost of the sale below.

Journal

Transactions	Dr.	Cr.
___ ___	_____	_____
	_____	_____

4. Recall from the previous frames that revenues from the sale on March 10 were $15,000 and that the merchandise sold had cost $8,000. Prepare the closing entries.

Journal

Transactions	Dr.	Cr.
___ ___	_____	_____
___ ___	_____	_____
	_____	_____

5. The following journal entries will be used in Frames 6 and 7. There is no response required in this frame.

Journal

Transactions		Dr.	Cr.
March 5	Inventory	6,000	
	Cash		6,000
March 10	Cash	6,000	
	Accounts Receivable	9,000	
	Revenues		15,000
March 10	Expenses	8,000	
	Inventory		8,000
March 31	Revenues	15,000	
	Retained Earnings		15,000
March 31	Retained Earnings	8,000	
	Expenses		8,000

6. Post the journal entries from the previous frame to the ledger accounts below.

Asset accounts:

Cash

Bal.	25,000	_____	
	_____		
Bal.	_____		

Accounts Receivable

Bal.	11,000	
	_____	
Bal.	_____	

Inventory

Bal.	40,000	_____	
	_____		
Bal.	_____		

Property and Plant

Bal.	30,000	

7. Post the journal entries from Frame 5 to the ledger accounts below.

Liability and Equity accounts:

Accounts Payable
	16,000 Bal.

Paid-in Capital
	60,000 Bal.

Revenues
———	———

Expenses
———	———

Retained Earnings
———	30,000 Bal.
	———
	——— Bal.

8. Complete the following table by selecting Debits or Credits.

	Debits	Credits
Increases in asset accounts are ....[Dr. / Cr.]		
Decreases in asset accounts are.............................[Dr. / Cr.]		
Increases in liability accounts are ....[Dr. / Cr.]		
Decreases in liability accounts are ....[Dr. / Cr.]		
Increases in equity accounts are............................[Dr. / Cr.]		
Decreases in equity accounts are...........................[Dr. / Cr.]		
Increases in revenue accounts are ....[Dr. / Cr.]		
Increases in expense accounts are ....[Dr. / Cr.]		

9. Refer back to Frames 6 and 7. Prepare a balance sheet for Kay Company as of March 31.

KAY COMPANY

Balance Sheet as of March 31

Assets		Liabilities and Equity	
Cash ....$_____		Accounts payable...$_____	
Accounts receivable....................................._____		Paid-in capital ...._____	
Inventory ...._____		Retained earnings..._____	
Property and Plant..............................._____			
Total......................................$_____		Total......................................$_____	

10. Refer back to Frame 7. Prepare an income statement for Kay Company for March.

_____ _____

_____ _____ for _____

_____ ....$_____

_____ ...._____

_____ ....$_____

11. A critic said that the company had $25,000 cash at the beginning of March and $25,000 at the end of March, and since its cash balance was unchanged, it couldn't be said to have any income in March. This criticism is [correct / incorrect].

12. The reason the criticism is incorrect is because income is an increase in _____ _____, not necessarily in _____. For example, the sales revenue of Kay Company in March was $15,000 and its income was $7,000 even though $9,000 was received in cash.

Lidija Perez—Part 3

Let's join Lidija again in the same case we saw in Part 2. This time Lidija needs help translating the transactions below into journal entries and T-accounts.

Six months after starting her business Lidija stares at a notebook filled with names and numbers. She has been working hard and business has been brisk, and yet the $45 she had at the end of her first day of business is now completely gone and she is about to slaughter her last pig. Lidija isn't quite sure what happened, but she knows that most of the problem is in the long list of people who have not yet paid.

Lidija hopes that she might be able to take out a second loan, but she knows that before she can approach the loan officer she is going to need to go through her records and bring her balance sheet up to date.

Lidija waited four months before slaughtering her first pig, so that it could be of good size and have plenty of meat. She thought that her family would be able to live during this time from what her husband would earn during the fishing season. However within two months he needed money for gas for the boat, and Lidija lent him $10 from the cash she had left. She is still waiting for repayment, but she knows he doesn't have the money so she isn't asking for it. And then when school started Lidija needed to buy shoes for her daughter, and that was another $8.

When Lidija did kill her first pig she was excited when she thought about the money that she would earn. But then after a long day of slaughtering, cooking, and walking door-to-door she found that most of her neighbors wanted to buy on credit. "I'll pay you next week," they said. Without refrigeration Lidija decided she had to sell her product, even though at the end of the day she only had the equivalent of $10 in cash and the beginning of her list of unpaid accounts. Totaling the numbers that night Lidija found that her neighbors owed her $35.

The next week Lidija killed another pig, gaining $5 in cash and another $30 from neighbors who didn't pay her. Lidija decided it was time to start repaying her loan so she took $25 of the money she had earned to the loan officer.

However, when Lidija killed her third pig suddenly it seemed like no one had money. She wasn't sure what had happened, but all she could do was sell $25 worth of meat, and all of that on credit. That night her children ate well, but Lidija was worried.

Lidija knew that she needed to buy more pigs if her business was going to continue. Her mother offered her a piglet for $20 and Lidija decided to go ahead and buy it with the last of her cash ($17) and a promise to pay $3 more.

Lidija then killed her fourth pig. She was able to earn another $50—$20 in cash and $30 in promises—but it was time to make another $25 payment on her loan. Lidija took the $20 she had to the loan officer, knowing that she was going to hear a lecture about the risks of selling on credit.

What does Lidija's balance sheet look like after she makes the $20 payment to the loan officer? What advice would you give Lidija as she thinks about the future of her business?

The Kenya Connection—Part 3

Mark stared at the papers in front of him. The good news was that sales had been brisk, but this meant that he needed to sort through all of the financial transactions that had accumulated during a few fairly busy days. He was grateful for the knowledge he now had about basic bookkeeping from the introductory course he just completed at his local community college.

During his three years with the Peace Corps Mark had lived in Kenya, and he had been amazed at the creativity and ingenuity of the people that he served. Animals carved from discarded flip-flops, colorful bowls woven out of telephone wires, and bookmarks made from recycled bottle caps were just some of the amazing handicrafts that Mark had found for sale in the marketplace. As he returned to the United States Mark decided that he would devote himself to providing the ability for artisans throughout Kenya to offer their products for sale on the global market.

Mark founded The Kenya Connection, an organization that featured and sold the work of Kenyan artisans. Most sales took place through Internet orders, which meant The Kenya Connection was open for business 24 hours a day, 7 days a week. He was proud of the fact that the artisans would finally be paid fair prices for their products.

Help Mark sort through the following financial transactions by first writing the records in the journal and then posting them to the ledger.

On September 21 Mark paid $250 for shipping supplies in preparation for Christmas orders. He also received two different shipments from Kenya. One shipment was from a group of Maasi women and it contained 20 beaded necklaces. Mark strongly wanted to support the artisans through fair trade practices and so (through his partners in Kenya) he paid the women $12 per necklace. The other shipment came from a rural community of Tabaka and it contained 30 soapstone ornaments, and Mark paid the artisans $3 each per ornament. That afternoon Mark received an order from a children's foundation for 3 animals carved from flip-flops. Since this was a new client, and as Mark had the animals in stock, he shipped them immediately, billing the foundation $195 to be paid within 30 days. The cost of the animals was $150 ($50 per animal) that had been paid directly to the artists who carved them sometime over the summer. Mark also had to pay $15 for shipping costs associated with the flip-flop animals.

On September 22 Mark received a series of orders. There was an order for 10 recycled bottle cap bookmarks, which Mark sold for $3 each, and for a set of 3 telephone wire bowls, which Mark sold for $20. Young unwed mothers living in Kisumu made the bookmarks and the bowls and they were paid $2 per bookmark and $5 per bowl. Another order was for 5 beaded Maasi necklaces, which Mark sold for $15. A different order was for 5 soapstone ornaments, which Mark sold for $4. And there was another order for 2 sets of telephone wire bowls, which Mark sold for $40 (total). Each of the orders was paid for by Mark's PayPal account, or with a credit card. As he went to UPS, Mark knew that the shipping costs for these 4 orders would total $25.

On September 23 Mark continued to prepare for the rush in orders that he expected to occur within the coming weeks. He asked his partner in Kenya to buy 40 sets of telephone wire bowls and 40 bottle cap bookmarks from the mothers in Kisumu, 10 flip-flop animals, 30 beaded necklaces from the Maasi women, and 50 soapstone ornaments. Since Mark wanted to pay the artisans immediately for their work he wired the money to his partner that afternoon. Wiring the money cost Mark another $12.

Mark would like help organizing the inventory he ordered and subsequently sold. Please complete the following tables and prepare a set of journal entries.

First Order:

#	Product	Cost	Selling Price	Sales
	Bookmarks			
	Bowls			
	Necklaces			
	Ornaments			

Second Order:

#	Product	Cost	Selling Price	Total Cost
	Bowls			
	Bookmarks			
	Animals			
	Necklaces			
	Ornaments			

1. The conservation concept states that increases in equity are recognized only when they are _____ _____, while decreases in equity are recognized as soon as they are _____ _____.

2. The materiality concept states: disregard _____ _____, but disclose all _____ _____.

3. What is the length of the usual accounting period? _____ _____. Financial statements prepared for shorter periods are called _____ statements.

4. Cash accounting reports items that increase or decrease cash. Accrual accounting reports items that change _____ or _____ _____, even though these changes may not affect cash.

5. Increases in equity associated with the entity's operations during a period are _____, and decreases are _____. The difference between them is labeled _____.

6. The realization concept states that revenues are recognized when goods or services are _____.

7. Hartwell Company manufactures a table in August and places it in its retail store in September. Bernard Guyer, a customer, agrees to buy the table in October, it is delivered to him in November, and he pays the bill in December. In what month is the revenue recognized? _____

8. The receipt of cash is a debit to Cash. What is the offsetting credit and (type of account) for the following types of sales transactions?

Account credited
(a) Cash received prior to delivery
   _____ ____ _____
   (a _____)
(b) Cash received in same period as delivery
   _____
(c) Cash received after the period of delivery
   _____ _____
   (an _____)

9. Similarly, revenue is a credit entry. What is the offsetting debit when revenue is recognized in each of these periods?

Account debited
(a) Revenue recognized prior to receipt of cash
   _____ _____
(b) Revenue recognized in same period as receipt of cash
   _____
(c) Revenue recognized in period following receipt of cash
   _____ ____ _____

10. In February, Hartwell Company agrees to sell a table to a customer for $600, and the customer makes a down payment of $100 at that time. The cost of the table is $400. The table is delivered to the customer in March, and the customer pays the remaining $500 in April. Give the journal entries (if any) that would be made in February, March, and April for both the revenue and expense aspects of this transaction.

February

_____   _____
_____ ____ _____   _____

March

_____ _____   _____
_____ ____ _____   _____
_____   _____

March

_____   _____
_____   _____

April

_____   _____
_____ _____   _____

11. At the end of 2008, Timber Company had accounts receivable of $200,000, and it estimated that $2,000 of this amount was a bad debt. Its revenue in 2008, with no allowance for the bad debts, was $600,000.

(a) What account should be debited for the $2,000 bad debt? _____

(b) What account should be credited?
_____ ____ _____
_____

(c) What amount would be reported as *net* accounts receivable on the balance sheet?
$_____

(d) What amount would be reported as revenue on the 2008 income statement?
$_____

12. In 2009, the $2,000 of bad debt was written off.

(a) What account should be debited for this write off? _____ ____
_____ _____

(b) What account should be credited?
_____ _____

Lidija Perez—Part 4

Lidija Perez decided to take an introductory financial management course offered by her local lending organization. She was surprised to learn that by doing some basic cash management she would not end up in such tight spots with respect to having enough cash to keep her small business running. (Please visit Parts 1, 2 and 3 for the introduction to Lidija's business.)

Lidija decided to set a firm price for her product and offered the people in her community a discount if they paid her in cash at the time they bought the meat. She said she would allow this only if their accounts were paid in full. Amazingly, she collected 90% of what had been owed to her. (See Part 3 Post-Test for Lidija's last balance sheet.)

She also decided to start breeding her own pigs so that she would not have to pay $25 or more for new ones. Lidija still had the piglet she bought from her mother and it was ready for a mate. She decided to buy another five pigs from the farmer, which were also ready for breeding. He agreed to sell them to her for the original price of $25 per pig. She paid the farmer $50 and promised to pay him the rest as soon as possible.

Several people heard about the expansion of Lidija's business and asked if they could place their orders for meat in advance. Lidija said they could do so and offered a discount if they paid in full ahead of time. She ended up with $200 worth of orders this way.

As Lidija's business grew, she knew she would be unable to sell all of her meat for cash. Some customers simply did not have cash available when they needed to buy meat from Lidija. Although she was willing to sell to them for a promise to pay, she estimated that approximately 3% of them might never pay her, and decided to be conservative and round this up to an average of $5 for this time period.

Lidija's pigs were healthy and they were producing meat for her to sell, as well as reproducing themselves! So far she was able to sell the meat from four more pigs without having to replenish her stock of pigs from the farmer, including the $200 worth of meat for which she took advanced orders. She delivered all of this in a single day to her customers, with help from the kids, ending up with $300 in cash and $100 in promises to pay for the sales beyond the advanced orders.

With some cash on hand, Lidija paid her mother back the $17 she owed her for the piglet and paid off the balance of her loan ($105). She knew she was in good shape now, but to keep growing she would have to make some new investments in buildings to house the growing family of pigs and the additional food and help to care for them. Beyond Lidija's imagination, she now had a thriving business. At this turning point, complete a balance sheet for her. Do you think Lidija is ready to expand?

The Kenya Connection II—Part 4

Mark's Kenya Connection (see Part 3) has grown. There has been so much interest among his U.S. customers in supporting the African artisan that Mark has expanded the business. His first Christmas season was a huge success. With some cash in the bank, Mark decided it was now OK to sell more items on credit. Further, since his partners in Kenya promised a steady supply of products, Mark began taking more orders, certain that he could deliver in a timely manner.

Mark kept his pricing the same as before the Christmas holidays because his costs for merchandise did not change. To recap, here is what he pays for his products, as well as what he charges. Shipping costs average $25 per order of merchandise he receives from Africa and $15 for each order sent out to his customers.

Product	Cost/Unit	Selling Price/Unit
Flip-flop carved animals	$50	$150
Telephone wire bowls	$5	$20
Bookmarks	$2	$3
Beaded necklaces	$12	$15
Soapstone ornaments	$3	$4

During April Mark sent a large order to the gift shop at the Museum of Modern African Culture. The museum gave him a deposit of $250 but asked for 60 days to pay for the rest of the bill for merchandise ordered. The museum ordered 4 animal sculptures, 20 beaded necklaces, 10 wire bowls, and 100 bookmarks. The shop still had some ornaments left from the holidays and hence did not order more.

Mark also received a check in the mail for a special order of beaded necklaces from the U.S. Olympics Committee to be given as gifts during the upcoming games. The colors were specific to various countries' flags and would take a few months to create. The order was for 200 necklaces of varying colors and represented 50% of the order. Mark was unsure how to account for this transaction.

Selling on credit was still new for Mark. Although he had no bad experiences to date, he fully expected not to collect 10% of what was owed to him. Before the April orders Mark had $550 in accounts receivable. He estimated his bad debts to be around 10% of what was outstanding. Mark still had shipping supplies left over from his holiday business.

Help Mark with the journal entries for his April transactions.

1. An expenditure occurs in the period in which goods or services are [acquired / consumed]. An expense occurs in the period in which goods or services are [acquired / consumed].

2. A certain asset was acquired in May. There was therefore an _____ in May. At the end of May, the item was either on hand, or it was not. If it was on hand, it was an _____; if it was not on hand, it was an _____ in May.

3. Productive assets are [expired / unexpired] costs. Expenses are [expired / unexpired] costs.

4. The matching concept states that _____ associated with the revenues of a period are _____ of that period.

5. Expenses of a period consist of:
   (a) _____ of the goods and services _____ during that period.
   (b) Other _____ that benefit _____ of the period.
   (c) _____

6. If Brown Company pays rent prior to the period that the rent covers, the amount is initially reported as a credit to cash and a debit to _____ Rent, which is a(n) [asset / liability] account. If Brown Company pays rent after the period covered, the amount is initially recorded as a debit to Rent Expense and a credit to _____ Rent, which is a(n) [asset / liability] account.

7. A brand new machine owned by Lily Company was destroyed by fire in 2008. It was uninsured. It had been purchased for $10,000 with the expectation that it would be useful for five years. The expense (i.e., loss) recorded in 2008 should be [$2,000 / $10,000].

8. Gross margin is the difference between _____ _____ and _____ _____ _____.

9. Give the numerator and denominator of the gross margin percentage:

   _____ _____
   _____
   _____ _____

10. The difference between revenues and expenses in an accounting period (or the amount by which equity [i.e., retained earnings] increased from operating activities during the period) is called _____ _____.

11. A distribution of earnings to shareholders is called _____.

12. Give an equation that used the terms
   (a) net income
   (b) dividends
   (c) retained earnings at the beginning of the period, and
   (d) retained earnings at the end of the period.
      ( ) = ( ) + ( ) – ( )

Tobo Construction Services I—Part 5

Tobyn Bowstrom worked as a carpenter in the construction industry for 15 years, and recently started his own company. He specialized in remodeling projects for small- and medium-size businesses, and most construction projects lasted at least 60 to 90 days. The typical invoicing for this industry was to bill customers at the end of each month for the amount of construction completed during the month. This was important to cash flow for the business, as construction workers are paid on a weekly basis.

Because monthly billings often meant that the entire construction project was not yet completed, Tobyn had to calculate a value for the work that was completed as of the time of invoicing. Work included any labor, materials, and subcontractor costs that were directly related to the project. There was also a need to charge for some amount of overhead, to help cover the general administration costs associated with the company. After years of working as a carpenter for someone else, Tobyn was surprised to find how challenging this part of running a business would be.

Tobo Construction's official first day of operations was October 2nd, and Tobyn began his first project (Job 1—Warehouse remodel for Celtic Manufacturing) on October 9th. The project was expected to last nine weeks, and Tobyn had hired a laborer and a carpenter to complete the work. Tobyn served as the project manager.

It was now October 31st and Tobyn needed to determine how much to invoice his customer. Thankfully he had taken a "record-keeping for small businesses" class a few months earlier and had kept precise records of the costs he incurred during the month.

Monday Oct 2nd

October Office Rent: $750

Friday Oct 6th

Payroll:

    T. Bowstrom (Owner, Project Manager): $1,000 (weekly salary)

Monday, Oct 9th

Lumber purchase for Job 1:

    Lori's Lumberyard: $1,500 (put on store credit account)

Demolition equipment rental for Job 1:

    Ace Rentals: $350 (put on store credit account)

Cleaning and containment supply purchase for Job 1:

    Central Supplies: $125 (paid with credit card)

Friday Oct 13th

Payroll:

    M. James (Laborer): $240 (demolition work—16 hours @ $15)—Job 1

    Z. Bell (Carpenter): $640 (site containment and framing—32 hrs @ $20)—Job 1

    T. Bowstrom (Owner, Project Manager)—$1,000 (weekly salary)

Friday Oct 20th

Payroll:

> M. James (Laborer): $480 (cleaning work and framing assistance—32 hours @ $15)—Job 1
>
> Z. Bell (Carpenter): $800 (framing work—40 hrs @ $20)—Job 1
>
> T. Bowstrom (Owner, Project Manager)—$1000 (weekly salary)

Friday Oct 27th:

Payroll:

> M. James (Laborer): $480 (cleaning work and framing assistance—32 hours @ $15)—Job 1
>
> Z. Bell (Carpenter): $800 (framing work—40 hrs @ $20)—Job 1
>
> T. Bowstrom (Owner, Project Manager)—$1000 (weekly salary)

October portion of staff payroll to be paid on Friday Nov 3rd:

> M. James (Laborer): worked last two days of October—$120 (8 hours)—Job 1
>
> Z. Bell (Carpenter): worked last two days of October—$320 (16 hours)—Job 1
>
> T. Bowstrom (Owner, Project Manager)—worked the last two days of October—$400 (2/5 of weekly $1,000 salary)

Other Bills Received:

> October telephone services (due Nov 5th): $35
>
> October utilities (due Nov 10th): $100
>
> Annual Membership to local Construction Association (due Nov 25th): $180

Tobyn, who works eight hours per day, calculated that he has spent about 50% of his time directly working on Job 1 (Celtic Manufacturing) during October. The remaining time was spent doing sales calls, completing bookkeeping activities and continuing to establish office systems. Tobyn also decided that he would charge a 20% overhead fee for his jobs, which would help him cover his indirect costs, and hopefully make a profit too. He would calculate the fee amount by multiplying 20% by the subtotal of any labor, materials and subcontractor costs associated with a project.

Help Tobyn by doing the following:

1. Draft his first invoice, billing the Celtic Manufacturing project for work completed in the month of October. Show labor, materials and the 20% overhead fee as separate line items. Although Job 1 did not start until October 9th, Tobyn felt it was fair to charge a portion of his salary for the first week of October to the job as he was preparing for it during that time.

2. Next, create a first month's income statement for Tobo Construction, allowing Tobyn to see whether his operations have been profitable.

3. Determine Tobo Construction's gross margin and net income percentage for October work.

Mike's Pizza Box Mulch III—Part 5

"I can't believe I'm a business owner!" Mike thought to himself. It was one year since college graduation and he was still a little amazed by how his inspiration for an environmental cause—preventing multitudes of pizza boxes from going into the garbage—had developed into a profitable business (See Parts 1 and 2 for the start of Mike's business.). When entering college he had never envisioned himself as an entrepreneur running a business; he had imagined working *for* some well-known environmental organization. He laughed as he thought of a bumper sticker he recently saw on a car, which said *"Think globally, Act locally."* He realized that was exactly what he was doing.

During his first two years of operation, the business was simple and Mike was fortunate to have Quinn, his college roommate, help him set up a basic financial system from the start. However, the business now had a wider variety of financial activities, including bank loan payments, machine maintenance, and business insurance, and the bookkeeping side of the business was starting to stretch Mike's skills. To be sure that he had posted everything accurately for his last operating period, he decided to email his transaction notes and income statement draft to Quinn for a quick review.

Quinn had just emailed him back the documents with a short message of *"Good news—your operations made more profit than you think! I'm leaving town for a work event… will call you this weekend if you have questions about my adjustments."*

Mike looked over the report with Quinn's changes and was happy to see that several expenses were reduced. But he was also confused about why these purchases would not be expenses.

Briefly explain for Mike why each of Quinn's adjustments is appropriate.

1. A dealer sells a television set for $800 cash. It had cost $600. Write journal entries for the *four* accounts affected by this transaction.

Dr. _____ _____

   Cr. _____ _____

Dr. _____ ____ _____ _____

   Cr. _____ _____

2. When using the perpetual inventory method, a record is kept for _____ _____, showing receipts, issues, and the amount on hand.

3. Write an equation that shows how the cost of sales is determined by deduction:

cost of sales = _____ _____

         + _____

         – _____ _____

4. Following is information about a certain product:

	Quantity	Unit Cost	Total Cost
Inventory, July 1	400	$1.00	$400
Purchases, July 15	200	$1.20	240
Total goods available	600		640
Inventory, July 31	300		

What was the cost of sales for July:

  (a) Under the FIFO method _____

  (b) Under the LIFO method _____

  (c) Under the average-cost method _____

5. In periods of inflation, many companies use the LIFO method in calculating their taxable income because LIFO gives a _____ cost of sales and hence a _____ taxable income.

6. A company discovers that the fair value of its inventory is $1,000 lower than its cost. What journal entry should it make?

Dr. _____ ____ _____ _____

   Cr. _____ _____

7. In a manufacturing business, what three elements enter into the cost of a manufactured item?

_____ _____, _____ _____, and _____.

8. Period costs become an expense during the period in which they were _____.

9. Product costs become an expense during the period in which the products were _____.

10. One type of overhead rate involves use of the total direct labor costs and total production overhead costs for a period. Write a ratio that shows how the overhead rate is calculated.

Total _____ _____ costs

——————————————————

Total _____ _____ costs

11. A given finished item requires $50 of direct materials and 5 hours of direct labor at $8 per hour. The overhead rate is $4 per direct labor hour. At what amount would the finished item be shown in inventory?

$_____ [= $_____ + $_____ + $_____]

12. An inventory turnover of 5 is generally [better / worse] than an inventory turnover of 4 because it indicates that [more / less] capital is tied up in inventory, and there is [more / less] risk that the inventory will become obsolete.

Tobo Construction Services II—Part 6

After reviewing the income statement from his first month of operations, Tobyn saw that the 20% overhead rate he used was not sufficient to cover all of his indirect costs. He decided to calculate some other methods for determining an overhead rate to find one that could be used to ensure he would not create an operating loss.

First Tobyn realized he would have to make some assumptions. He assumed that his indirect costs of rent, utilities, telephone, and membership fees would not change in the near future, and that he would continue to spend about 50% of his time on activities not directly related to any one job.

Using these assumptions and the figures from his October operations (*below*), calculate the following overhead rate possibilities for Tobyn. After making your calculations, provide any other factors Tobyn would be wise to consider before deciding on what to use as an overhead rate.

- Rate per Labor Dollar

- Rate per Labor Hour

- Rate as % of Direct Costs (that would provide for at least breakeven)

Tobo Construction Services
Operational Costs—October

Direct Costs

	Wage Rate	Hours	Total Cost
Laborer wages	$15	88	$1,320
Carpenter wages	$20	128	$2,560
Project management wages	$25	88*	$2,200
Materials			$1,975
Total **Direct** Costs/Hours		304	$8,055
Total **Direct Labor** Costs			**$6,080**

Indirect/Overhead Costs			
Owner salary (non-job related)	$25	88	$2,200
Rent			$750
Telephone			$35
Utilities			$100
Membership fees			$15
Total **Indirect**/OH Costs			**$3,100**

*Assume a 40-hour workweek.

Blue Jeans by the Pound—Part 6

Katherine couldn't believe her good fortune at being offered a six-month internship with a local blue jean distributor, *Blue Jeans by the Pound.* As college senior studying fashion retail, Katherine believed this would be a dream job. How could there be a dull moment in the world of designers, fabric, fashion trends and international manufacturing? She began to doubt her excitement, however, as she sat across from her supervisor who was explaining that she would begin her internship in the accounting department. It was her supervisor's philosophy that interns should be exposed to *all* aspects of the business, especially the critical part of how revenues and expenses were managed to keep the company profitable. The supervisor believed this aspect of the garment industry was often overlooked by starry-eyed fashion students, and Katherine would be well served to have a better understanding of how it worked. Katherine was going to start by helping with the quarterly inventory accounting. She would help take the physical inventory figures to determine the cost of goods sold over the past three months for the "Cowboy Jeans" brand line. She was happy to learn that the work only required a basic ability with algebra and spreadsheets. Katherine and the inventory manager, Ryan, collected the following data:

"Cowboy Jeans" Line

	# of Units	Cost per Unit	Value
Beginning Inventory Balance	3,500	$13.10	$45,850
Purchases	# of Units	Cost per Unit	Value
April 5	1000	$13	$13,000
April 27	600	$12.75	$7,650
May 12	700	$12.70	$8,890
May 29	1500	$12.55	$18,825
June 23	1750	$12.40	$21,700
Total Value (BB + Purchases)			**$115,915**

Ending physical inventory at June 30th: **3,800**

As a training piece, Ryan explained three different ways the value of remaining inventory and the cost of goods sold could be determined (FIFO, LIFO, Average Cost). He said that the method used by *Blue Jeans by the Pound* was selected to meet the following financial goal: to have the lowest income tax expense. This meant the company wanted to have the lowest taxable income, which happens when the company shows the lowest profits.

Based on this goal, he asked Katherine to do the following:

• Calculate the total number of units sold during the quarter

• Determine the value of the remaining inventory using FIFO and LIFO

• Calculate the COGS under each method

• Guess which method the company was using in order to meet its tax goals.

1. The amount at which a new property, plant, and equipment (PPE) asset is recorded in the accounts includes its purchase price plus _____ _____ incurred to make the asset ready for its intended use (such as transportation and installation).

2. A PPE asset is acquired in 2008. It is expected to be worn out at the end of 10 years and to become obsolete in 5 years. What is its service life? _____ years

3. Ordinarily, land [is / is not] depreciated because its _____ _____ is indefinitely long.

4. A PPE asset is acquired in 2008 at a cost of $20,000. Its estimated service life is 10 years, and its estimated residual value is $2,000:

(a) The estimated depreciable cost of the asset is $ _____

(b) If the straight-line depreciation method is used, the depreciation rate for this asset is _____%.

(c) What amount will be recorded as depreciation expense in each year of the asset's life? $_____

(d) What account will be debited and what account will be credited to record this depreciation expense?

Dr. _____ _____

Cr. _____ _____

(e) After five years have elapsed, how would this asset be reported on the balance sheet?

(1) _____ $_____

(2) ____ _____ _____ $_____

(3) ____ _____ $_____

5. A machine is purchased on January 2, 2008, for $20,000 and it has an expected life of five years and no estimated residual value.

(a) If the machine is still in use six years later, what amount of depreciation expense will be reported in for the sixth year? _____

(b) What amount, if any, will be reported on the balance sheet at the end of the sixth year?

[ ] (1) It will not be reported.

[ ] (2) It will be reported as follows:

_____ $_____

_____ _____ $_____

_____ _____ $_____

6. A machine is purchased on January 2, 2008, for $50,000. It has an expected service life of 10 years and no residual value. Eleven years later it is sold for $3,000 cash.

(a) There will be a [loss / gain] of $_____

(b) What account will be debited and what account credited to record this amount?

Dr. _____

Cr. _____ on _____ of _____

7. Give an example of each of the following types of assets, and give the name of the process used in writing off the cost of the second and third type.

Asset type	Example	Write-off process
PPE Asset	m_____,	Depreciation
	b_____	
Wasting asset	c_____, o_____ _____	
	m_____	
Intangible asset	g_____	_____
	t_____	

8. Shell Company purchased a producing oil property for $10,000,000 on January 2, 2008. It estimated that the property contained one million barrels of oil and that the property had a service life of 20 years. In 2008, 40,000 barrels of oil were recovered from the property. What amount should be charged as an expense in 2008? $_____

9. Wasting assets and intangible assets are reported on the balance sheet in a different way than building, equipment, and similar plant assets. The difference is that wasting assets are reported at the _____ _____ and plant assets are reported at _____, _____ _____, and _____ _____.

10. In calculating its taxable income, a company tries to report its income as _____ as it can. In calculating its financial accounting income, a company tries to report its income as _____ as it can.

11. As compared with straight-line depreciation, accelerated depreciation writes off [more / the same / less] depreciation in the early years of an as-

set's life and [more / the same / less] in the later years. Over the whole life of the asset, accelerated depreciation writes off [more / the same / less] total cost as straight-line depreciation.

12. Companies usually use accelerated depreciation in tax accounting because it [increases / reduces] taxable income and hence income tax in the early years.

13. Assume an income tax rate of 40%. If a company calculated its financial accounting income (before income taxes) in 2008 as $6 million and its taxable income as $4 million, what amount would it report as income tax expense on its 2008 income statement? $_____

14. Fill in the missing name on the following table:

Income tax expense	$100,000
Income tax paid	−60,000
_____ _____ _____	$ 40,000

The $40,000 would be reported on the balance sheet as a(n) [asset / liability].

Iceberg Pure H₂O-I—Part 7

With an exploding consumer market for bottled water and intense producer competition, companies work to differentiate their water as being of premium quality to command higher prices. Although many advertise their specialty water sources of unique wells and springs, few can match the claims of the new Alaskan company *Iceberg Pure H₂O*. As the name implies, this company harvests its water from an Alaskan iceberg, creating bottled water that is said to be the absolute purest because it is "10,000 years old—frozen long before any pollutants tainted the earth." Company founder and president Helen Holmes, an Alaskan native, got the idea after boating in local waters and watching icebergs cleave into manageable-sized chunks. She arranged to buy the rights to an iceberg and then bought a small canning plant and converted it into a state-of-the-art water-bottling factory. She bought the iceberg for $25,000, after estimating that it held at least 750,000 liters of water, and that she would be able to sell Iceberg's 500-ml water bottles for $3.00 each. The following table outlines her initial business calculations, showing an incredible profit potential and the ability to meet her operating expenses with the actual water only costing less than 2 cents per bottle. With some initial market research and retail contracts, Helen expected to sell **550,000 bottles per year.**

Iceberg Cost	Iceberg Capacity (liters)	Cost per Liter	# Bottles Capacity (500-ml size)	Cost per 500 ml	Estimated Revenue (@ $3.00 bottle)
$25,000	750,000	$0.03	1,500,000	$0.015	$4,500,000

Helen believed *Iceberg Pure H₂O* would be a big hit and had great growth potential. She knew that having excellent financial records would be essential if she were to need future bank loans, or consider selling the company to a larger corporation. This especially meant she needed to have a proper accounting for the usage of the actual iceberg, which was her primary asset.

Advise Helen on what kind of asset the iceberg is and what accounting method is appropriate for expensing its use. Using her current projections, help her establish an annual expense projection and total useful life for the iceberg.

Iceberg Pure H$_2$O-II—Part 7

In addition to the iceberg, *Iceberg Pure H$_2$O* had a few other long-term assets; its three (3) water-melting tanks, the bottling machine, and the actual plant building. Now that she had determined how to account for the iceberg (see Iceberg Pure H$_2$O-I), Helen turned her attention to these.

WATER TANKS

She purchased the stainless steel water-melting tanks for $4,500 each and they seemed to be built to last forever. It cost another $3,100 to have the tanks installed and plumbed.

BOTTLING MACHINE

The bottling machine was a great deal because an old friend was vice president for the manufacturer (another reason she decided to start the *Iceberg Pure H$_2$O* business in the first place). Even though the machine had a retail price of $42,000, she was able to buy it at cost plus 15%, which was $28,500. The machine would easily produce her expected volume of 550,000 bottles per year, and had additional capacity up to another 150,000 per year. Including delivery, labor, electrical and plumbing needs, the installation of the machine cost $12,000.

PLANT BUILDING

Being in northern Alaska was advantageous for real estate costs (although shipping of the actual product was more expensive!). The plant building cost only $19,000, plus a $600 agent fee and $7,000 in improvements to make it functional. She also bought a cool neon sign to install on the front of the building for $500. It was a great effect in the snowy environment and no one in the area would fail to see it. The plant gave plenty of room for the tanks, bottling, and storage of product inventory.

To determine her depreciation for these items, Helen knew she needed a "service life" for each of them. She also knew that she was projecting to make incredible profits on her business, so she would pay less income tax if she had more expenses to match against her revenues. Since depreciation was an operating expense, the faster she could depreciate her equipment, the more tax advantage she would have.

Provide Helen with a total cost for each asset (assuming no residual value for any of them) so she knows how much is available to be depreciated. Then provide the reasons Helen must consider when deciding the service life for these long-term assets.

1. The term *working capital* means the difference between _____ _____ and _____ _____.

2. The two principal sources of a company's permanent capital are _____ and _____.

3. Bonds obligate the company to make regular payments of _____ and _____. Bonds are [never / sometimes / always] current liabilities.

4. The two principal sources of equity capital are _____-____ _____ from _____ and _____ _____ (income not paid out as dividends).

5. A corporation issues 1,000 shares of $1 par value common stock in exchange for $10,000 cash. Complete the journal entry for this transaction:

Dr. Cash 10,000

   Cr. _____ _____ ....   _____

       _____ _____-__ _____ ....   _____

6. The equity section of a balance sheet is as follows:

Common stock (1,000 shares, no par value) $10,000

Other paid-in capital...20,000

Retained earnings 40,000

Total equity..$70,000

(a) The stated value per share is [$10 / $30 / $70 / can't tell].

(b) The company received from its shareholders [$10,000 / $30,000 / $70,000 / can't tell].

(c) The shareholders' equity is worth [$10,000 / $30,000 / $70,000 / can't tell].

(d) The company has cash of at least [$10,000 / $30,000 / $70,000 / can't tell].

(e) The company's income to date has totaled [$40,000 / at least $40,000 / can't tell].

(f) If the company is liquidated, the shareholders will receive at least [$10,000 / $30,000 / $70,000 / can't tell].

7. The dollar amount reported for common stock on the balance sheet is the amount for the number of shares [authorized / issued]. This amount is called the amount _____.

8. Kay Company had 200,000 shares of stock authorized. It issued 150,000 shares. It later bought back 10,000 shares. The 10,000 shares are called _____ stock. The total shareholder equity on the balance sheet would be the amount for _____ shares.

9. Preferred shareholders usually have preference as to _____ and also in the event of liquidation they have preference as to _____ _____.

10. A cash dividend [increases / decreases / does not change] shareholder equity. A stock dividend [increases / decreases / does not change] shareholder equity. A stock dividend [increases / decreases / does not change] the number of shares of stock outstanding.

11. Select the correct words in the following table, which shows the principal differences between debt capital and equity capital.

	Bonds (Debt)	Stock (Equity)
Annual payments are required.	[Yes / No]	[Yes / No]
Principal payments are required.	[Yes / No]	[Yes / No]
Therefore, risk to the entity is	[Higher / Lower]	[Higher / Lower]
But its cost is relatively	[Higher / Lower]	[Higher / Lower]

12. Matthew Company has the following permanent capital:

Debt capital ....$ 80,000

Equity capital..20,000

   Total $100,000

(a) Its debt ratio is _____%.

(b) The company is said to be highly

     _____.

13. Able Company owns 51% of the stock of Charlie Company, 50% of the stock of David Company, and 49% of the stock of Eastern Company. Able is the _____ company. The accounts of _____ _____ and _____

_____ would be consolidated in consolidated financial statements. The equity of the shareholders who own 49% of the stock of Charlie Company would be reported as the item _____ _____ on the consolidated balance sheet.

14. Able Company's income statement reported revenue of $1,000,000, of which $10,000 was sales to Charlie Company. Charlie Company's income statement reported revenue of $500,000, of which $20,000 was sales to Able Company. Revenue on the consolidated income statement would be reported as $_____.

Olive's Organics—Part 8

Olive scanned rows of milk jugs as her baby dropped his pacifier on the floor. The jugs had white caps, pink caps, and green caps, but Olive couldn't find the distinctive green boxes of organic whole milk. With a sigh, she pushed her cart past the aisles of socks, antifreeze, and birthday cards as she went searching for organic applesauce.

As she wandered through Sam's Save More, Olive realized that what harried, concerned mothers needed was a store that sold only organic foods. She decided it was time to start her own business and Olive's Organics was born.

The next week Olive went to the bank for a loan. However, she quickly learned that no one was willing to lend to a business started by a young mother with a degree in social work. So Olive formed a partnership with her brother, a wealthy and eccentric accountant who lived by the conservatism concept and the motto "never a borrower or lender be."

Five years later Olive sat at her desk and stared at the papers that told her Sam's Save More had just purchased a significant part of the stock in Olive's Organics. She picked up the phone and called her brother. "Explain to me what happened," she said, "in terms that I can understand."

Please explain what you see happening in the balance sheets for Olive's Organics that might be enticing for a competitor. Should Olive be worried?

Olive's Organics (000s)

Balance Sheet

	31-Dec-09	31-Dec-08	31-Dec-07
Assets			
Current Assets			
Cash and Cash Equivalents	55,230	340,440	301,050
Accounts Receivables	110,200	95,300	87,020
Inventory	160,500	150,400	124,750
Total Current Assets	**325,930**	**586,140**	**512,820**
Long-Term Investments	365,110	147,260	106,560
Property Plant and Equipment ...	969,400	680,000	576,090
Other Assets	5,000	4,900	4,700
Total Assets	**1,665,440**	**1,418,300**	**1,200,170**

Liabilities

Current Liabilities . . . .

Accounts Payable	250,600	310,500	179,900
Short-Term Debt	800	5,700	6,200
Total Current Liabilities	**251,400**	**316,200**	**186,100**
Long-Term Debt	8,400	10,600	9,070
Total Liabilities	**259,800**	**326,800**	**195,170**

Stockholder's Equity . . . .

Paid-in Capital	400,000	400,000	400,000
Common Stock	590,700	390,700	330,000
Retained Earnings	414,940	300,800	275,000
Total Stockholder's Equity	**1,405,640**	**1,091,500**	**1,005,000**
Total Liabilities plus Equity	**1,665,440**	**1,418,300**	**1,200,170**

Satellite Streak—Part 8

Dinner conversations with friends are usually interesting, but they can get weary when a pair becomes locked in an argument over something as "exciting" as whether bonds or stock should be issued. Such was the evening for Matteo, who sat sipping his coffee and considering the energetic debate of his friends Donna and Walter. It centered on the *Satellite Streak* company, a communication satellite parts manufacturer in which both Donna and Walter owned stock. The expanding world of satellite-supported technology (e.g., phones, radio, television, Internet, and GPS systems) was definitely a profitable market and *Satellite Streak* was supposedly a hot company with no shortage of orders to fill. What it possibly lacked was additional capital to support new growth. Donna insisted that the company should set up another production facility and simply issue some of its treasury stock to raise the needed capital. Walter also believed the company should build more manufacturing capacity, but said the capital should be raised by borrowing via a bond issue.

Matteo, quietly listening to the argument go back and forth, realized that his friends were really arguing about the future value of their stock if the company could grow. Neither mentioned anything about the risk associated with their proposed options. This didn't surprise Matteo much, as neither Donna nor Walter had a background in finance and both were new to their interest in investing. Matteo decided that he wanted to shift the conversation away from this subject, and decided to "wrap it up" by explaining that the choice was first about company risk, and then about future market stock prices.

What could Matteo say to his friends about the basic risk associated with bonds *(debt capital)* versus stock *(equity capital)* that a company would consider when raising capital?

1. The preparation of a statement of cash flows is [recommended / required] by U.S. accounting rules.

2. The income statement reports net income on a(n) _____ basis. The statement of cash flows adjusts net income to a(n) _____ basis.

3. The three sections of the statement of cash flows are:

cash flow from _____ _____

cash flow from _____ _____

cash flow from _____ _____

4. At December 31, 2008, XYZ Corp. had accounts receivable of $70,000. At December 31, 2009, the company's accounts receivable balance was $65,000. This $5,000 decrease of accounts receivable [decreased / had no effect on / increased] net income adjusted to a cash basis.

5. Accounts payable for XYZ Corp. decreased by $3,000 between December 31, 2008 and December 31, 2009. This change [decreased / had no effect on / increased] net income adjusted to a cash basis.

6. The change in XYZ Corp.'s cash balance from the end of 2008 to the end of 2009 [is / is not] part of the changes in current assets used to calculate "cash flow from operating activities."

7. XYZ Corp. had $2,000 in depreciation expense in 2009. This [was / was not] a cash flow during that year.

8. To adjust XYZ Corp.'s net income to a cash basis, the $2,000 in depreciation expense should be [added to net income / subtracted from net income / ignored].

9. Complete the "cash flow from operating activities" section of XYZ Corp.'s statement of cash flows. Assume accounts receivable decreased by $5,000, accounts payable decreased by $3,000, and depreciation expense was $2,000. There were no other changes in current assets.

Net income	$50,000
Depreciation expense	$_____
Decrease in accounts receivable	$_____
Decrease in accounts payable	($_____)
Total cash flow from operations	$_____

10. What kind of activity is described by each of the events of the transactions below?

(a) Jones Co. buys a piece of equipment for $40,000.

[operating / investing / financing]

(b) Jones Co. borrows $50,000 from a bank, signing a long-term note payable.

[operating / investing / financing]

(c) Jones Co. pays $20,000 of its outstanding accounts payable.

[operating / investing / financing]

(d) Smith Corp. arranges $10,000 in new short-term borrowings from the bank.

[operating / investing / financing]

(e) Smith Corp. issues 1,000 of its common stock for $10 per share.

[operating / investing / financing]

(f) Smith Corp. sells one of the buildings it used for operations for $500,000.

[operating / investing / financing]

(g) Smith Corp. receives interest revenue on invested funds. [operating / investing / financing]

(h) Smith Corp. pays dividends to its investors.

[operating / investing / financing]

Olive's Organics II—Part 9

Five years later, as Olive and her brother discussed why Sam's Save More was purchasing their stock at a steady rate, Luigi Ciaccia, their financial manager, phoned Olive on her cell phone. He was quite alarmed about the rate at which the cash balance was declining. Luigi had just finished preparing the pro forma (projected) financial statements for 2010 and he wanted to meet with Olive and her brother immediately.

Dissatisfied that Luigi brought only the projected income statement and balance sheets for 2009–2010, Olive decided to try her hand at constructing the statement of cash flows. She had just completed the financial accounting course that was part of her graduate studies in business. What will Olive learn from her analysis of the statement of cash flows that might help her strategic planning?

Olive's Organics (000s)

Balance Sheet	Pro Forma 31-Dec-10	31-Dec-09	Pro Forma Income Statement period ending 31-Dec-2010		Pro Forma Statement of Cash Flows 2010		
Assets							
Current Assets			Total Revenue	$ 4,300,500	**Operating Activities**		
Cash and Cash Equivalents	$ 2,640	$ 55,230	Cost of Revenue	2,800,000	Surplus		
Accounts Receivables	310,200	110,200	**Gross Profit**	**1,500,500**	Add back depreciation		
Inventory	260,300	160,500			Change in A/R		
Total Current Assets	**573,140**	**325,930**	Research and Development	250000	Change in Inventory		
Long Term Investments	639,500	365,110	Selling General and Administrative	900,700	Change in A/P		
Property Plant and Equipment	1,500,400	969,400	Depreciation	53,000	**Cash Flows from Operating Activities**		
Other Assets	6,700	5,000	Total Operating Expenses	1,203,700			
Total Assets	**$ 2,719,740**	**$ 1,665,440**					
			Operating Income or Loss	**296,800**			
			EBIT	296,800			
Liabilities			Interest Expense	4,200	**Investing Activities**		
Current Liabilities			Income Before Tax	292,600	Change in Long Term Investments		
Accounts Payable	$ 412,600	$ 250,600	Income Tax Expense	116,500	Change in PPE (net of depreciation)		
Short-term Debt	4,800	800			Change in Other Assets		
Total Current Liabilities	**427,400**	**251,400**	**Net Income**	**$ 176,100**	**Cash Flows from Investing Activities**		
Long-term Debt	710,600	8,400					
Total Liabilities	**$ 1,138,000**	**$ 259,800**			**Cash Flows from Financing Activities**		
					Change in short-term debt		
Stockholder's Equity					Change in long-term debt		
Paid-in Capital	400,000	400,000			**Net Cash Flows from Financing Activities**		
Common Stock	590,700	590,700					
Retained Earnings	591,040	414,940			**Net Change in Cash**		
Total Stockholder's Equity	**$ 1,581,740**	**$ 1,405,640**			Beginning Cash	$	55,230
					Ending Cash	$	2,640
Total Liabilities plus Equity	**$ 2,719,740**	**$ 1,665,440**					

The Investment Dilemma—Part 9

Your cousin Thomas has been telling you about a great investment he made with *Lawman Security*. It is a regional company specializing in surveillance equipment, both selling wholesale and doing installation work. Thomas says the company has been growing and even has some government contracts, which he believes is an indicator that the company will continue to expand nationally and be even more profitable. This means its cheap stock price is bound to keep climbing. You've been talking investments with family and friends because you've just sold some and have

$3,500 to reinvest. This *Lawman Security* sounds really interesting, but you also know that companies that grow too quickly without good financial management can get themselves into trouble (you've lost on such stock scenarios in the past!). Besides *Lawman,* you are also seriously considering *Solar-Us,* a solar panel manufacturer that a friend told you is another rising star company. You've decided to do more research on selecting one of these companies because they are both definitely in business sectors with lots of growth potential. Unfortunately this decision is getting tough, because both companies also have strong balance sheets, income statements showing profitability, and good ROE ratios. You're now looking at their third important financial statement, the most recent *Statement of Cash Flows.* Based on what you see in the following reports, which company has indicators of cash management that fit with your desire for stable growth, and why?

Solar-US Company Statement of Cash Flows —Yr End 2009		Lawmen Security Company Statement of Cash Flows—Yr End 2009	
Cash Flow from Operating Activities		**Cash Flow from Operating Activities**	
Net income	65,000	Net income	78,000
Depreciation expense	25,000	Depreciation expense	15,000
Increase in accounts receivable	(75,000)	Increase in accounts receivable	(80,000)
Increase in inventory	(45,000)	Increase in inventory	(55,000)
Increase in accounts payable	67,000	Increase in accounts payable	71,000
Net Cash Flow from Operating Activities	**37,000**	*Net Cash Flow from Operating Activities*	**29,000**

Cash Flow from Investing Activities		**Cash Flow from Investing Activities**	
Purchase of equipment	(75,000)	Purchase of equipment	(20,000)
Net Cash Flow from Investing Activities	**(75,000)**	*Net Cash Flow from Investing Activities*	**(20,000)**

Cash Flow from Financing Activities		**Cash Flow from Financing Activities**	
Bank loan (long-term)	75,000	Bank loan (short-term line of credit)	20,000
Dividends paid *	(15,000)	Dividends paid *	-
Net Cash Flow from Financing Activities	**60,000**	*Net Cash Flow from Financing Activities*	**20,000**

Net Increase in Cash	22,000	Net Increase in Cash	29,000
Plus: Beg. Balance of Cash	25,000	Plus: Beg. Balance of Cash	28,000
Equals: Ending Balance Cash @ 12/31/2009	**47,000**	**Equals: Ending Balance Cash @ 12/31/2009**	**57,000**

*Although dividends are often considered a financing activity, it is common to see *dividends paid* in "Cash Flows from Operating Activities."

1. Use the following data:

Inventory	20	Sales revenue	100
Total current assets	100	Cost of sales	60
Total assets	220	Gross margin	40
Current liabilities	40	EBIT	30
Noncurrent liabilities	80	Net income	10
Equity	100		

(a) The current ratio was:

$$\frac{\rule{2cm}{0.4pt}}{\rule{2cm}{0.4pt}} = \rule{1.5cm}{0.4pt}$$

(b) The inventory turnover was:

$$\frac{\rule{2cm}{0.4pt}}{\rule{2cm}{0.4pt}} = \rule{1.5cm}{0.4pt} \text{ times}$$

(c) The profit margin percentage was:

$$\frac{\rule{2cm}{0.4pt}}{\rule{2cm}{0.4pt}} = \rule{1.5cm}{0.4pt} \%$$

(d) The debt ratio (to the nearest percent) was:

$$\frac{\rule{2cm}{0.4pt}}{\rule{2cm}{0.4pt}} = \rule{1.5cm}{0.4pt} \%$$

(e) The return on equity investment was:

$$\frac{\rule{2cm}{0.4pt}}{\rule{2cm}{0.4pt}} = \rule{1.5cm}{0.4pt} \%$$

(f) The EBIT margin was:

$$\frac{\rule{2cm}{0.4pt}}{\rule{2cm}{0.4pt}} = \rule{1.5cm}{0.4pt} \%$$

(g) The capital turnover (to one decimal place) was:

$$\frac{\rule{2cm}{0.4pt}}{\rule{2cm}{0.4pt}} = \rule{1.5cm}{0.4pt} \text{ times}$$

(h) The pretax return on permanent capital (to the nearest percent) was:

$$\frac{\rule{2cm}{0.4pt}}{\rule{2cm}{0.4pt}} = \rule{1.5cm}{0.4pt} \%$$

2. The pretax return on permanent capital can also be calculated by multiplying the c_____ t_____ by the _____ margin.

3. A company can decrease its equity by:
(a) [increasing / decreasing] its assets.
(b) [increasing / decreasing] its liabilities.

4. Liquidity means a company's ability to meet its _____ obligations.

5. Solvency means a company's ability to meet its _____-_____ _____ obligations.

6. The DuPont system of ratios breaks down ROE in three components.

_____ _____

_____ _____

_____ _____

7. Profit margin is a measure of _____ efficiency. Asset turnover is a measure of _____ _____ efficiency. The equity multiplier is a measure of financial _____.

8. Accounting cannot provide a complete picture of the status or performance of an entity because:
(a) Accounting deals only with events that can be reported in m_____ terms.
(b) Financial statements report only p_____ events.
(c) Balance sheets do not show the f_____ v_____ of assets.
(d) The accountant and management have [some latitude / no choice] in choosing among alternative ways of recording an event (e.g., LIFO, FIFO, or average cost).
(e) Accounting amounts are affected by e_____.

9. Analysts often attempt to evaluate the q_____ of e_____ for a company. All other things equal,

(a) A conservative accounting policy is characteristic of [higher / lower] quality of earnings.

(b) Net income from one-time, high impact events is characteristic of [higher / lower] quality of earnings.

(c) Sales revenues that give rise to cash inflows in the near term are characteristic of [higher / lower] quality of earnings.

10. The name of the law passed in 2002 to strengthen corporate governance and restore investor confidence is called the S_____ -O_____ Act.

11. The Sarbanes-Oxley Act helps to protect w_____ b_____ or those who might be able to expose undesirable or unlawful behavior by companies.

Olive's Organics and Sam's Save More—Part 10

Sam scowled as he stared at the pro forma (projected) financial statements in front of him. Ground was being broken for a new Olive's Organics store in front of his corporate office, and Sam knew he needed to get to the bottom of what was going on. He had led the effort for his company, Sam's Save More, to purchase almost 50% of the stock of Olive's last year. Now he was having second thoughts. Olive's Organics had relatively little debt at the time and it was a fast-growing company. These were the primary reasons Sam thought it was a wise acquisition at the time.

Looking at the projected balance sheets for 2009 and 2010, as well as the statement of cash flows for 2010, for both Olive's Organics and Sam's Save More, help Sam analyze and compare the financial condition of these two operations.

Olive's Organics (000s)

Balance Sheet	Pro Forma 31-Dec-10	31-Dec-09	Pro Forma Income Statement period ending 31-Dec-2010			Pro Forma Statement of Cash Flows 2010	
Assets							
Current Assets			Total Revenue	$ 4,300,500		**Operating Activities**	
Cash and Cash Equivalents	$ 2,640	$ 55,230	Cost of Revenue	2,800,000		Surplus	$ 176,100
Accounts Receivables	310,200	110,200	**Gross Profit**	1,500,500		Add back depreciation	53,000
Inventory	260,300	160,500				Change in A/R	-200,000
Total Current Assets	573,140	325,930	Research and Development	250,000		Change in Inventory	-99,800
Long Term Investments	639,500	365,110	Selling General and Administrative	900,700		Change in A/P	162,000
Property Plant and Equipment	1,500,400	969,400	Depreciation	53,000		**Cash Flows from Operating Activities**	$ 91,300
Other Assets	6,700	5,000	Total Operating Expenses	1,203,700			
Total Assets	$ 2,719,740	$ 1,665,440				**Investing Activities**	
			Operating Income or Loss	296,800		Change in Long-Term Investments	-274,390
			EBIT	296,800		Change in PPE (net of depreciation)	-584,000
Liabilities			Interest Expense	4,200		Change in Other Assets	-1,700
Current Liabilities			Income Before Tax	292,600		**Cash Flows from Investing Activities**	$ (860,090)
Accounts Payable	$ 412,600	$ 250,600	Income Tax Expense	116,500			
Short-term Debt	14,800	800				**Cash Flows from Financing Activities**	
Total Current Liabilities	427,400	251,400	**Net Income**	$ 176,100		Change in short-term debt	14,000
Long-term Debt	710,600	8,400				Change in long-term debt	702,200
Total Liabilities	$ 1,138,000	$ 259,800				**Net Cash Flows from Financing Activities**	$ 716,200
Stockholder's Equity						**Net Change in Cash**	$ (52,590)
Paid-in Capital	400,000	400,000				**Beginning Cash**	$ 55,230
Common Stock	590,700	590,700				**Ending Cash**	$ 2,640
Retained Earnings	591,040	414,940					
Total Stockholder's Equity	$ 1,581,740	$ 1,405,640					
Total Liabilities plus Equity	$ 2,719,740	$ 1,665,440					

Sam's Save More (000s)

Balance Sheet	31-Dec-10	31-Dec-09	Income Statement period ending	31-Dec-10		Statement of Cash Flows 2010	
Assets							
Current Assets			Total Revenue	$41,367,000		**Operating Activities**	
Cash and Cash Equivalents	$ 340,500	$ 290,885	Cost of Revenue	29,250,000		Surplus	$ 1,115,000
Accounts Receivables	677,900	555,240	**Gross Profit**	12,117,000		Add back depreciation	1,472,800
Inventory	2,897,700	3,010,340				Change in A/R	(122,660)
Total Current Assets	3,916,100	3,856,465	Research and Development	345,000		Change in Inventory	112,640
Long-Term Investments	890,600	773,900	Selling General and Administrative	8,432,070		Change in A/P	261,655
Property Plant and Equipment	10,980,000	9,884,200	Depreciation	1,472,800		**Cash Flows from Operating Activities**	2,839,435
Other Assets	912,980	890,670	Total Operating Expenses	10,249,870			
Total Assets	$ 16,699,680	$ 15,405,235	**Operating Income or Loss**	1,867,130			
Liabilities			EBIT	1,867,130		**Investing Activities**	
Current Liabilities			Interest Expense	326,000		Change in Long-Term Investments	(116,700)
Accounts Payable	$ 3,987,000	$ 3,725,345	Income Before Tax	1,541,130		Change in PPE (net of depreciation)	(2,568,600)
Short-Term Debt	877,480	723,090	Income Tax Expense	550,400		Change in Other Assets	(22,310)
Total Current Liabilities	4,864,480	4,448,435				**Cash Flows from Investing Activities**	$(2,707,610)
Long-Term Debt	4,285,000	4,716,000	**Net Income**	$ 1,115,000			
Other Liabilities	865,400	671,000				**Cash Flows from Financing Activities**	
						Change in short-term debt	154,390
Total Liabilities	$ 10,014,880	$ 9,835,435				Change in long-term debt	(431,000)
						Change in other liabilities	194,400
Stockholder's Equity						**Net Cash Flows from Financing Activities**	$ (82,210)
Common Stock	4,800	4,800					
Retained Earnings	6,680,000	5,565,000				**Net Change in Cash**	$ 49,615
						Beginning Cash	$ 290,885
Total Stockholder's Equity	6,684,800	5,569,800				**Ending Cash**	$ 340,500
Total Liabilities plus Equity	$ 16,699,680	$ 15,405,235					

The Savvy Silkworm—Part 10

The Savvy Silkworm, formed in early 2007, pledged to abide by the International Labor Organization core labor standards in its operating practices. The corporation also promised it would only grow and harvest the mulberry leaves eaten by the silkworms according to sustainable and environmentally sound practices. And, above all else, it guaranteed that it would treat the silkworms humanely, allowing them to grow their cocoons in their natural habitats.

However, Beth knew that these commitments didn't necessarily mean that The Savvy Silkworm should be added to her socially responsible investment portfolio. While fair treatment and sound environmental practices were important to her, she also needed to make sure that the companies in which she invested were financially viable and capable of providing an acceptable return on her investment.

Advise Beth on how to think about whether or not to invest in The Savvy Silkworm based on the information contained in the following balance sheets.

BALANCE SHEETS FOR THE SAVVY SILKWORM			
Assets	**31-Dec-09**	**31-Dec-08**	**31-Dec-07**
Cash	20,500	22,670	15,670
Accounts Receivable	26,788	12,340	4,300
Inventory	78,231	96,350	34,560
Total Current Assets	**125,519**	**131,360**	**54,530**
Property, Plant, and Equipment	120,999	45,400	20,240
Intangible Assets	2,175	1,430	670
Other Assets	33,950	15,810	7,000
Total Assets	**282,643**	**194,000**	**82,440**
Liabilities			
Accounts Payable	41,676	31,060	10,560
Current Portion of Long-Term Debt	98,556	35,620	12,450
Other Current Liabilities	567	450	420
Total Current Liabilities	**140,799**	**67,130**	**23,430**
Long-Term Debt	82,756	78,515	35,510
Total Liabilities	**223,555**	**145,645**	**58,940**
Equity			
Common Stock	55,433	45,500	23,000
Retained Earnings	3,655	2,855	500
Total Equity	**59,088**	**48,355**	**23,500**
Total Liabilities plus Equity	**282,643**	**194,000**	**82,440**
Return on Equity	1.4%	4.9%	2.1%
Debt Ratio	58.3%	61.9%	60.2%
Current Ratio	0.89	1.96	2.33

POST-TEST 11

1. Nonprofit entities have three basic financial statements:

statement of _____ _____

statement of _____

statement of _____ _____

2. In a nonprofit organization the difference between revenues and expenses is called a _____.

3. The surplus is not always the appropriate measure of _____ in a nonprofit.

4. In many instances the m _____ and g _____ of nonprofit organizations are very different from for-profits. Therefore, different _____ of performance are required.

5. There are three types of net assets that must be reported on a nonprofit's statement of financial position:

_____ _____

_____ _____

_____

6. The classification of net assets depends on the intention of the _____.

7. The gains and losses on investments held by nonprofits must be reported as _____ in the current accounting period.

8. The cash or investment portion of a nonprofit's assets derived from permanently restricted donations is called an _____.

9. When restricted funds are eventually used for their intended purpose, they show up on the financial statements as _____.

10. The reason that ROE may be an inappropriate measure of financial performance for a nonprofit organization is:

_____

_____.

Jasper's House I—Part 11

Jasper's House, a nonprofit organization providing support activities for families of children with muscle disorders, finally hired a new financial officer. The position had been vacant for four months and the Board of Directors was anxious to see a set of current financial reports. The new financial officer, Erin Norton, had built a career working in the banking industry as a business loan officer. As with any new business she came across, her first step was to get acquainted with the past financial reports of Jasper's House. After years of monitoring profit margins, return on equity (ROE), and dividend payments to shareholders, she was surprised to see no reference to these in the reports. The move to Jasper's House was her first time working for a nonprofit organization, and she now realized her existing financial perspective was going to need an adjustment.

How would you explain to Erin the absence of her core financial indicators (profit margin, ROE, and dividend payments) on the Jasper's House financial reports?

Jasper's House II—Part 11

After gaining more understanding of the different financial perspectives of nonprofit and for-profit organizations, Erin finished reviewing the available monthly financial reports for Jasper's House, and is now ready to create financials for the past four months. Many of the transactions she posts are familiar to her, especially in the area of expenses. However, the revenue structure of Jasper's House is more complicated. Although families come to use the facility equipment, attend educational classes, and receive counseling support, they are not required to pay for these services. If a family can pay, there is a requested monthly fee of $30 for unlimited services. Yet many families are already financially exhausted by providing for their child's medical needs, so not all families pay the fee, and some only pay it occasionally. These fees-for-service account for only about 15% of total revenue, leaving Jasper's House to rely on individual donors, an annual fundraising luncheon, and grants to generate enough revenue to provide its services. Erin has found that some of the recent donations came with specific requests, such as *"to support your upcoming music therapy series"* and *"to buy additional walkers for kids aged 4 yrs & older."* She also had a $12,000 grant that was *"in support of general operating activities,"* as well as a $5,000 grant to *"fund two internships for graduate students in occupational therapy."* Given her background in for-profit industries, Erin was used to posting revenue transactions as services were provided. These special donations and grants were a little confusing.

Can Erin simply post these revenues transactions as she would all other fee-for-service and general donations received?

POST-TEST 12

1. IFRS stands for:

_____ _____ _____ _____

2. U.S. accounting practice is based on _____, while the proposed set of international standards, IFRS, is based on _____.

3. The two accounting concepts that are embraced by the IFRS framework are:

    a. _____-_____ concept

    b. a_____ accounting

4. G_____ financial reporting will depend on a single set of accounting standards that all countries will adopt.

5. The current names of financial statements may be revised to the following:

    a. Balance Sheet = _____

    b. Income Statement = _____

    c. Statement of Cash Flows = _____

6. One potential difference between GAAP and IFRS is on the measurement called f_____ v_____.

7. The four qualitative characteristics of IFRS are:

    a. u _____

    b. r _____

    c. r _____

    d. c _____

Answers for Post-Tests

ANSWERS FOR POST-TEST 1

1. (a) assets

(b) cash

(c) liabilities

(d) equity

2. liabilities

equity

3. at a point in time

4. Assets = Liabilities + Equity

5. Dual-aspect concept

6. monetary amounts

7. money-measurement concept

8. no better or worse off; less; entity

9. entities; persons

10.

LEWIS CORPORATION

Balance Sheet as of December 31, 2008

Assets		Liabilities and Equity	
Cash	$12,000	Liabilities	$10,000
Other assets	25,000	Equity	27,000
Total	$37,000	Total	$37,000

11. entity; indefinitely

12. fair value; cost

13. Yes: (a), (e), (f)

No: (b), (c), (d)

14. purchased

15. one year

16. one year

17. current; noncurrent

18. True; False

19. current assets

20. noncurrent assets

21. inventory; noncurrent asset

22. F (a, b, c, d, e) Note: All the statements are false. Assets must have been acquired at a measurable cost. Neither the amount reported as paid-in capital nor the amount of total equity has any necessary relation to fair value or what the entity is worth. Retained earnings is not cash; cash is an asset on the left-hand side of the balance sheet.

Lighter Light Solutions—Part 1 Answer

- The following items appear on the balance sheet since they represent assets owned or controlled by the entity, with future economic benefits, or liabilities owed by the entity to others. Remember that items that appear on the balance sheet must be able to be expressed in monetary value too: 1, 4, 8, 11, 12.

- The following items might be of information to others, but they would not appear on the balance sheet in the forms noted above, although some of these might appear in a set of notes to formal financial statements as items of interest: 2, 3, 5, 6, 7, 9, 10, 13.

Pizza Box Mulch—Part 1 Answer

Mike's Pizza Box Mulch
Balance Sheet

Assets:		Liabilities & Equity:	
Cash	$200	Paid-in Capital	$500
Other Assets (machine)	$300		
Total Assets	**$500**	**Total Liabilities and Equity**	**$500**

Lidija Perez—Part 1 Answer

Lidija Perez
Balance Sheet

Assets		Liabilities and Equity	
Cash	45	Loans payable	150
Inventory	125		
		Paid-in capital	20
Total Assets	**170**	**Total Liabilities and Equity**	**170**

Cash: 150 + 20 − 125

Inventory: 25 × 5 pigs

ANSWERS FOR POST-TEST 2

1.

BROWN COMPANY

Balance Sheet as of January 31

Assets		Liabilities and Equity	
Cash	$11,500	Notes payable	$15,000
Accounts receivable	2,500	Paid-in capital	5,000
Inventory	2,000	Retained earnings	3,000
Automobile	7,000		
Total	$23,000	Total	$23,000

BROWN COMPANY

Income Statement for January

Revenue	$6,000
Expense	2,000
Income	$4,000

2. f

3. No; asset-measurement; cost; fair value

4. receivable; payable

Pizza Box Mulch—Part 2 Answer

The $1070 in surplus was added to the amount that was in retained earnings from the previous year. Therefore, we can assume that the business had a $1000 profit in the first year and a $1070 profit in the second year, for a total of $2070 in retained earnings.

The two parts of the balance sheet show very different things. Assets show what the business owns and has available for its use. Liabilities and equity show the source of these assets. The $1620 cash in the bank is an asset that the business can use. The $2070 in retained earnings indicates the accumulation of profits from the first two years since the business began. The $500 Mike originally contributed has also been used as a source in obtaining a portion of these assets.

Lidija Perez—Part 2 Answer

Lidija Perez Business
Balance Sheet

Assets		Liabilities and Equity	
Cash	0	Notes payable	3
Accounts receivable	120	Loans payable	105
Inventory	45		
		Retained earnings	55
		Paid-in capital	2
Total Assets	**165**	**Total Liabilities and Equity** . . .	**165**

Cash:

1. Beginning balance = $45
2. Loans money to husband and buys shoes for daughter = –$18
3. Gets $10 and then $5 for her product = $15
4. Pays the lender $25 = –$25
5. Buys another piglet from her mother = –17
6. Gets $20 from her sales = $20
7. Pays the lender = –$20

Accounts Receivable:

1. Neighbors buy on credit and promise to pay = $35 + $30 + $25 + $30

Inventory:

1. Beginning balance = $125

2. Kills and sells 4 pigs over this period of time = $25 × 4 = –$100

3. Buys the piglet = $20

Notes Payable:

1. Buys the piglet from her mother and promises to pay later = $3

Loans Payable:

1. Beginning balance = $150

2. Pays the lender twice during this period = $25 + $20 = $45

Retained Earnings (Sales – Expenses):

1. Sales of her products during this time period = $45 + $35 + $25 + $50 = $155

2. Expenses of her products during this time period = $25 + $25 + $25 + $25 = $100

ANSWERS FOR POST-TEST 3

1.

JOURNAL

March 5	Inventory	6,000	
	Cash		6,000

2.

JOURNAL

March 10	Cash	6,000	
	Accounts Receivable	9,000	
	Revenues		15,000

3.

JOURNAL

March 10	Expenses	8,000	
	Inventory		8,000

4.

JOURNAL

March 31	Revenues	15,000	
	Retained earnings		15,000
March 31	Retained earnings	8,000	
	Expenses		8,000

5. No response

6.

Cash

Bal.	25,000	6,000
	6,000	
Bal.	25,000	

Accounts Receivable

Bal.	11,000	
	9,000	
Bal.	20,000	

Inventory

Bal.	40,000	8,000
	6,000	
Bal.	38,000	

Property and Plant

Bal.	30,000	

7.

Accounts Payable

	16,000 Bal.

Paid-in Capital

	60,000 Bal.

Revenues

15,000	15,000

Expenses

8,000	8,000

Retained Earnings

8,000	30,000 Bal.
	15,000
	37,000 Bal

8.

	Debits	Credits
Increases in asset accounts are	X	
Decreases in asset accounts are		X
Increases in liability accounts are		X
Decreases in liability accounts are	X	
Increases in equity accounts are		X
Decreases in equity accounts are	X	
Increases in revenue accounts are		X
Increases in expense accounts are	X	

9.

KAY COMPANY

Balance Sheet as of March 31

Assets		Liabilities and Equity	
Cash	$25,000	Accounts payable	$16,000
Accounts receivable	20,000	Paid-in capital	60,000
Inventory	38,000	Retained earnings	37,000
Property and plant	30,000		
Total	$113,000	Total	$113,000

10.

KAY COMPANY

Income Statement for March

Revenues	$15,000
Expenses	8,000
Income	$ 7,000

11. incorrect

12. retained earnings; cash

Lidija Perez—Part 3 Answer

JOURNAL ENTRIES

From Part 1:

1.	Dr. Cash	150		Takes out a loan
	Cr. Liabilities		150	
2.	Dr. Cash	20		Invests her own money
	Cr. Paid-in Capital		20	
3.	Dr. Inventory (Pigs)	125		Buys the pigs
	Cr. Cash		125	

From Part 2:

4.	Dr. Paid-in Capital	10		Loans money to her husband
	Cr. Cash		10	
5.	Dr. Paid-in Capital	8		Takes cash to buy shoes for her daughter
	Cr. Cash		8	
6.	Dr. Cash	10		First sale
	Dr. Accounts Receivable	35		
	Cr. Sales Revenue		45	
7.	Dr. Cost of Sales	25		Cost of the first pig sold
	Cr. Inventory		25	
8.	Dr. Cash	5		Second sale
	Dr. Accounts Receivable	30		
	Cr. Sales Revenue		35	
9.	Dr. Cost of Sales	25		Cost of the second pig sold
	Cr. Inventory		25	
10.	Dr. Loans Payable	25		First payment to loan officer
	Cr. Cash		25	
11.	Dr. Accounts Receivable	25		Sales of third pig, all on credit
	Cr. Sales Revenue		25	
12.	Dr. Cost of Sales	25		Cost of the third pig sold
	Cr. Inventory		25	
13.	Dr. Inventory	20		Purchase of the piglet partially with a loan
	Cr. Cash		17	
	Cr. Notes Payable		3	

14. Dr. Cash   20   Sale of the fourth pig
    Dr. Accounts Receivable   30
        Cr. Sales Revenue   50

15. Dr. Cost of Sales   25   Cost of the fourth pig sold
        Cr. Inventory   25

16. Dr. Loans Payable   20   Second payment to loan officer
        Cr. Cash   20

T-ACCOUNTS

CASH		ACCOUNTS RECEIVABLE		INVENTORY	
(1) 150	125 (3)	(6) 35		(3) 125	25 (7)
(2) 20	10 (4)	(8) 30		(13) 20	25 (9)
(6) 10	8 (5)	(11) 25			25 (12)
(8) 5	25 (10)	(14) 30			25 (15)
(14) 20	17 (13)				
	20 (16)				
0		**120**		**45**	

NOTES PAYABLE		LOANS PAYABLE		PAID-IN CAPITAL	
	3 (13)	(10) 25	150 (1)	(4) 10	20 (20)
		(16) 20		(5) 8	
	3	**105**		**2**	

SALES REVENUE		EXPENSES		RETAINED EARNINGS	
	45 (6)	25 (7)		100	155
	35 (8)	25 (9)			
	25 (11)	25 (12)			
	50 (14)	25 (15)			
	155	**100**		**55**	

The Kenya Connection—Part 3 Answer

#	Product	Cost	Selling Price	Sales
10	Bookmarks	$ 2	$ 3	$30
3	Bowls	$ 5	$20	$60
5	Necklaces	$12	$15	$75
5	Ornaments	$ 3	$ 4	$20
2	Bowls	$ 5	$20	$40

#	Product	Cost	Selling Price	Total Cost
40	Bowls	$ 5	$ 20	$200
40	Bookmarks	$ 2	$ 3	$ 80
10	Animals	$50	$150	$500
30	Necklaces	$12	$ 15	$360
50	Ornaments	$ 3	$ 4	$150

JOURNAL ENTRIES

9/21

1. Dr. Supplies Inventory   250   Purchases shipping supplies
      Cr. Cash   250

2. Dr. Inventory   224   Buys 20 necklaces at $12 each
      Cr. Cash   224

3. Dr. Inventory   90   Buys 30 ornaments at $3 each
      Cr. Cash   90

4. Dr. Accounts Receivable   195   Sale of 3 carved animals
      Cr. Sales Revenue   195

5. Dr. Cost of Sales   150   Cost of the 3 carved animals
      Cr. Inventory   150

6. Dr. Expenses   15   Shipping expense
      Cr. Supplies inventory   15

9/22

7. Dr. Cash   225   Sales made
      Cr. Sales Revenue   225

8. Dr. Cost of Sales   120   Cost of above sales
      Cr. Inventory   120

9. Dr. Expenses   25   Shipping expense

     Cr. Supplies Inventory   25

9/23

10. Dr. Inventory   1290   Purchase of additional inventory

     Cr. Cash   1290

11. Dr. Expenses   12   Shipping expense

     Cr. Supplies Inventory   12

ANSWERS FOR POST-TEST 4

1. reasonably certain

reasonably possible

2. trivial matters

important matters

3. one year; interim

4. equity; retained earnings

5. revenues; expenses; income

6. delivered

7. November

8. (a) Advances from customers (a liability)

(b) Revenue

(c) Accounts receivable (an asset)

9. (a) Accounts receivable

(b) Cash

(c) Advances from customers

10.

February	Cash	100	
	Advances from customers		100
March	Accounts receivable	500	
	Advances from customers	100	
	Revenue		600
March	Expenses	400	
	Inventory		400
April	Cash	500	
	Accounts receivable		500

11. (a) Revenue

(b) Allowance for doubtful accounts

(c) $198,000

(d) $598,000

12. (a) Allowance for doubtful accounts

(b) Accounts receivable

Lidija Perez—Part 4 Answer

JOURNAL ENTRIES

1.	Dr. Cash	108		Collects 90% of $120
	Cr. Accounts Receivable		108	
2.	Dr. Inventory	125		Buys 5 more pigs
	Cr. Cash		50	
	Cr. Accounts Payable		75	
3.	Dr. Cash	200		Receives advance orders
	Cr. Advances from Customers		200	
4.	Dr. Advances from Customers	200		Delivers the meat from advanced orders
	Cr. Sales Revenues		200	
5.	Dr. Cash	300		Sells the rest of the meat from 4 pigs
	Dr. Accounts Receivable	100		
	Cr. Sales Revenues		400	
6.	Dr. Cost of Sales	100		Expenses of selling the 4 pigs
	Cr. Inventory		100	
7.	Dr. Notes Payable	3		Pays back her mother and loan officer
	Dr. Loans Payable	105		
	Cr. Cash		108	
8.	Dr. Bad Debt Expense	5		To account for the expected bad debts
	Cr. Allowance for Doubtful Accounts		5	

T-ACCOUNTS

	CASH		ACCOUNTS RECEIVABLE		ALLOWANCE FOR DOUBTFUL ACCOUNTS		INVENTORY	
BB 0	50 (2)	BB 120	108 (1)		5 (8)	BB 45	100 (6)	
(1) 108	108 (7)	(5) 100				(2) 125		
(3) 200								
(5) 300								
450		**112**			**5**	**70**		

	ACCOUNTS PAYABLE		ADVANCES FROM CUSTOMERS	
75 (2)	(4) 200	200 (3)		
75		**0**		

	NOTES PAYABLE		LOANS PAYABLE		PAID-IN CAPITAL	
(7) 3	3 BB	(7) 105	105 BB	2 BB	
0		**0**		**2**	

	SALES REVENUE		EXPENSES		RETAINED EARNINGS	
	200 (4)	(6) 100	55 BB	
	400 (5)	(8) 5	495	
600		**105**	**550**	

The Kenya Connection—Part 4 Answer

Mark's Order:

#	Product	Cost	Selling Price	Cost	Sales
4	Animals	$50	$150	$200	$600
20	Necklaces	$12	$ 15	$240	$300
10	Bowls	$ 5	$ 20	$ 50	$200
100	Bookmarks	$ 2	$ 3	$200	$300

JOURNAL ENTRIES

April

1. Dr. Cash 250   First order in April

 Dr. Accounts Receivable 1150

  Cr. Sales Revenue 1400

2. Dr. Cost of Sales 690   Cost of first April sales

  Cr. Inventory 690

3. Dr. Expenses 15   Cost of shipping

  Cr. Supplies Inventory 15

4. Dr. Cash 1500   Advance order

  Cr. Advances from 1500

  Customers

5. Dr. Bad Debt Expense 165   ($500 + $1150) × 10%

  Cr. Allowance for 165

  Doubtful Accounts

ANSWERS FOR POST-TEST 5

1. acquired; consumed

2. expenditure; asset; expense

3. unexpired; expired

4. costs; expenses

5. (a) costs; delivered

   (b) expenditures; operations

   (c) losses

6. Prepaid; asset
   Accrued; liability

7. $10,000

8. sales revenue; cost of sales

9. Gross margin
   Sales revenue

10. net income (or income)

11. dividends

12. (d) = (c) + (a) − (b)

Tobo Construction Services I— Part 5 Answer

ANSWER 1

Invoice for Celtic Manufacturing project:

October Project Costs		Price
Laborer (88 hours)		$1,320
Carpenter (128 hours)		$2,560
Project Management (4 weeks plus 2 days)		$2,200
Materials		$1,975
	Subtotal	$8,055
Overhead Charge (@ 20%)		$1,611
	Total Due:	**$9,666**

ANSWER 2

First month's Income Statement for Tobo Construction:

Tobo Construction Services

Income Statement—**Month End** *October*

Revenue

Celtic Manufacturing—Job 1	$9,666	
Total Revenue		$9,666

Expenses		
Payroll		
Laborer	$1,320	
Carpenter	$2,560	
Owner	$4,400	
Materials	$1,975	
Rent	$750	
Telephone	$35	
Utilities	$100	
Membership fees	$15	
Total Expenses		$11,155
Profit/(Loss)		($1,489)

The net result of Tobo Construction operations for October was a *loss* of $1,489.

ANSWER 3

Tobo Construction's Gross Margin and Net Income percentage:

Construction Sales Revenue		$9,666
Construction Direct Costs		
Laborer wages	$1,320	
Carpenter wages	$2,560	
Project management wages	$2,200	
Materials	$1,975	
Total Direct Costs		$8,055
Gross Margin		**$1,611**
Gross Margin %		**16.7%**
Administrative/Overhead Costs		
Owner salary (non-job related)	$2,200	
Rent	$750	
Telephone	$35	
Utilities	$100	
Membership fees	$15	
Total Admin/OH Costs		$3,100
Net Income/(Loss)		**($1,489)**
Profit Margin %		**−15.4%**

Pizza Box Mulch—Part 5 Answer

There is a difference between an *expenditure* (when Mike's Mulch *spends or borrows* to acquire a good or service) and an *expense* (when Mike's Mulch *uses or consumes* a good or service in its operations). Mike's Mulch's current income statement should only include the amounts of transactions that were actually used up during the June 2008– June 2009 period. The other portion of the transaction is still an asset that can be used for future operations, and these items will be listed under future expenses only when they are consumed. This is true for each of Quinn's adjustments, with the exception of the bank loan payment, because the bank loan is not acquiring a good or service, it is acquiring funds in order to buy goods or services for operations. Specific transaction explanations are as follows.

Mike's Pizza Box Mulch

Income Statement—*Adjustment Explanations* June 2008–June 2009			Mike's Amount	Quinn's Adjusted Amount
1-Jun-08	**Deposit**	To be reimbursed at end of occupancy	~~250~~	0

The deposit is not a current expense because it was not used/consumed in current operations. It is an intangible asset (a prepaid expense) that will show on the Balance Sheet until the time it is either reimbursed or used.

20-Jun-08	**License fee**	4-year license for domain name 'mikespizzamulch.com'	~~40~~	10

Only 1/4 of the expenditure is a current expense because only 1/4 of the useful life of the license has been consumed during the current period. The remaining $30 is another intangible asset (also a prepaid expense) on the Balance Sheet.

1-Sep-08	**Bank loan payment**		~~50~~	0

Payment of a bank loan is not an expense—it is a reduction of a liability and would therefore be reflected on the Balance Sheet.

10-Oct-08	**New mulch machine**	#3 machine—paid cash - target to last 4 years	~~400~~	100

Mulching machine is an asset with a useful life of 4 years so only 1/4 of the useful life is "used up" each year. This would equal an annual expense of $100 (called a "Depreciation" expense).

1-Nov-08	**Maintenance agreement plan**	One year—covers all 3 machines for Dec08–Dec09	~~300~~	150

The maintenance agreement is a pre-paid expense for services covering 12 months, from Dec. 2008–Dec. 2009. Only 50% has been used up and should be listed as an expense because the Income Statement report is as of June 2009, leaving 6 months remaining on the maintenance agreement. The remaining $150 is an asset on the Balance Sheet.

30-June-09	**Business liability insurance**	Coverage for July 2009–2010	~~150~~	0

Insurance coverage is for the months of July 2009–July 2010; therefore none of the coverage has been used in the current operating period (June 2008–June 2009). It is a pre-paid expense that will be listed on the Balance Sheet until it is actually used.

	Total Expenses		~~10,072~~	9,142

Adjusted "Total Expenses" is the new sum of all adjusted and unadjusted expenses.

	Net Income		~~903~~	$1,833

Adjusted "Operating Profit" reflects Revenue minus the adjusted Total Expenses.

ANSWERS FOR POST-TEST 6

1. Dr. Cash   800

    Cr. Revenue   800

  Dr. Cost of Sales   600

    Cr. Inventory   600

2. each item

3. Cost of sales = beginning inventory + purchases – ending inventory

4.

	Cost of Sales
(a) FIFO	$300
(b) LIFO	340
(c) Average-cost	320

5. higher; lower

6. Dr. Cost of Sales   1,000

    Cr. Inventory   1,000

7. Direct materials, direct labor, and overhead.

8. incurred

9. sold

10. Total production overhead costs
      Total direct labor costs

11. $110 [= $50 + $40 + $20]

12. better; less; less

Tobo Construction Services II— Part 6 Answer

Rate per Labor *Dollar:* Total Overhead Costs / Total Direct Labor Dollars

$3100 / $6080 = **$0.51 per labor dollar**

Rate per Labor *Hour:* Total Overhead Costs / Total Direct Labor Hours

$3100 / 304 hours = **$10.20 per labor hour**

Rate as *% of Direct Costs:* Total Overhead Costs / Total Direct Costs

$3100 / $8055 = **38.4% overhead rate**

Some other factors to consider when making the overhead rate decision:

• Would these overhead rates make the price of his services too high?

• Are these rates realistic given they are based on his first month of operations and may not reflect a typical volume of labor dollars or hours? If his labor dollars or hours increase in future months, his rates could significantly decrease.

• With the assumption that Tobo Construction's indirect costs will remain constant in the near future, they are considered a fixed cost. As a fixed cost, they will not change with volume. Therefore if Tobyn could increase his volume and have more than one construction project going, he may be able to cover his indirect costs without charging a higher overhead rate.

• Are there any ways Tobyn could reduce his indirect costs so that they are more in line with the 20% rate? Could Tobyn do some of the carpenter work himself, allowing him to charge a higher percent of his salary dollars to direct costs?

Blue Jeans by the Pound— Part 6 Answer

Total number of units sold during the quarter

Beginning Inventory Balance:	3,500
+ Purchases:	5,550
– Ending Inventory Balance:	3,800
Total Units Sold:	**5,250**

Under FIFO

Value of the remaining 3,800 inventory would be *based on most recent purchase prices*

Remaining units of 3,800

			Value (Units × Cost)
May 12	550	$12.70	$ 6,985
May 29	1500	$12.55	$ 18,825
June 23	1750	$12.40	$ 21,700
Totals	**3800**	**-**	**$ 47,510**

Cost of Goods Sold = Total Value of Inventory – Remaining Inventory Balance

$115,915 – $47,510 = <u>$68,405</u> Cost of Goods Sold **under FIFO**

Under LIFO

Value of the remaining 3,800 inventory would be *based on oldest purchase prices*

Remaining units of 3,800

			Value (Units × Cost)
Beg. Balance	3500	$13.10	$ 45,850
April 5	300	$13.00	$ 3,900
Totals	**3800**	**-**	**$ 49,750**

Cost of Goods Sold = Total Value of Inventory – Remaining Inventory Balance

$115,915 – $49,750 = <u>$66,165</u> Cost of Goods Sold **under LIFO**

Guess which method the company is using.

- Based on the goal of tax minimization, *Blue Jeans by the Pound* uses the FIFO method to value inventory because it results in the higher COGS expense. When the COGS expense is subtracted from revenue, it would give the company a lower profit level and lower taxable income amount.

- FIFO is also a good method based on the assumption that fashion styles change and thus it is better to get rid of older inventory first, before it becomes unfashionable and possibly unable to be sold, which would cause the company to have to "write down" the inventory to recognize the loss.

The reason FIFO results in better tax results in this case is the continuously lower costs the company has in buying its inventory. If the company's costs were continuously *increasing,* then the LIFO method would give the company the higher COGS and better tax advantage.

ANSWERS FOR POST-TEST 7

1. all costs

2. five

3. is not; service life

4. (a) $18,000

    (b) 10

    (c) $1,800

    (d) Depreciation expense

        Accumulated depreciation

    (e) (1) Plant.................................. $20,000

        (2) Less accumulated

            depreciation 9,000

        (3) Book value......................... $11,000

5. (a) zero

    (b) [x] (2) It will be reported as follows:

Machine $20,000

    Accumulated depreciation 20,000

                    Book value 0

6. (a) gain; $3,000

    (b) Dr. Cash

        Cr. Gain on disposition (or sale) of assets

7.

	Example	Write-off process
Plant asset	machine, building	
Wasting asset	coal, oil, minerals	Depletion
Intangible asset	goodwill, trademark	Amortization

8. $400,000 (40,000 barrels @ $10 per barrel, not $50,000)

9. net amount; cost; accumulated depreciation; net amount

10. low; fairly

11. more; less; the same

12. reduces

13. $2,400,000

14. Deferred income tax; liability

Iceberg Pure H₂O I—Part 7 Answer

- The iceberg is a **wasting asset**—the **depletion method** would be used, calculating the amount of the iceberg depleted each year to determine the depletion expense for each year.

- Depletion expense = Quantity of Iceberg Used Each Year $\times$ Cost per Unit

- Total Iceberg Cost / Total # of Bottles => \$25,000 / 1,500,000 => \$0.015 per bottle

- # Bottles Produced Each Year $\times$ Cost per Bottle => 550,000 $\times$ \$0.015 = **\$8,250 depletion expense per year**

- Estimated Service Life of Iceberg = Total Iceberg Cost / Annual Depletion Expense => **\$25,000 / \$8,250 = 3 years**

- The iceberg is estimated to have a useful life of three years.

Iceberg Pure H₂O II—Part 7 Answer

Water Tanks: Total Depreciable Cost = (\$4,500 $\times$ 3) + \$3,100 = **\$16,600**

Bottling Machine: Total Depreciable Cost = \$28,500 + \$12,000 = **\$40,500**

Plant Building: Total Depreciable Cost = \$19,000 + \$7,000 + \$600 = **\$26,600**

(Note: the neon sign would not be part of the total depreciable cost because it is not a permanent part of the asset, but the agent's fee is considered part of the acquisition cost.)

Depreciation is meant to recognize the total usefulness of the assets, so the service life is determined by either how long before it is expected to wear out or how long before it becomes obsolete. After this timeframe the company would have to replace the asset, so Helen would choose whichever of the two was a shorter time period.

For *Iceberg Pure H₂O* to maximize its tax advantage, it would want to use accelerated depreciation for some or all of these assets (if it is possible considering IRS tax code).

ANSWERS FOR POST-TEST 8

1. current assets; current liabilities

2. debt; equity

3. interest; principal; sometimes

4. paid-in capital; shareholders; retained earnings

5. Common stock   1,000
     Other paid-in capital   9,000

6. (a) $10
  (b) $30,000
  (c) can't tell (equity does not represent "worth")
  (d) can't tell (equity has no relation to cash)
  (e) at least $40,000 (it exceeds $40,000 by the amount of the dividends)
  (f) can't tell (equity does not show liquidation value)

7. issued; outstanding

8. treasury; 140,000

9. dividends; par value

10. decreases; does not change; increases

11. Yes   No
     Yes   No
     Higher   Lower
     Lower   Higher

12. (a) 80 percent
  (b) leveraged

13. parent; Able Company, Charlie Company; minority interest

14. $1,470,000 (= $1,000,000 − 10,000 + 500,000 − 20,000)

Olive's Organics—Part 8 Answer

If Olive looks at her low levels of debt compared to her equity (as per the conservatism of her brother), she will see why another company might want to own a controlling share in her company.

> *If one corporation owns more than 50% of the stock in another corporation, it can control the affairs of that corporation because it can outvote all other owners. Many businesses consist of a number of corporations that are legally separate but, because they are controlled by one corporation, are part of a single "family."*

The calculation of the debt ratio is: $$\frac{\text{Debt Capital}}{\text{Total Permanent Capital}}$$

We can see that for the years represented, her ratios indicate a very low debt ratio.

2007: 0.9%

2008: 1.0%

2009: 0.6%

Satellite Streak—Part 8 Answer

Shareholders could potentially benefit from either option for raising capital, if the capital investment does result in company growth and increased profitability. However, there is a basic difference in the amount of potential risk associated with the two options.

BONDS

Issuing bonds to raise capital is a form of debt and will create two financial obligations for *Satellite Streak*. The company must pay interest to bondholders and pay back the principal once the bonds become due. The interest is an expense of each accounting period in which the bonds are still outstanding, and the bonds create a long-term liability on the balance sheet (assuming the bond period is for more than one year). The risk of issuing bonds is that if things do not go well and the company is unable to pay its debt (either interest or principal), the bondholders could force the company into bankruptcy. But if *Satellite Streak* has good cash flows and minimal long-term debt already, using a bond to finance a long-term production asset *may* be a relatively low-risk option.

STOCK

Issuing stock does not create a financial obligation for *Satellite Streak*. Instead, each new shareholder who purchases the stock becomes a partial owner in the company and, although the shareholders expect to receive dividends and have the market value of the stock appreciate, *Satellite Streak* has no absolute obligation to pay them, as it does with bondholders. If *Satellite Streak* can finance additional productive assets without assuming more long-term debt, this would be a low-risk option.

ANSWERS FOR POST-TEST 9

1. required

2. accrual; cash

3. operating activities; investing activities; financing activities

4. increased

5. decreased

6. is not

7. was not

8. added to net income

9. 2,000
  5,000
  (3,000)
 $54,000

10. investing (a, f)
  financing (b, d, e)
  operating (c, g, h)
  (Remember that GAAP suggests dividend payments show in the operating section although many consider them to be a financing activity.)

Olive's Organics II—Part 9 Answer

Olive was relieved to see that her operating activities would still provide cash to the organization. However, it was not nearly enough cash to cover the investing activities projected for 2010. She remembered that for every current asset account that had increased from the previous period, there was a corresponding negative impact on cash. And, when current liabilities increased, the impact on operating cash flows would be positive. Further, there were positive impacts on cash from increased long-term borrowing, but Olive knew that those sources of cash are not always a sign of financial health.

On further investigation, Olive realized that she was probably planning on investing too much in inventory and extending too much credit, while relying on her vendors in the short term. She certainly did not want to damage her good relationship with them. She thought too that Luigi had planned on too much long-term borrowing for the level of investment in property, plant, and equipment planned and that she could even cut back on that. Some borrowing would be OK, since she had relied so little on debt financing in the past, but this would be a sudden leap. All in all, Olive was grateful that she could do this type of analysis prior to the operating period. Olive, Luigi, and Olive's brother would have to sit down and plan differently for the coming year.

Olive's Organics (000s)							
Balance Sheet	**Pro Forma**		**Pro Forma** **Income Statement**		**Pro Forma** **Statement of Cash Flows 2010**		
	31-Dec-10	**31-Dec-09**	period ending 31-Dec-2010				
Assets							
Current Assets			Total Revenue	$ 4,300,500	**Operating Activities**		
Cash and Cash Equivalents	$ 2,640	$ 55,230	Cost of Revenue	2,800,000	Surplus		$ 176,100
Accounts Receivables	310,200	110,200	**Gross Profit**	**1,500,500**	Add back depreciation		53,000
Inventory	260,300	160,500			Change in A/R		-200,000
Total Current Assets	**573,140**	**325,930**	Research and Development	250,000	Change in Inventory		-99,800
Long Term Investments	639,500	365,110	Selling General and Administrative	900,700	Change in A/P		162,000
Property Plant and Equipment	1,500,400	969,400	Depreciation	53,000	**Cash Flows from Operating Activities**		**$ 91,300**
Other Assets	6,700	5,000	Total Operating Expenses	1,203,700			
Total Assets	**$ 2,719,740**	**$ 1,665,440**			**Investing Activities**		
			Operating Income or Loss	**296,800**	Change in Long Term Investments		-274,390
			EBIT	296,800	Change in PPE (net of depreciation)		-584,000
Liabilities			Interest Expense	4,200	Change in Other Assets		-1,700
Current Liabilities			Income Before Tax	292,600	**Cash Flows from Investing Activities**		**$(860,090)**
Accounts Payable	$ 412,600	$ 250,600	Income Tax Expense	116,500			
Short-term Debt	4,800	800			**Cash Flows from Financing Activities**		
Total Current Liabilities	**427,400**	**251,400**	**Net Income**	**$ 176,100**	Change in short-term debt		14,000
Long-term Debt	710,600	8,400			Change in long-term debt		702,200
Total Liabilities	**$ 1,138,000**	**$ 259,800**			**Net Cash Flows from Financing Activities**		**$ 716,200**
Stockholder's Equity					**Net Change in Cash**		**$ (52,590)**
Paid-in Capital	400,000	400,000			**Beginning Cash**		**$ 55,230**
Common Stock	590,700	590,700			**Ending Cash**		**$ 2,640**
Retained Earnings	591,040	414,940					
Total Stockholder's Equity	**$ 1,581,740**	**$ 1,405,640**					
Total Liabilities plus Equity	**$ 2,719,740**	**$ 1,665,440**					

The Investment Dilemma—
Part 9 Answer

With both companies already having other strong financial indicators (balance sheet, profitability, and ROE ratio), it appears both could be a good investment because they also show very similar cash flows and indicators of stable cash management. Both companies:

- Are generating cash from operations.

- Are using cash to invest in equipment (which would be expected with growth).

- Are borrowing cash (to fund equipment purchases).

- Have an increased amount of cash to start the 2010 fiscal year.

- Have similar outstanding accounts receivable and accounts payable (AP) and inventory increases.

However, there are a few slight differences that could indicate that *Solar-Us* could be the safer investment:

Solar-Us

- Borrowing (long-term debt) to fund an equipment purchase (long-term asset) is a smart matching of debt to life-of-asset.

- Paid dividends to its investors (shareholders).

- Had it not paid dividends to shareholders, it would have had a higher ending cash balance than *Lawmen Security*.

Lawmen Security Co.

- Is generating less cash from operating activities than *Solar-Us*.

- Borrowed using a line of credit (short-term debt) to fund an equipment purchase (long-term asset).

- Will have to use current cash to pay off the line of credit, for an asset that will be expensed (depreciated) over several years. This indicates an unwise matching of debt to life-of-asset.

- Did *not* pay dividends to investors (shareholders).

ANSWERS FOR POST-TEST 10

1. (a) $\dfrac{100}{40} = 2.5$

$(\dfrac{60}{20} = 3$ times

(c) $\dfrac{10}{100} = 10\%$

$(\dfrac{80}{180} = 44\%$

(e) $\dfrac{10}{100} = 10\%$

$(\dfrac{30}{100} = 30\%$

(g) $\dfrac{100}{180} = 0.6$ times

(h) $\dfrac{30}{180} = 17\%$

2. capital turnover; EBIT

3. (a) decreasing

(b) increasing

4. current

5. long-term debt

6. profit margin

asset turnover

equity multiplier

7. operating

asset use

leverage

8. (a) monetary

(b) past

(c) fair value

(d) some latitude

(e) estimates

9. quality of earnings

higher

lower

higher

10. Sarbanes-Oxley

11. whistle blowers

Olive's Organics and Sam's Save More—Part 10 Answer

Looking at the pro forma financial statements, it is clear that Olive's Organics is growing at a rapid pace. The figures for 2009 and 2010 show that in the one year alone, the organization's total assets increased by 63%. Inventory increased by 62%, and property, plant, and equipment increased by 55%. This is far greater than any growth during the same time period for Sam's Save More.

However, during this year there was a comparable increase in accounts payable (65%) and an even more dramatic increase in accounts receivable (181%), so there is reason to wonder about the sustainability of this growth. It is unknown if Olive's Organics is increasing accounts payable as a form of a free loan, and it is unknown if the business will be able to collect such a large amount in accounts receivable.

Comparing the two businesses more directly with respect to profitability, we can see that Sam's Save More has a return on equity (ROE = Net Income/Equity) of 16.7% during 2010. We can then compare this with Olive's Organics, which has an ROE of 11.13%. So, Sam's Save More appears to be a more attractive company if measured by ROE.

Liquidity is another story. We are concerned for both organizations. While Olive's Organics has more current assets than current liabilities during both 2009 and 2010, in 2010 a smaller portion of the current assets is in cash and a greater portion is in the less readily available forms of accounts receivable and inventory. This is a cause for some concern, as a large amount of funding will be due immediately to cover accounts payable. Sam's Save More is in a more grave position. The business has not had enough current assets to cover current liabilities for two years, and a good portion of the current assets for Sam's Save More is also found in accounts receivable and inventory. Sam knew from experience that profitability could be strong without liquidity, but he was not prepared for the direction in which both companies seem to be going. Further, the situation could be exaggerated due to competition with each other.

Looking at the statement of cash flows for Olive's Organics, we can see that the business was generating cash from operations, which is an important sign of financial health. The business also brought in cash from financing activities (more specifically, increases in long-term debt), which was poured into long-term investments and investments in property, plant, and equipment. It cannot be discerned from the financial statements if this was a wise strategy or not, but it has committed the business to a trajectory of growth that must be sustained to cover the increased long-term debt obligations. In comparison, looking at the statement of cash flows for Sam's Save More, we can see that the business generated cash from operations, and this was what funded a comparable increase in property, plant, and equipment.

The Savvy Silkwork—Part 10 Answer

There are a number of factors (in addition to her desire to be socially responsible) that Beth should consider as she decides whether to invest in The Savvy Silkworm.

The first concern would be profitability and return on equity (ROE). The organization does not look appealing here. While we do not have income statements for the three years, looking at the relatively small increases in retained earnings from year to year shows that the profits are relatively low. Furthermore, if we look at ROE, it fluctuates a bit, but does it look much better for Beth than investing in something less risky, such as a simple bank deposit account? For the most recent year ROE is only 1.4%. With just a little research Beth would find that other comparable socially responsible clothing lines have an ROE above 10%.

The next concern might be risk associated with debt. The ratio of debt capital to total permanent capital (see Part 8 to review this ratio), sometimes called the *debt ratio,* indicates high levels of debt as part of permanent capital structure. This is higher risk than an organization would have with a lower debt ratio.

Finally, Beth should be concerned about the organization's liquidity, or lack thereof. While historically the organization has had enough current assets available to cover current liabilities, in 2009 we can see that the situation is beginning to change. The current ratio has gone from 2.33 in 2007 to 0.89 in 2009, which is a notable change in a short time span. Furthermore, it is important to note what the current assets are. In 2009, over 60% of the current assets are inventory, which is far less readily available than cash. However, in this same year the current liabilities are almost entirely due in the immediate or very near future (and a large portion of long-term debt will be payable in the coming year), so it is questionable whether the organization will be able to sell the inventory quickly enough to make these payments.

Due to these concerns, it would be best if Beth continued looking until she found another business to add to her portfolio.

ANSWERS FOR POST-TEST 11

1. Statement of Financial Position
   Statement of Activities
   Statement of Cash Flows

2. surplus

3. performance

4. mission; goals; measures of

5. permanently restricted
   temporarily restricted
   unrestricted

6. donor

7. income

8. endowment

9. transfers

10. Nonprofit organizations do not have owners and hence, they don't have equity.

Jasper's House I—Part 11 Answer

- Nonprofit organizations do not have profit maximization as their primary goal. They have nonmonetary considerations (mission and goals) that are key indicators in determining success. Just looking at financial "profits" would tell an incomplete story of whether the organization is effective.

- In nonprofit organizations, any revenues in excess of expenses are usually a "surplus" instead of a "net income" or "profit."

- Nonprofit organizations have no owners and no shareholders.

- Equity implies ownership, so it is not used in nonprofit-sector financial statements. The term "net assets" is used instead.

- There are no shareholders, so there are no dividend payments (although you can see the term "dividend" under Revenues, which is a reference to payments the nonprofit organization receives from its own stock investments).

- Financial reports often have different titles in nonprofit organizations. A "Balance Sheet" may be referred to as a *Statement of Financial Position,* and an "Income Statement" may be referred to as a *Statement of Activities.*

Jasper's House II—Part 11 Answer

Only the $12,000 grant for "general operating activities" can be posted as general revenue (unrestricted funds), just as with fee-for-service and general donations. The other three transactions cannot simply be posted as general revenue because each one has been restricted in some way by the donor/grantor. They must be posted as "temporarily restricted" funds and remain there until the specific activity has occurred. At that time the funds can be "transferred"—moved from "temporarily restricted" to "unrestricted" funds.

ANSWERS FOR POST-TEST 12

1. International Financial Reporting Standards

2. rules, principles

3. going-concern, accrual

4. Global

5. Statement of Financial Position, Statement of Comprehensive Income, Statement of Cash Flows

6. fair value

7. userability, relevance, reliability, comparability

Glossary

Note: The definitions here are brief and are intended as an introduction to the meaning of the terms. They do not encompass all the nuances or qualifications. For a more full discussion, the concepts are defined in the text.

Accelerated depreciation: A method of depreciation that charges off more of the original cost of a plant asset in the earlier years than in the later years of the asset's service life. Used mainly in calculating taxable income.

Account: A record in which the changes for a balance sheet or income statement item are recorded.

Account payable: The amount that the entity owes to a supplier, not evidenced by a note.

Account receivable: An amount that is owed to the business, usually as a result of the ordinary extension of credit to one of its customers.

Accountability: Demonstrating accountability for budgetary compliance is a distinguishing objective of government financial reporting.

Accounting income: Income measured according to accounting principles. Contrast with taxable income.

Accounting period: The period of time over which an income statement summarizes the changes in equity. Usually the official period is one year, but income statements are also prepared for a shorter, or interim, period.

Accrual accounting: Accounting for revenues in the period in which they are earned and for expenses in the period in which they are incurred. This is normal accounting practice. Cash accounting, which accounts only for cash receipts and payments, is usually not acceptable.

Accrued expense: Another term for Accrued liability. Note that this is a liability account, not an expense account.

Accrued liability: A liability that arises because an expense occurs in a period prior to the related cash payment. Example: accrued wages payable.

Accrued pensions: The amount a company owes its employees for the benefits they accumulated under a pension plan. The liability is measured as the benefits accumulate.

Accumulated depreciation: An account showing the total amount of an asset's depreciation that has been accumulated to date. It is subtracted from the cost of the asset; the difference is the asset's book value.

Additional paid-in capital: The amount paid by investors in excess of the par or stated value of the stock.

Advances from customers: A liability account showing the amount due customers who have paid for goods or services in advance of their delivery. Sometimes called deferred revenue, precollected revenue, or unearned revenue.

Allowance for doubtful accounts: The amount of estimated bad debts that is included in accounts receivable. This amount is subtracted from accounts receivable on the balance sheet.

Amortization: The process of writing off the cost of intangible assets. Sometimes used as a name for expensing the cost of all assets.

Asset: A valuable item that is owned or controlled by the entity and that was acquired at a measurable cost.

Asset-measurement concept: Accounting focuses on the fair value of monetary assets and on the cost of nonmonetary assets.

Asset turnover: Sales revenue divided by assets.

Auditing: An examination of accounting records by independent, outside public accountants.

Authorized stock: The total number of shares of stock that a corporation is permitted to issue. (The total number actually issued is usually a smaller amount.)

Available for sale: The sum of beginning inventory and purchases during the period.

Average-cost method: Finding cost of sales by taking the average cost per unit of the beginning inventory plus purchases.

Bad debt: An account receivable that never will be collected.

Bad debt expense: The estimated amount of bad debts applicable to an accounting period.

Balance: The difference between the totals of the two sides of an account. An account has either a debit balance or a credit balance.

Balance sheet: A financial statement that reports the assets, liabilities, and equity of a company at one point in time. Assets are listed on the left and liabilities and equity on the right.

Benchmarking: Comparing an entity's performance against the performance of the company thought to be the best managed in the industry.

Bond: A written promise to repay money furnished the business, with interest, at some future date, usually more than one year hence.

Book value: The difference between the cost and the accumulated depreciation of a depreciable asset.

Calendar year: The year that ends on the last day of the calendar, December 31. The accounting period for many entities is the calendar year, but some use the natural business year.

Capital: In general, the amount of funds supplied to an entity. Also used as the name for paid-in capital in a proprietorship or partnership.

Capital-intensive: Characterizes a company that has a large capital investment in relation to its sales revenue.

Capital lease: An item the entity controls by a lease agreement that extends over almost the whole life of the item. A capital lease is an asset.

Capital stock: A balance sheet account showing the amount that the shareholders contributed in exchange for stock. This plus retained earnings equals equity in a corporation.

Capital turnover: A ratio obtained by dividing annual sales by the amount of permanent capital.

Cash: The name for money, whether in currency or in a bank account.

Cash flow statement (also, Statement of Cash Flows): A financial statement reporting the sources and uses of cash during an accounting period.

Cash-basis accounting: An accounting system that does not use the accrual basis; it records only cash receipts and payments. Usually not an acceptable basis for accounting.

Charge (verb): To debit an account.

Claim: Amount owed to creditors or others who have provided money or have extended credit to a business.

Closing entries: Journal entries that transfer the balances in revenue and expense accounts for a period to retained earnings.

Common stock: Stock whose owners are not entitled to preferential treatment with regard to dividends or to the distribution of assets in the event of liquidation. Its book value is not related to its market value.

Comparisons, bases of: Performance can be compared with past performance, with performance of other entities, or with a judgmental standard.

Concepts: Accounting concepts are presented throughout the book.

Conservatism concept: Recognize increases in equity only when they are reasonably certain; recognize decreases as soon as they are reasonably possible.

Consolidated statements: Financial statements prepared for a whole corporate family as an entity. The family consists of a parent and its subsidiaries.

Contra-asset account: An account whose balance is subtracted from that of the corresponding asset account.

Conversion cost: The labor and overhead costs of converting raw material into finished products.

Cost: A monetary measure of the amount of resources used for some purpose. Product costs and acquisition costs are among those presented in the book.

Cost accounting: The process of identifying and accumulating manufacturing costs and assigning them to goods in the manufacturing process.

Cost of goods sold: Same as cost of sales.

Cost of sales: Cost of the same products whose revenues are included in sales revenue.

Credit (noun): The right-hand side of an account or an amount entered on the right-hand side of an account. Abbreviated as Cr.

Credit (verb): To make an entry on the right-hand side of an account. Rules for debit and credit are summarized in the book.

Creditor: A person who lends money or extends credit to an entity.

Current assets: Cash and assets that are expected to be converted into cash or used up in the near future, usually within one year.

Current liabilities: Obligations that become due within a short period of time, usually one year.

Current ratio: The ratio obtained by dividing the total of the current assets by the total of the current liabilities.

Days' sales uncollected: The number of days of sales that are tied up in accounts receivable as of the end of the accounting period. Sales per day is found by dividing annual credit sales by 365, and accounts receivable is divided by sales per days to find the days' receivables.

Debit (noun): The left-hand side of an account or an amount entered on the left-hand side of an account. Abbreviated as Dr.

Debit (verb): To make an entry on the left-hand side of an account. Rules for debit and credit are summarized in the book.

Debt capital: The capital raised by the issuance of debt securities, usually bonds.

Debt ratio: The ratio of debt capital to total permanent capital.

Deduction method: Finding cost of sales by adding the beginning inventory and purchases and subtracting the ending inventory.

Deferred income taxes: The difference between the actual income tax for the period and income tax expense.

Deferred revenue: Revenues received as cash in advance of the time period in which the services are provided. See also Advances from customers.

Depletion: The process of writing off the cost of a wasting asset, such as natural gas, coal, oil, or other minerals.

Depreciable cost: The difference between the cost of a plant asset and its estimated residual value.

Depreciation expense: The portion of the estimated net cost of plant assets (e.g., buildings, equipment) that becomes an expense in a given accounting period.

Depreciation rate: The percentage of the cost of an asset that is an expense each year. In the straight-line method, the rate is 1 divided by the service life.

Derivative: An instrument issued by a financial institution that promises to pay interest, for example, derived from underlying obligations such as mortgages. Some companies obtain funds by issuing such instruments backed by other instruments. Also, any type of transaction whose value depends, at least in part, upon the value of a related asset or liability.

Direct labor or materials: The labor or material that is used directly on a product.

Disposition of plant, gain or loss on: The difference between book value and the amount actually realized from a sale of a plant asset.

Dividend: The funds generated by profitable operations that are distributed to shareholders. Dividends are not an expense.

Double-entry system: A characteristic of accounting in which each transaction recorded causes at least two changes in the accounts.

Dual-aspect concept: The total assets of an entity always are equal to its total liabilities and equity.

DuPont Identity: Separates the components of Return on Equity (ROE) into three distinct ratios: profit margin, asset turnover and the equity multiplier (leverage ratio).

Earnings: Another term for net income.

Earnings before interest and taxes (EBIT): An amount used in calculating return on permanent capital.

Earnings per share: A ratio obtained by dividing the total earnings for a given period by the number of shares of common stock outstanding.

EBIT margin: Earnings before interest and income taxes as a percentage of sales revenue.

Entity: A business or other organization for which a set of accounts is kept.

Entity concept: Accounts are kept for entities, rather than for the persons who own, operate, or are otherwise associated with those entities.

Entry: The accounting record made for a single transaction.

Equation, fundamental accounting: Assets = Liabilities + Equity.

Equity: Capital supplied by (1) equity investors and (2) the entity's retained earnings. Also, claims against the entity by equity investors.

Equity capital: The capital supplied by owners, who are called equity investors.

Equity multiplier: Sometimes called the leverage ratio; part of the DuPont system of ratios. Equals assets divided by equity.

Exchange transactions: Occur when a customer exchanges money for a good or service from a business. See also Nonexchange Transactions.

Expenditure: The decrease in an asset or increase in a liability associated with the acquisition of goods or services. Do not confuse with expense, which represents the use of goods and services and which may occur after the expenditure.

Expense: A decrease in equity resulting from operations during an accounting period; that is, resources used up or consumed during an accounting period. Example: wage expense. Concepts discussed in the book include assets that will become expenses and expenses that create liabilities.

Expensing: The process of charging the cost of an asset to expense.

Expired cost: Another name for expense.

External basis of comparison: Comparing an entity's performance with the performance of other entities.

Face amount: The total amount of a loan that must be repaid, specified on the face of a bond.

Fair value: The amount for which an asset can be sold in the marketplace.

FASAB: The Federal Accounting Standards Advisory Board establishes accounting principles for federal entities in the United States.

FASB: The Financial Accounting Standards Board regulates the accounting practices for private and nonprofit entities.

FIFO (first-in, first-out) method: Finding cost of sales on the assumption that the oldest goods (those first in) were the first to be sold (first out).

Financial statements: See the three required financial statements: balance sheet, income statement, statement of cash flows.

Fiscal year: See Natural business year.

Fixed assets: Tangible, noncurrent assets

Free cash flow: The amount remaining after special needs for cash in the coming period is subtracted from the cash flow expected from operating activities.

Fringe benefits: Benefits, principally monetary, beyond wages; owed to an employee because of his or her service to the company.

Fund reporting: The means by which a relationship is established between current financial resource flows and the modified accrual basis of accounting for government entities.

GAAP: Generally Accepted Accounting Principles refers to the standard framework of guidelines for financial accounting for all transactions necessary to prepare the financial statements.

Gain (or loss) on disposition of plant: The difference between book value and the amount actually realized from a sale of a plant asset.

GASB: The Government Accounting Standards Board is the regulatory agency for state and local government accounting in the United States.

Going-concern concept: Accounting assumes that an entity will continue to operate indefinitely.

Goods available for sale: The sum of the beginning inventory plus purchases during the period.

Goodwill: An intangible asset; the amount paid in excess of the value of a company's identifiable net assets, representing an amount paid for a favorable location or reputation. Goodwill is an asset only if it was purchased.

Gross margin: The difference between sales revenue and cost of sales.

Gross margin percentage: Gross margin as a percentage of sales revenue.

Historic cost concept: See Cost concept.

Historical basis of comparison: Comparing an entity's performance with its own performance in the past.

IFRS: International Financial Reporting Standards.

Income: The amount by which equity increased as a result of operations during a period of time.

Income statement: A statement of revenues and expenses, and the difference between them, for an accounting period; a flow report. It explains the changes in equity associated with operations of the period.

Income tax: A tax levied as a percentage of taxable income. See Taxable income.

Intangible asset: An asset that has no physical substance, such as goodwill or the protection provided by an insurance policy.

Interest: The amount paid for the use of money. A loan requires payment of both interest and principal.

Interest expense: The entity's cost of using borrowed funds during an accounting period.

Interest revenue: Revenue earned from permitting someone to use the entity's money. Revenue from the "rental" of money. Often but erroneously called interest income.

Interim statements: Financial statements prepared for a period shorter than one year, such as a month or a quarter.

Intrafamily transactions: Transactions between the corporations in a consolidated family. These transactions are eliminated in preparing consolidated financial statements.

Inventory (noun): Goods being held for sale, and material and partially finished products that will be sold upon completion.

Inventory (verb): To conduct a physical observation and count of inventory.

Inventory turnover: A ratio that shows how many times inventory was totally replaced during the year; calculated by dividing the average inventory into cost of sales.

Investments: Securities that are held for a relatively long period of time and are purchased for reasons other than the temporary use of excess cash. They are noncurrent assets.

Issued stock: The shares of stock that have been issued. Issued stock less treasury stock equals outstanding stock. Contrast with authorized stock.

Journal: A record in which transactions are recorded in chronological order. It shows the accounts to be debited or credited and the amount of each debit and credit. Transactions are posted to the ledger.

Judgmental basis of comparison: Comparing an entity's performance with our personal judgment.

Land, life of: Except in rare cases, land retains its usefulness indefinitely.

Lease: An agreement under which the owner of property permits someone else to use it. The owner is the lessor. The user is the lessee.

Ledger: A group of accounts. Entries are posted to the ledger from the journal.

Leverage: The proportion of debt capital to total permanent capital. A company that obtains a high proportion of its permanent capital from debt is said to be highly leveraged.

Leverage ratio: Assets divided by equity. Part of the DuPont system of ratios.

Liability: The equity or claim of a creditor.

LIFO (last-in, first-out) method: Finding cost of sales on the assumption that the goods most recently purchased (last in) were the first to be sold (first out).

Limitations on financial statement analysis: There are many pieces of information one might want when analyzing an organization. The financial statements do not provide all of it.

Liquidity: An entity's ability to meet its current obligations. Often measured by the current ratio.

Losses: Expenses resulting from assets whose future benefit has expired during a period, for example, from fire or theft, and liabilities occurring in a period, for example, from lawsuits. See also Gain (or loss).

Manufacturing company: A company that converts raw materials into finished, salable products and then sells these products. There are accounting practices specifically for inventory in a manufacturing company.

Manufacturing overhead: See Production overhead cost.

Marketable securities: Securities that are expected to be converted into cash within a year; a current asset.

Matching concept: Costs that are associated with the revenues of a period are expenses of that period.

Materiality concept: Disregard trivial matters, but disclose all important matters.

Measurable cost: An item whose amount is known, usually because the item was acquired from an outside party.

Merchandising company: A company that sells goods that it has acquired from other businesses; for example, a retail store or a wholesaler.

Minority interest: The equity of those shareholders in a subsidiary other than the equity of the parent. Reported as an equity item on the consolidated balance sheet.

Monetary assets: Cash and promises by an outside party to pay the entity a specified amount of money.

Money-measurement concept: Accounting records report only facts that can be expressed in monetary amounts. Accounting therefore does not give a complete record of an entity.

Mortgage: A pledge of real estate as security for a loan.

Mortgage payable: The liability for a loan that is secured by a mortgage.

Natural business year: A year that ends on the day that activities are at a relatively low level. For some entities, the accounting period is the natural business year, rather than the calendar year. Also called the fiscal year.

Net: The amount remaining after something has been subtracted from a gross amount. Example: accounts receivable, net.

Net assets: In a nonprofit organization, the portion of the balance sheet occupied by equity in a for-profit organization. Alternatively, assets–liabilities. Net assets may be unrestricted, temporarily restricted or permanently restricted.

Net income: The amount by which total revenues exceed total expenses for an account period; the "bottom line." In a nonprofit organization, the surplus.

Net income percentage: Net income expressed as a percentage of sales revenue.

Net loss: The amount by which total expenses exceed total revenues in an accounting period; negative net income. In a nonprofit organization, the deficit.

Net worth: Another (but misleading) name for equity.

Nonbusiness organizations: Municipalities, hospitals, religious organizations, and other organizations that are not operated for the purpose of earning a profit.

Noncurrent asset: An asset that is expected to be of use to the entity for longer than one year.

Noncurrent liability: A claim that does not fall due within one year. Similar to Debt capital.

Nonexchange transactions: When governments receive value from citizens without directly giving equal value in exchange.

Nonprofit or not-for-profit: An entity with no ownership or shareholders. The regulations to determine nonprofit status vary from state to state.

No-par-value stock: Common stock that does not have a par value. It is recorded at its stated value.

Note: A written promise to pay.

Note payable: A liability evidenced by a written promise to pay.

Obsolescence: A loss in the usefulness of an asset because of the development of improved equipment, changes in style, or other causes not related to the physical condition of the asset. It is one cause of depreciation; the other cause is wearing out.

Opinion or Opinion letter: The report in which the auditor gives his or her opinion as to the fairness of the financial statements.

Other post-employment benefits (OPEB): Health care or other fringe benefits, besides pensions, owed to an employee after his or her employment ends.

Outstanding stock: Shares of stock held by investors. Consists of issued stock less treasury stock.

Overhead: See Production overhead cost.

Overhead rate: A rate used to allocate overhead costs to products.

Owners' equity: The claims of owners against the assets of a business. In a corporation, owners' equity consists of capital stock plus retained earnings.

Package of accounting reports: See Report package.

Paid-in capital: The amount paid by investors in exchange for stock. The amount in excess of the stock's par or stated value is called additional paid-in capital.

Par value: The specific amount printed on the face of some stock certificates. No longer significant in accounting.

Parent: A corporation that controls one or more other corporations because it owns more than 50 percent of their stock. The controlled corporations are its Subsidiaries.

Partnership: An unincorporated business with two or more owners.

Patent: A grant that gives an inventor the exclusive right, for 17 years, to produce and sell an invention.

Percentage: A number obtained by dividing one number by another (which is the base, or 100 percent), and multiplying by 100. Income statement items are often expressed as percentages of sales revenue.

Performance, measures of: Often analyzed using ratios, overall measures of performance can be compared to other organizations or to the same organization over its history.

Period costs: Costs associated with general sales and administrative activities. Contrast with product costs.

Permanent account: An account for a balance sheet item, so called because it is not closed at the end of the accounting period. Contrast with temporary account.

Permanent capital: The sum of noncurrent liabilities and equity.

Permanently restricted net assets: In a nonprofit organization, assets donated for specific purposes which cannot be used in other ways.

Perpetual inventory: A record of the cost of each item in inventory showing the quantity and the cost of receipts, issues, and the amount on hand, updated nearly simultaneously for each day's activity.

Physical inventory: The amount of inventory currently on hand, obtained by making a physical count.

Plant assets: All tangible, noncurrent assets except land.

Posting: The process of transferring transactions from the journal to the ledger.

Precollected revenue: See Advances from customers.

Preferred stock: Stock whose owners have a preferential claim over common stockholders for dividends and for assets in the event of liquidation.

Prepaid expenses: The general name for intangible assets that will become expenses in future periods when the services they represent are used up. Example: prepaid insurance.

Price-earnings ratio: A ratio obtained by dividing the average market price of the stock by the earnings per share.

Principal: The amount that must be repaid on a loan. The total repayment consists of principal plus Interest.

Product: Goods or services sold or to be sold. Sometimes refers only to tangible goods.

Product costs: The direct materials, direct labor, and production overhead costs of a product. Contrast with period costs.

Production overhead cost: Product costs other than direct materials and direct labor. Includes, for example, supervision, building maintenance, and power. See also Overhead rate.

Profit: Another name for income or surplus.

Profit and loss statement: Another name for income statement.

Profit margin: Net income divided by sales revenue.

Proprietorship: An unincorporated business with a single owner.

Quality of earnings: Some characteristics include consistent and conservative accounting policies, income from recurring activities, revenues and net income that are stable, predictable and indicative of future cash flow, and appropriate levels of debt.

Ratio: The result of dividing one number by another. See, for example, Current ratio.

Real earnings: Earnings that generate cash from year to year and are part of normal, recurring operating activities.

Realization concept: Revenue is recognized when goods or services are delivered, in an amount that is reasonably certain to be realized.

Reasonably certain: A criterion for deciding on the amount to be entered for an asset or liability account.

Recognition: The act of recording a revenue or expense item as being applicable to a given accounting period. Revenue recognition is governed by the realization concept.

Red flags: Warning signals about a company's financial condition that might give hints about the quality of earnings. See also Quality of Earnings.

Rental revenue: Revenue earned from permitting someone to use a building or other property.

Report, Auditors': See Opinion.

Report package: Consists of a balance sheet for the beginning and end of the accounting period and an income statement for the accounting period.

Residual claim: The claim of equity investors.

Residual value: The amount for which a company expects to be able to sell a plant asset for at the end of its service life.

Retained earnings: The increase in equity that has resulted from the operations of the entity. It is an equity item, not an asset.

Return on equity (ROE): A ratio obtained by dividing net income by the amount of equity.

Return on investment (ROI): Earnings before interest and taxes divided by noncurrent liabilities plus equity. (Some people calculate it in other ways.)

Return on permanent capital: Another name for return on investment.

Revenue: The increase in owners' equity resulting from operations during a period of time, usually from the sale of goods or services.

Sales income: Sometimes used to mean sales revenue; a misleading term because income is the difference between sales revenue and expenses.

Sales revenue: Revenue from the delivery of goods or services.

Sarbanes-Oxley Act: 2002 law passed to help ensure compliance with accounting regulations and transparency in financial reporting.

Security: An instrument such as a stock or bond. Securities give the entity that owns them valuable rights from the entity that issued them.

Service: An intangible product. Examples are personal services, rent, and insurance protection.

Service life: The period of time over which an asset is estimated to be of service to the entity.

Service revenue: Revenue from the performance of services.

Shareholder equity: The equity section of a corporation's balance sheet. Also called stockholder equity. See also Equity.

Shareholders: The owners of a corporation. Also referred to as stockholders.

Shrinkages: Goods that have been stolen or spoiled and hence are no longer in inventory.

Sole proprietorship: See Proprietorship.

Solvency: An entity's ability to meet its long-term obligations. Often measured by the debt ratio.

Specific identification method: A way of calculating cost of sales by keeping track of the specific item (e.g., an automobile) sold.

Stated value: The amount at which no-par-value stock is reported on the balance sheet, as voted by the directors.

Statement of activities: In a nonprofit organization, the statement of revenues and expenses, or the statement which describes the change in net assets.

Statement of cash flows (also Cash Flow Statement): A financial statement reporting the sources and uses of cash during an accounting period.

Statement of comprehensive income: Another name for an income statement.

Statement of financial position: Another name for a balance sheet.

Stewardship: The notion of stewardship involves being responsible for more than just the reporting of the financial data.

Stock: See Capital stock, Common stock, Preferred stock.

Stock dividend: A dividend consisting of shares of stock in the corporation.

Stock split: An exchange of the number of shares of stock outstanding for a substantially larger number.

Stockholders: See Shareholders.

Straight-line depreciation: A depreciation method that charges off an equal fraction of the estimated depreciable cost of a plant asset over each year of its service life.

Subsidiary: A corporation that is controlled by another corporation, the parent, which owns more than 50 percent of its stock.

Surplus: In a nonprofit organization, the equivalent of profit, income, or earnings.

T-account: The simplest version of an account.

Tangible assets: Assets that can be touched; they have physical substance. Noncurrent tangible assets are often referred to as property, plant, and equipment.

Tax depreciation: The depreciation used in calculating taxable income.

Taxable income: The amount of income subject to income tax, computed according to the rules of the Internal Revenue Service. There can be a difference between taxable income and accounting income due to the treatment of depreciation.

Temporarily restricted net assets: In a nonprofit organization, assets donated for specific purposes in a designated accounting period.

Temporary account: A revenue or expense account. A temporary account is closed at the end of each accounting period. Contrast with Permanent account.

Trademark: A distinctive name for a manufactured good or a service.

Transaction: An event that is recorded in the accounting records; it always has at least two elements.

Transfer: In a nonprofit organization, as funds are used for their intended purposes they are transferred from temporarily restricted funds to the unrestricted category on the statement of activities.

Treasury stock: Previously issued stock that has been bought back by the corporation.

Unearned revenue: See Advances from customers.

Unexpired cost: The cost of assets on hand now that will be consumed in future accounting periods.

Units-of-production method: A depreciation method. A cost per unit of production is calculated, and depreciation expense for a year is found by multiplying this unit cost by the number of units that the asset produced in that year.

Unrealized gain: Gains on invested funds, whether such investments are sold for cash or held for the future by an organization.

Unrestricted activities: In a nonprofit organization, those activities reported on the statement of activities matched with unrestricted revenues.

Unrestricted net assets: In a nonprofit organization, net assets that result from profitable operating activities or from donations with no restrictions.

Wasting assets: Natural resources, such as coal, oil, and other minerals. The process of charging wasting assets to expense is called depletion.

Whistle blower: Those who publicly expose undesirable or unlawful behavior by companies to call attention to the objectionable practices.

Working capital: The difference between current assets and current liabilities.

Write down: To reduce the cost of an item, especially inventory, to its market value.

Write-off of bad debt: To remove a bad debt from accounts receivable.